THIRD EDITION

Evidence In Context

A Trial Evidence Workbook

THIRD EDITION

Evidence In Context

A Trial Evidence Workbook

Robert P. Burns

Steven Lubet

James H. Seckinger

The National Institute for Trial Advocacy

Adapted with permission and gratitude from materials from the National Institute for Trial Advocacy by James H. Seckinger

ISBN-55681-849-1
Burns, Robert P., and Steven Lubet, *Evidence in Context: A Trial Evidence Workbook, Third Edition* (NITA, 2004).
5/04

CONTENTS

PART TWO—CASE ONE: MURDER
State v. Mitchell

Part Three—Case Two: Defamation
MacIntyre v. Easterfield

INTRODUCTION

These problems, questions, and exercises are based mainly on *State v. Mitchell* and *MacIntyre v. Easterfield*. (You will notice that the earlier problems are based mainly on *State v. Mitchell* and the later ones mainly on *MacIntyre v. Easterfield*.)

The problems contain different sorts of instructions. Most often you are asked to "argue" an issue. When you are asked to argue an issue, you should think through and be ready to present, in role, the best arguments for your designated side's point of view, as if you were arguing an objection at trial. The student presenting the objection to admissibility (the "opponent") should speak first, addressing the teacher as judge, and stating the objection(s). The student who is the "proponent" of the evidence should then respond to the objection(s). The opponent will then respond to the proponent's response. This portion of the class will be strictly "in role," but it won't take long for you to get the hang of it. The class will then consider the issues and questions that each argument raises. (It is usually possible to identify precisely what the issue is and what the relevant arguments are. The "answer" is sometimes more elusive.) Students must be present and prepared to present the arguments.

Working through these problems for yourself is a principal, perhaps the principal, way of actually learning the law of evidence. This requires doing the reading and thinking the problems through before class—something more active than just letting the class discussion roll over you. Note, too, that the topics are cumulative—you cannot understand hearsay unless you understand relevancy.

Sometimes you are asked to "consider" an issue. In those cases you are to think through the issues raised in light of the Rules and the Text and be prepared to discuss those issues.

Sometimes you are asked to perform a small segment of a witness examination. In those cases you are to ask precisely those questions you would ask the witness at trial on the topic indicated.

RELEVANCE

1. Read *State v. Mitchell* as a detective or historian might. Who did it? Why do you think so? (Several students may be assigned "adversary" roles as advocates to criticize the opinions and reasoning of our detectives/historians.)

2. Prosecutors tell a short (two-minute) story showing Brooke Thompson's deep affection for Leslie. Defense counsel tell a short (two-minute) story showing Brooke's indifference or hostility to Leslie. What makes one story more plausible than the other? [*Mitchell*]

3. Argue the relevance of the reduction of Brooke Thompson's income in October 1999, of the terms of the life insurance policy on Leslie, and the terms of the trust. Consider how relevance is related to theory of the case. [*Mitchell*]

4. Argue the relevance of Porter's hearing brakes screeching outside her window after 10 P.M. [*Mitchell*]

5. Consider the importance for the choice of prosecution theory of Joe's reaction to the news of his wife's shooting (page 14), agitation on the way to the station (page 16), of his excited insistence that 1751 Madison was not Leslie's home, and his statement, the substance of which was that Leslie should not have been at that address that night. [*Mitchell*]

6. Consider the relevance, under any theory of prosecution or defense, of the testimony that Leslie left her key on her bedroom table. What are you doing when you so consider?

7. Argue the relevance of Slyviak's observation of "a mark on the door post where the bullet might have struck and then dropped to the step . . ." (pages 13–14). [*Mitchell*]

8. Brooke Thompson offers "direct" (not circumstantial) evidence against Joe Mitchell. Are there any propositions, other than the propositions constituting the direct evidence, that you must believe in order to accept this "direct" evidence as true? If so, what reasons do you have for accepting those general propositions as true? What kinds of reasons are those? [*Mitchell*]

9. Assume for a moment that Chris Ravenna would testify that while Joe was in his shop, Sam went into the back of the store to get Joe's newly serviced revolver. As he was returning to the front of the store, he thought he caught a glimpse of Joe moving furtively away from a gun cabinet in which a number of .38 caliber revolvers were stored. An hour or two later he looked in that cabinet and noticed that a .38 on display was missing. He had checked it last the morning before, when he had found the .38 present. During the course of yesterday, there had been perhaps ten persons in the store, none of whom did he see near in the cabinet. Argue admissibility of the hypothetical testimony. [*Mitchell*]

10. Assume you are at a hearing on a motion to suppress Mitchell's statements made at the boarding house. The material fact presently at issue is whether a reasonable person in Mitchell's situation would have felt free to leave the officers' presence. Argue the relevance of Slyviak's testimony that the officers were instructed merely to "contact . . . Joe Mitchell, to inform him of the shooting and ask him to come to headquarters for further investigation. If he refuses, just leave." Prosecutors argue it is relevant; defense argues that it is not. [*Mitchell*]

11. In *MacIntyre*, argue the relevance of Jesse's attempts to borrow money in June and July 2002 (pages 21, 27).

12. Argue the relevance of Leslie's fear of Joe expressed to Quinn Washington, and Leslie's interpretation of Joe's letter of September 9, 2002 (pages 42, 73). Disregard hearsay issues. [Mitchell]

13. Consider the admissibility of the terms of the insurance policy that the Easterfields had on the missing brooch and their understanding as to the disposition of the proceeds. [MacIntyre]

14. Consider the relevance of such "background facts" as Joe's service in the Marines, Ross Easterfield's war record, Leslie Thompson's schooling and employment history. Such facts would normally be admitted simply to fill in the background of the story, though careful trial lawyers know how important they may be to some jurors. [MacIntyre and Mitchell]

15. Prosecutors argue the relevance of each of the pictures in the Mitchell file. Defense counsel argue the irrelevance of each of the pictures. What material proposition ("fact that is of consequence to the determination of the action") does each picture make more or less probable than it would be without the picture? Why? [You should be prepared to answer the equivalent questions for each problem in which relevance is at issue.] [Mitchell]-

16. Argue the relevance of Brooke Thompson's negative opinion of Joe if offered by the prosecution. Argue the relevance if offered by the defense. Put aside for now the opinion's admissibility under Rule 701. [Mitchell]

17. Argue the relevance of Joe's not stopping to say hello to Porter on his way up the stairs at 9:40–9:55 (page 48). Consider the relevance of Brooke's giving Leslie a ring on the night Leslie was shot (page 9). [Mitchell]

18. For each of the following pieces of evidence argue the relevance if offered by your side and the irrelevance if offered by your opponent: [Mitchell]

    a. The "first thought that flashed" through Brooke Thompson's mind after the shooting was that Joe had shot Leslie.

    b. Joe's drinking and blood alcohol level.

    c. Brooke's owning the .38 and its disappearance.

    d. Brooke's having seen Joe hundreds of times before at the same time and place.

19. Argue the relevance of Easterfield's encounter with Kelly Emerson at the time Kelly was eavesdropping outside the Easterfields' bedroom (pages 30, 51). Each side should argue its relevance for its case and its irrelevance for the other side's case. How can the same piece of evidence be arguably relevant for both sides? [MacIntyre]

20. Plaintiff in MacIntyre seeks to introduce Jesse's testimony concerning Ross Easterfield: "I had seen him jump up and shake a temporary maid who had spilled coffee on him at breakfast. He's a big man and he really shook her hard. I was afraid" (page 13). Argue relevancy. What if Jesse had included a claim for assault for Easterfield's threatening behavior in the library? Would the argument be easier? Why or why not?

21. Argue the relevance of the fact that Ross Easterfield is one of the richest men in the city. Argue the relevance of the fact that he is rumored to be one of the richest men. [MacIntyre]

22. Consider this: If questions of "logical relevance" are issues of logic and human experience and not of law, why should the judge be given the role of deciding them? If the doctrine of relevance exists mainly as a concession to the shortness of life, why not simply allocate time to the two sides and allow them to decide what is most relevant? In an adversary system, they should present the most relevant evidence, shouldn't they?

23. Consider this: If the judge in Mitchell makes every arguable (i.e., probably not reversible) relevance determination against you, will the jury see a "fair" picture of the evidence? [Mitchell]

24. Consider whether it would be more troubling if the "man who is telling the truth" letter (page 25) and the testimony with regard to Jerry Young (pages 16–17) were both excluded or if either one was excluded and the other admitted. If you think it would be more troubling, do the rules of evidence take into account your scruples about excluding both pieces of evidence? [Mitchell]

25. Argue the relevance of Brooke Thompson's racial attitudes. [Mitchell]

26. Argue the relevance of the fact that Ross Easterfield's club does not admit Catholics, Jews, or Blacks. [MacIntyre]

27. Argue the relevance of Brooke Thompson's landlording practices, including her willingness to take advantage of her relationship to her dead husband, the judge, for business purposes. [Mitchell]

28. Argue the relevance of Joe's membership in Men Angry About Divorce (page 29). [Mitchell]

29. Argue the relevance of Joe's barroom fight four years ago (page 27). [Mitchell]

30. Argue the relevance of Joe's shooting at the motorist (page 28). [Mitchell]

31. Argue the relevance of Mrs. Thompson's shooting in self-defense (page 5). [Mitchell]

32. Argue the relevance of the letter Slyviak describes (page 18). Consider Rule 104 issues. [Mitchell]

33. Jesse testifies on direct that she was not aware that Frank Holman planned to rob the gas station (pages 18–19). Consider the relevance of Frank Holman's having a criminal record at the time he attempted the armed robbery for which Jesse was imprisoned. Are there Rule 104 issues? [See pages 82–83.] [MacIntyre]

34. Argue the relevance of Brooke's statement to Leslie, "That man's a loser. I'd rather die than see you go back to him," and of Joe's "reaction" (page 9). Consider Rule 104 issues. [Mitchell]

35. Argue the relevance of Joe's walking toward the front door of the police station before he was arrested (pages 16, 34). Are there Rule 104 issues? [Mitchell]

36. Argue the relevance of Joe's aggravated assault case (page 28). Consider Rule 104 issues. [Mitchell]

37. Argue the relevance of the death of Joe's first wife (page 27). Are there Rule 104 issues? Assume for the moment that Joe had pled guilty to the shooting death of his first wife after a heated argument during their walk in the woods in Wisconsin and served eight years in prison. Now argue admissibility. [Mitchell]

38. Assume for the moment that Joe's grandparents left a will in which the family house was bequeathed to one of Joe's uncles. Joe was enraged that the house in which he grew up was left to someone else. After the reading of the will, he said to his uncle, "You've screwed me out of what is rightfully mine. If I can't have the house, no one will." Three days later the house mysteriously burned down. The police determined that the fire was set. Joe had an airtight alibi and their usual contacts did not yield any evidence Joe had paid someone to set the fire. Argue admissibility in this case. [Mitchell]

39. Defense offers to prove Joe's practice of listening to The Shadow regularly (pages 33, 48). Defense should conduct the segment of Joe's direct examination that would support admissibility (the "foundation"). Prosecution objects. Argue the legal relevance. [Mitchell]

40. Argue the relevance in MacIntyre of Jesse's placing money found around the house in the video cassette of Jesse James Rides Again.

41. Plaintiff in MacIntyre seeks to prove Mrs. Easterfield's "habit" of misplacing jewelry through the general testimony of Kelly Emerson (page 50). Any objection? Consider whether the plaintiff may ask Emerson to describe the incident recounted on pages 50–51 in order to prove the "habit."

42. Prosecution offers to prove through Chris Ravenna that Joe is a fast driver (page 53). Argue the relevance. [Mitchell]

43. Plaintiff in MacIntyre seeks to prove that the letter on page 93 was sent. Argue its logical relevance.

44. Easterfield denies receiving it. Taylor says that the church secretary sent the letter. Assume the secretary has no specific recollection of sending the letter. Consider whether the plaintiff is stuck. [MacIntyre]

45. Assume that Mr. Easterfield had a serious discussion with his wife in the presence of Kelly Emerson a week after Jesse left their employ. During that discussion he said, "From now on under no circumstances are you to discuss missing jewelry or anything else you cannot find with the house staff. No accusations . . . no questions . . . nothing. Come to me and me alone about such problems." Plaintiff offers to prove the conversation. Argue the objection. [MacIntyre]

46. Assume that Joe made bail while awaiting his trial. During the time he was out of jail (without telling his lawyer, who was not pleased) he began attending a weekly support group at a local community center called "Controlling Your Rage: Practical Techniques." Argue admissibility. [Mitchell]

47. In ultimately unsuccessful settlement negotiations in MacIntyre, the defendant's attorney said: "So, Easterfield despises your client and would like to see her suffer over this. That's why he contacted the loan company . . . So what?" Easterfield then made an offer of $30,000, which was rejected. Assume that Easterfield's lawyer has the authority to make admissions for him and there is thus no hearsay problem. Is the offer admissible as an admission of liability? Is the statement admissible if offered by the plaintiff to show malice? [MacIntyre]

48. Plaintiff seeks to inquire on Easterfield's cross-examination into his attempt to convince the Loan Company to prosecute Jesse criminally (page 31), contending that it provides evidence of malice, which is relevant both to the qualified immunity defense and to punitive damages. Defense objects under Rule 408, asserting that during settlement negotiations Easterfield offered to drop those efforts if she would accept $5,000 to dismiss the case. For the plaintiff, respond. [MacIntyre]

49. Plaintiff in *MacIntyre* seeks to admit the fact that the defendants have made no settlement offers at all. Argue the relevancy.

50. Assume that Jesse MacIntyre's criminal conviction is admissible under Rule 609. MacIntyre's lawyer argues that because Jesse pled guilty, the evidence is barred by Rule 410. For Easterfield, respond. [*MacIntyre*]

51. Consider the admissibility under Rule 411 of the insurance policy that Brooke had on Leslie (page 5). Assume that the homeowner's insurance policy that the Easterfields had in effect on July 17, 2002, excluded intentional torts. Defamation is an intentional tort. Consider the admissibility. [*Mitchell*]

52. Assume that the homeowners' policy does cover intentional torts, and Paul Pirro, the investigator who obtained the statement of Reeve Winsor (page 103), testifies that Winsor carefully went over the statement to make sure it was accurate before signing it. Winsor tells a rather different story (page 57). Plaintiff seeks to reveal the existence of the liability policy on cross-examination of Pirro. Permissible? [*MacIntyre*]

53. In what ways does Rule 412 treat "character-type" evidence differently than do Rules 404 and 405? Is one approach superior to the other for all cases where a defendant offers to present evidence of a victim's character or past behavior? What is there about sex offense cases that justifies a different approach?

Rule 412 excludes evidence that given defendants (whose defense is consent) may deem logically relevant under the very liberal standard of Rule 401. Could this exclusion result in the false conviction of some defendants? Are other rules of exclusion any different? If so, does that justify Rules 413–415?

Sexual offenses are dramatically under reported and some of the under reporting results from victims' fear of the public humiliation that the traditional rule permitted. Assume that many more perpetrators go unpunished than defendants could be falsely convicted because of the operation of Rule 412. Does that assumption justify the provisions of Rule 412? What kind of justification is appropriate? Do all evidentiary rules of exclusion rely on this kind of justification? If so, does that justify Rules 413–415?

54. Prosecution seeks to admit the results of the ballistics tests (page 80). Defendant seeks to admit only those results described in the first paragraph under "Ballistics Test." Argue admissibility. [*Mitchell*]

55. Prosecution seeks to admit the results of the skid mark tests (page 79). Defendant objects. Argue admissibility. [*Mitchell*]

56. Assume that evidence technicians found bloodstains on a jagged piece of metal on the fire escape leading up to Joe's room. A blood analysis showed it to be in the blood group A and to be Rh negative. Joe's blood belongs to that blood group and is Rh negative. Argue admissibility based on the following additional facts: [*Mitchell*]

   (1) Mr. Peter Sanguin, a biochemist, testifies. He testifies that 2 percent of the world's population is in group A, and about 10 percent have Rh negative blood. By the rule of compound probabilities, multiplying the two individual probabilities together allows one to determine the probability of the concurrence of the two variables. In this case it is under .25 percent. That means that fewer than 1 in 400 people have this concurrence. Argue admissibility.

   (2) Assume that the defense is aware of Dr. Sanguin's likely testimony. Before he is allowed to testify, the defense asks for a voir dire hearing outside the hearing of the jury to submit additional evidence. At the hearing, the defense proves the following facts:

(a)   A physical exam of Joe upon his arrest found no cuts or scrapes and Joe testifies that he was not on the fire escape and had no cuts or scrapes. Argue admissibility of Sanguin's testimony now.

(b)   A workman was on that fire escape on the afternoon of September 10. He remembers cutting himself on that same jagged piece of metal and

   (i)   his blood type is A and Rh negative.

   (ii)   his blood type is O and Rh negative.

Consider admissibility of Sanguin's testimony assuming (a) and (b)(i) or (b)(ii).

(c)   A workman whose blood type is A and Rh negative was on the fire escape on September 10 but does not remember cutting himself. Consider admissibility of Sanguin's testimony assuming (a) and (c).

(d)   By an odd coincidence, three of the six people who live at Porter's have the concurrence of A and Rh negative. Consider admissibility of Sanguin's testimony assuming (1) and (3).

IMPEACHMENT

57. Consider the admissibility of Slyviak's testimony in *Mitchell* concerning his ability to see his partner from the porch of the Thompson home on September 10.

58. Argue the admissibility of Chris Ravenna's testimony in *Mitchell* concerning his ability to see Joe Mitchell as Joe left the gun shop on September 10 (page 52.

59. Mrs. Easterfield will not testify for the defendant in *MacIntyre*. Argue whether Kelly Emerson may testify that Mrs. Easterfield had an alcoholic beverage for breakfast on July 17 (page 33).

60. Mrs. Easterfield does testify. Argue whether she may be asked on cross-examination whether she had an alcoholic beverage for breakfast. If she denies having the drink, may Kelly Emerson testify that she did indeed have the drink? [*MacIntyre*]

61. Argue the admissibility of Reverend Taylor's testimony that Jesse called Kerry Easterfield "Isadore Easterfield" and her reaction to his inquiry as to where she had last seen the brooch (page 44). [*MacIntyre*]

62. In *Mitchell*, assume Raleigh Porter gives testimony favorable to Mitchell. Consider the admissibility of her having allowed Joe to fall behind on his rent while still living at the boarding house (page 45).

63. In *MacIntyre*, assume that Lee Marlow gives testimony favorable to Ross Easterfield. Argue the admissibility, on cross-examination, of Marlow's deposition testimony concerning the fate of the previous executive director of the club (page 63).

64. Reverend Taylor testifies for Jesse. Defendant seeks to cross-examine Reverend Taylor on the lunch with Jesse in order to show his bias in her favor (page 53). Defendant knows that Taylor and Jesse will deny any such meeting. Consider whether she may so inquire on the cross-examination of Taylor. If Taylor and Jesse deny the meeting, consider whether defendant may call Emerson to elicit her testimony on this matter. Are there Rule 104 issues? [*MacIntyre*]

65. Mrs. Easterfield has testified. On rebuttal, plaintiff recalls Kelly Emerson to testify that Mrs. Easterfield was thought by her house staff to be something of a liar (page 50). Argue admissibility. [*MacIntyre*]

66. The testimony in problem 65 is permitted. The defense seeks to cross-examine Emerson as to the incident Emerson described in her deposition in which Mrs. Easterfield took the blame for the botched dinner party (page 50). Argue the permissibility of the cross-examination. Assume Emerson cannot remember the incident. Assuming for the moment that the cross is permissible, how may the cross-examiner use the deposition transcript? Assume alternatively that Emerson denies that Mrs. Easterfield took the blame. May the defense cross-examine her as to whether she gave the description recorded on page 50? If she denies having said that at her deposition, what, if anything, may the defense do? [*MacIntyre*]

67. May Reverend Taylor testify that Jesse's reputation for honesty and veracity is good? If so, on cross-examination may the defendant ask Taylor about the incident in which the two twenty-dollar bills disappeared from the collection (page 46) and about her encounter with the T-Mart security official (page 20)? Argue the propriety of the cross-examination. [*MacIntyre*]

68. Mrs. Easterfield will testify for the defendant. Kelly Emerson says nothing about Mrs. Easterfield's veracity during Emerson's direct during the plaintiff's case. On cross, the defendant wishes to elicit Emerson's opinion that Mrs. Easterfield is a "truthful person" (page 50). Argue admissibility. [MacIntyre]

69. Kelly Emerson testifies for the plaintiff. On cross-examination the defendant wishes to question her concerning her statement to Mr. Easterfield that she had no knowledge of the fate of Easterfield's lobsters, a statement she admitted in her deposition to have been deceptive (page 51). Argue the permissibility of the impeachment. If she denies having deceived Easterfield, may she be impeached with the deposition statement? If she denies having made the statement in her deposition, may the court reporter be called to "complete the impeachment"? If the latter were permitted but the court reporter who recorded the deposition had no memory about what had been said, how could you complete the impeachment? (Assume, as is usual, the court reporter made and kept an audiotape cassette of the deposition and also took the deposition using the shorthand machine commonly used.) [MacIntyre]

70. Jesse testifies in plaintiff's case. On cross, no mention is made of the loan application on page 85. Plaintiff rests. Assume that the loan application on page 85 is properly authenticated and offered by defendant and that Jesse's statements on it are admissions of a party opponent and so not hearsay. There is a relevancy objection to the application and the judge asks the proponent what the relevancy is. He answers that it is offered to show Jesse's dishonesty since she has testified on direct that her income at the time she made the application was only $120 and that she did have debts at that time. Argue admissibility. Consider the applicability of Rules 608 and 613. [MacIntyre]

71. Is there any theory on which the loan application could be admitted? If there is, but the proponent relies on the "wrong" theory, will the opponent be able successfully to urge error on appeal?

72. Ross Easterfield has testified. Argue the admissibility of Winsor's testimony concerning Easterfield's reputation in the real estate world of Nita City ("a very aggressive deal-maker and a very hard, even slick, bargainer . . . Willing to conceal material information and even misrepresent facts") as described by Winsor (page 56). [MacIntyre]

73. Argue the logical and legal relevance in MacIntyre of Mrs. Easterfield's abortion offered by the plaintiff:

(1) if Mrs. Easterfield has said nothing about the Easterfields' not having children on direct;

(2) if Mrs. Easterfield has testified during her introductory testimony that "God hasn't blessed us" and

(a) plaintiff seeks to cross-examine Mrs. Easterfield about the abortion;

(b) after Mrs. Easterfield denies the abortion on cross, plaintiff seeks to call the doctor who performed the procedure; [Ignore privilege issues.]

(c) without mentioning the abortion on the cross of Mrs. Easterfield, plaintiff calls the doctor who performed the procedure; [Again, ignore privilege issues.]

(d) Mrs. Easterfield indignantly denies the abortion on cross and plaintiff recalls Jesse to impeach Mrs. Easterfield by testifying to the conversation between the Easterfields that she overheard (page 20);

(e) plaintiff does not ask Mrs. Easterfield about the abortion on cross, but simply seeks to recall Jesse and to elicit the testimony from Jesse.

Assume you believe that all the impeaching "extrinsic" evidence (evidence that is not merely an admission on cross) is inadmissible, may you still ask Mrs. Easterfield about the abortion on cross, assuming, too, that you believe it is relevant? [*MacIntyre*]

74. Argue the admissibility on the cross of Easterfield of the contents of his talk at the real estate brokers' convention described on page 57. [*MacIntyre*]

75. Consider the admissibility of Winsor's testimony concerning the rumors about Easterfield's business practices in the small Ohio city he worked in before he came to Nita (page 56). [*MacIntyre*]

76. Chris Ravenna testifies that it is his opinion that Joe has a good character for truthfulness and should be trusted as a witness. May the prosecution cross-examine using any of the incidents described on pages 27 and 28 of the *Mitchell* file?

77. Assume that Easterfield is a witness in the case. Marlow testifies that Easterfield has the highest reputation for honesty, integrity, and fair dealing (page 64). On cross-examination, consider whether plaintiffs may question Marlow about any facts which they could not otherwise put before the jury. [*MacIntyre*]

78. Jesse testifies. May you confront her on cross-examination with the incident at the T-Mart? If she denies it, may you call the security guard? [*MacIntyre*]

79. Assume the impeachment of Reverend Taylor concerning the missing twenty-dollar bills is permitted and Taylor denies that entire incident occurred, may you impeach him with his deposition as a prior inconsistent statement? Assume the impeachment with the prior inconsistent statement is allowed, and Taylor denies saying that in his deposition. Defendant seeks to call the court reporter to impeach Taylor. For the plaintiff, make the objection. [*MacIntyre*]

80. Assume that the school record on page 121 is an official record and therefore, once authenticated, that it falls under an exception to the hearsay rule. Argue its admissibility offered by the defendant to prove that Jesse is "dishonest." [*MacIntyre*]

81. Argue the admissibility on Winsor's direct of testimony concerning the two successful civil suits against Easterfield. [*MacIntyre*]

82. Argue the admissibility on Winsor's direct of (1) Easterfield's criminal conviction described on pages 56–57, (2) the details of the crime to which he pled guilty, and (3) the circumstances surrounding the reception of the guilty plea. [*MacIntyre*]

83. In *Mitchell*, Porter testifies for Joe Mitchell. Argue the admissibility of her criminal conviction.

84. In *MacIntyre*, Marlow testifies that it was the settled policy of the club not to hire ex-convicts. Argue the admissibility on Marlow's cross of Reverend Taylor's conversation with Marlow described on pages 46–47. Consider Rule 104 issues. May the plaintiff examine Taylor concerning the conversation with Marlow without raising it on the cross-examination of Marlow?

85. Plaintiff in *MacIntyre* testifies that she was innocent of the attempted armed robbery with which she was charged. In rebuttal, defendant seeks to admit the stipulation of Mr. Johnson, MacIntyre's lawyer, recounted on page 80. Argue admissibility.

86. Jesse testifies consistently with her deposition as to the events of July 17. Defendants wish to impeach Jesse with the statement in her complaint, "On Sunday, July 19, Mr. Easterfield said within the hearing of Kelly Emerson, 'Miss MacIntyre has stolen a diamond brooch'" as they did in her deposition (pages 13–14). Is this tactically wise? Is this permissible impeachment? [MacIntyre]

87. Marlow testifies favorably for Easterfield. Marlow tells the jury the club has a long-standing policy prohibiting the hiring of ex-convicts. Pursuant to the policy, as soon as she learned that Jesse was an ex-convict she could not hire her. On cross-examination her attention is directed to the conversation with Reverend Taylor in which, according to Taylor, she seemed open to hiring of ex-convicts (pages 46–47). It is also suggested on cross that Marlow is afraid of Ross Easterfield and wants to please him. She denies Taylor's account of the conversation (page 63). Taylor then is allowed to testify to his conversation with Marlow concerning the club's willingness to hire ex-convicts (pages 46–47). On rebuttal, Marlow is recalled and seeks to testify to her statement to Mrs. Easterfield (page 63) that the club would never hire someone with a criminal record. Argue admissibility of the latter statement. [MacIntyre]

88. Reverend Taylor is the witness. Argue the admissibility of the conversation between Reverend Taylor and Ross Easterfield in which Easterfield told Taylor that he was not willing to employ another young woman from the St. James Home (page 44). For now, ignore privilege issues. [MacIntyre]

89. Assume that Ross Easterfield is asked on direct why he hired Jesse and he answers, "My only motive was pure Christian charity. No good deed goes unpunished, I guess." Now argue the admissibility of the conversation. [MacIntyre]

90. Argue the admissibility of Dr. Steinfels' opinion of Jesse's likely truthfulness as a witness (page 118). [MacIntyre]

91. Argue the admissibility of Dr. Steinfels' opinion of Jesse's likelihood to misperceive and misinterpret events (page 118). [MacIntyre]

92. Argue the admissibility of Dr. Steinfels' opinion of Jesse's propensity to steal (pages 117–118). Put aside any problems that stem from Steinfels' claim to be testifying as an expert. [MacIntyre]

PRESUMPTIONS AND BURDENS OF PROOF

93. At the end of all the evidence, Mitchell moves for a directed verdict ("judgment as a matter of law"). What standard will the judge employ in deciding whether to allow the case to go to the jury? Defendant makes the same motion in *MacIntyre*. Is the standard any different? [*MacIntyre* and *Mitchell*]

94. At the end of the prosecution case in *Mitchell* the judge concludes that no reasonable person could conclude beyond a reasonable doubt that Joe received the retraction letter from his publisher nor that he was trying to escape from custody at the police station. Must he or she direct a verdict of acquittal? For the prosecution, argue the directed verdict motion.

95. The Nita Criminal Code places the burden of proof, by a preponderance of the evidence, of sanity on the prosecution and the burden of going forward on the defense. Nita courts often say that Nita recognizes the "presumption of sanity." The prosecution puts on its case in *Mitchell* without any direct evidence of sanity. At the end of the prosecution case the defense moves to dismiss on the ground that the prosecution has not carried its burden of proving sanity by a preponderance. For the prosecutor, respond.

96. Jerry Young's widow has filed a civil action to require payment on his life insurance policy. Nita recognizes a presumption that a person is dead upon proof that he had disappeared from his home, was absent for a period of seven years during which time no tidings were received from him by his immediate family, and diligent efforts to establish his whereabouts were made and were unsuccessful. The death of the covered individual is an element in Mrs. Young's action against the insurance company. Nita has adopted Rules 301 and 302. How should the court direct the jury on the element of the death of the covered individual in each of the following situations: [*MacIntyre*]

    A.. Mrs. Young testifies that she is the only member of Young's immediate family, that he disappeared from their house nine years ago, and that she had not heard anything from him for all those nine years, and that she searched ceaselessly for Jerry. No evidence to the contrary is presented.

    B. Mrs. Young testifies as in A, but admits on cross that she did not attempt to contact members of any New York organized crime family to inquire as to Jerry's whereabouts. Given the large scope of Mrs. Young's other efforts, you do not believe that this omission would permit a reasonable juror to conclude that Mrs. Young's efforts had not been "diligent."

    C. Mrs. Young testifies as in A and B, but also testifies that she made no attempt to contact Jerry's cousins and aunts. You regard this omission as being sufficiently important to permit a reasonable juror to conclude that Mrs. Young's efforts were not "diligent."

    D. Mrs. Young testifies as in A. The defense calls George Watson, a man who was an acquaintance of Jerry's in Nita City. He testifies that while vacationing in Miami three years ago, he saw a man who "bore some resemblance to Young." He never approached the man, who was within his sight for perhaps five seconds. You regard this evidence as insufficient to permit a reasonable juror to conclude that Young is still alive.

E. Mrs. Young testifies as in A. The insurance company calls Peg Parker who had met Jerry in Nita City once before he disappeared and whose son works for the defendant insurance company. Parker testifies that she met Jerry Young in a bar in Orlando three years ago. Parker had been engaged in small talk with this fellow for about fifteen minutes when Parker exclaimed, "You're Jerry Young, aren't you?" Parker's conversation partner smiled, winked, and said, "Keep a lid on it." He then left the bar. You regard this testimony as sufficient evidence to permit, though not require, a reasonable juror to find that Young is still alive.

F. Mrs. Young testifies as in A and B, but also testifies that she received an unsigned handwritten letter four years ago which said only, "I will always love you." She testified that the handwriting "looked like Jerry's but I couldn't be sure." You regard this as evidence sufficient to permit, but not require, a reasonable juror to conclude that Mrs. Young received tidings from Jerry and/or that he is still alive.

Assume that Mrs. Young's action was a diversity action filed in federal district court in California. The federal court will apply Nita insurance law in deciding the case. California's version of the above presumption would shift the burden of proving that Young was still alive to the defendant and its conflicts law would apply its own version if the claim based on Nita law were being tried in a California state court. How should the court determine which law to apply? [MacIntyre]

97. Joe Mitchell is on trial. "Capital murder" in Nita requires that the state prove that the defendant specifically intended the death "of the person killed or another person." Relying on authoritative studies of the statistical relationships between higher caliber and lethal effect, the Nita legislature has enacted the following presumption: "A person who shoots and kills another person with a gun of caliber of .38 or higher shall be presumed to intend the death of the person killed." Nita also has enacted the following presumption, potentially applicable to Joe's letter from the Wilson Studios: "Any letter received and opened by a person shall be presumed to be read by that person." [Mitchell]

Nita has enacted Standard 303.

A. Are Nita's presumptions constitutional in criminal cases?

B. Slyviak testifies that the Wilson Studios letter was found open. Joe does not testify whether or not he read the Wilson Studios letter, and no other evidence is submitted. At the end of the case, the prosecutor asks that the court direct the jury to find that Joe had read the letter. How should the court rule? [Mitchell]

C. At the end of all the evidence, putting aside the presumption, the judge is not convinced that a reasonable juror could find that Joe specifically intended to kill, rather than to wound or scare, his wife or Brooke. May the court submit the issue to the jury based on the force of the presumption? [Mitchell]

D. How should the judge instruct the jury as to the effect of the presumption concerning the reading of mail? [Mitchell]

E. How should the judge instruct the jury as to the effect of the presumption concerning intent to kill? [Mitchell]

98. Ross Easterfield is a very influential man. He has decided to seek legislative change to relieve the defendant of the burden of proving truth of a defamatory statement. His lawyers tell him that such a "merely procedural" change would control cases not yet tried. According to the bill that a friendly legislator is introducing for him, the plaintiff in a defamation action would have the burden of proving that the allegedly defamatory statement is untrue. Plaintiff and defendant both send lawyers to the legislative committee considering the bill. Testimony before the legislative committee is limited to two minutes. Make your arguments for and against the change in the allocation of the burden of proof. [MacIntyre]

RULINGS ON EVIDENCE

99. The following dialogue occurs on cross-examination of Joe in the trial court:

    Q.   Tell the jury how your first wife met her death.

    MR. JONES: OBJECTION.

    THE COURT: OVERRULED. ANSWER THE QUESTION.

    A.   She was shot in the chest by a rifle.

    Joe is convicted. May he raise the issue of the introduction of this evidence on appeal, based on the above dialogue? [*Mitchell*]

100. Defense counsel is cross-examining Brooke Thompson. She asks, "And what did you do with Leslie's possessions after her death?" The relevancy objection is sustained. Do what is necessary to preserve the error. [*Mitchell*]

101. The defense in Mitchell offers the letter on page 25. There is an objection based on inadequate authentication which is sustained. As if you were in the trial court, do what is necessary to preserve the issue of the letter's exclusion for appeal.

102. The prosecution in *Mitchell* calls an usher at the Palace Theater. He testifies without objection to Washington's words to Joe on the night Leslie was killed: "Joe, what have you done to Leslie? Why don't you leave her alone? She's afraid of you, Joe" (page 42). The prosecution then calls Ms. Washington and asks her what she said to Joe on the night of the killing. This time there is a hearsay objection which is overruled. Assume that the hearsay objection was valid. Consider whether the defense may obtain reversal predicated on the admission of Washington's testimony.

103. The prosecution in *Mitchell* finds and calls Maria Pietro (page 21). The defense objects, under Rules 404, 405, and 403, to the prior bad act evidence. The objections are overruled and Pietro testifies to her encounter with Joe as she did in his trial. Assume the objections were valid and were erroneously overruled. The defense then vigorously cross-examines Pietro and introduces extrinsic evidence that Pietro told the emergency room nurse that she was the aggressor and Joe acted in self-defense. The nurse remembers the incident well and is definite and credible. Pietro is not.

    Joe is convicted. May the defense obtain reversal predicated on the erroneous admission of Pietro's testimony? [*Mitchell*]

104. The appellate panel is considering the appeal under the circumstances described in problem 103. The panel reaches consensus on the truth of the following proposition: If we put aside the evidence of Joe's attack on Pietro, there is still adequate evidence independently sufficient to support the verdict. Should the panel hold that the trial court's ruling is harmless error? What if the panel determines that the evidence against Joe is "overwhelming"? [*Mitchell*]

105. Defendant in *Mitchell* seeks to elicit testimony from Brooke Thompson that she shot and killed one of her tenants. There is an objection as to relevancy and improper character evidence. When asked for his response, the proponent tells the court that the evidence is being introduced in order to show Brooke is a violent person. The objection is then sustained. Assume that, under the law of the jurisdiction, the evidence should have been received to show Brooke's knowledge of the use of firearms. May the defendant urge the court's failure to receive the evidence as error on appeal?

106. The objection to the evidence in problem 86 is improperly overruled. Would the prosecution be able to urge that erroneous ruling as reversible error on appeal?

107. Jesse is on the stand. She seeks to testify that Kelly Emerson told her that she, Kelly, had just found the brooch in the library. Defendant objects that the evidence violates the Best Evidence Rule since Kelly would offer better evidence on the subject. The objection is erroneously sustained. The proper objection is hearsay, though the proponent might be able to lay a foundation for a present sense impression exception to the hearsay rule. May the proponent urge error on appeal? [*MacIntyre*]

108. Jesse's lawyers lose a motion in limine to exclude her school records, which are clearly inadmissible. However, they fail to object when those records are offered at trial, relying on the earlier ruling. May plaintiff urge error on appeal? (*MacIntyre*]

109. Jesse's lawyer objects to the introduction of her criminal conviction to impeach her under Rule 609. His objections are overruled. In closing argument, he argues extensively that Easterfield's accusations were especially cruel given Jesse's previous conviction and incarceration, justifying a higher award of punitive damages. Assume that the use of the conviction to impeach would be reversible error. May the plaintiff urge that error on appeal? [*MacIntyre*]

110. Make the same assumption as in problem 109, but assume that Jesse offers evidence only that she did not, in fact, know about Holman's intention to commit the robbery. May she urge the trial court's admission of the conviction as error? (*MacIntyre*]

111. The defense in *MacIntyre* offers lay opinion evidence that Jesse had a strong propensity to steal and manipulate her benefactors. The defense does not object, but seeks to offer evidence from a worker at the St. James Home that Jesse has often had the opportunity to steal while living and working there and has never taken a penny. Should the rebuttal evidence be permitted? [*MacIntyre*]

112. Slyviak is describing the trip from the boarding house to the station. He is asked, "What happened next?" Slyviak testifies, "Well, Joe said that he hoped that we wouldn't hold the shooting death of his first wife against him." What should defense do? Prosecution argues on appeal that whatever the defense did was untimely, since they did not object to the question. Respond. [*Mitchell*]

AUTHENTICATION AND THE BEST EVIDENCE RULE

The following problems ask you to consider issues of authentication and the applicability of the so-called "Best Evidence Rule," probably better described as the "Original Document Rule." Many of the problems also raise hearsay issues, and so we will return to those problems when we reach hearsay. For the moment, you should put aside hearsay issues.

Authentication

113. How can the bullet recovered by Slyviak from the porch of the Thompson home be authenticated? [*Mitchell* at 13–14, 75.]

114. How can the textbook, Modern Physics by Henry P. MacIntyre, be authenticated? What relevance does the actual textbook recovered from the library of the Easterfield home have? [*MacIntyre* at 52.]

115. How can the theater ticket taken from Joe Mitchell be authenticated? [*Mitchell* at 75.]

116. How can the three photographs of the Easterfield home be authenticated? Are they relevant? [*MacIntyre* at 69–73.]

117. Can the four photographs of the Thompson front porch be authenticated? How? Are they admissible? [*Mitchell* at 63–71.]

118. Can the not-to-scale floor plan of the Easterfield home be authenticated for admission as evidence? If not, what is the foundation necessary for using the document solely as a demonstrative aid? [*MacIntyre* at 67.]

119. Is the not-to-scale diagram of the front of the Thompson home more problematic as evidence than is the floor plan of the Easterfield home? Can it be authenticated for admission as evidence? Used as a demonstrative aid? [*Mitchell* at 57.]

120. How might the not-to-scale diagram of the streets around the Thompson home be authenticated? Should it be admitted? [*Mitchell* at 55.]

121. What must you do to authenticate the Nita Country Club ad from the Nita City Tribune? [*MacIntyre* at 123.]

122. How can you authenticate Joe's handwritten note to Leslie? [*Mitchell* at 73.]

123. What must you do to authenticate the certified copy of the Nita Transit Authority Bus Schedule? [*MacIntyre* at 75–76.]

124. Specify the witness(es) and ask precisely the series of questions best calculated to support the authenticity of the letter that purports to be from Jesse to Reverend Taylor. Should the document be admitted? [*MacIntyre* at 91.]

125.   Specify the witness(es) and ask precisely the series of questions best calculated to support the authenticity of the anonymous letter to the Police Department described by Officer Slyviak. Is the case for its admissibility weaker or stronger than that for the admissibility of the document in the last problem? [*Mitchell* at 18, 25.]

Best Evidence Rule

126.   Rather than introducing Joe's handwritten note, may the prosecution simply ask Brooke Thompson what the letter said? [*Mitchell* at 73.]

127.   Assume that the copy of the St. James Parish Schedule of Masses [*MacIntyre* at 77–78] is a photocopy of a document originally prepared on a word processor in the beginning of the summer of 2002. Any problems under the Best Evidence Rule?

128.   Rather than offer the copy of the letter to Joe Mitchell from the Wilson Studios [*Mitchell* at 23] may the prosecution simply ask Slyviak what the letter said?

129.   Ross Easterfield's bank statement was obtained from him in discovery. He received it in the mail from the bank. Does the Best Evidence Rule preclude its admission? [*MacIntyre* at 105–106.]

130.   The ABC Employment Agency record was made from notes created earlier. Is it admissible under the Best Evidence Rule? [*MacIntyre* at 55–56, 115.]

131.   Are there problems with the admissibility under the Best Evidence Rule of the copy of the section map of Nita City containing annotations by the Deputy City Engineer? Any solutions to those problems? Assume that the map itself is an official record admissible as an exception to the hearsay rule. [*Mitchell* at 59–61.]

Hearsay

The next set of problems will deal with the rule against hearsay evidence and the exclusions from and exceptions to the rule. In each of the problems you must be prepared to address two questions. Is the "statement" hearsay? If it is, does it fall under any exception recognized by the Federal Rules? (Do not pass too quickly to the second question.) Where the instructions are to argue an issue you must consider whether you have an argument relating to each of those questions. If you do, you should prepare to present it. In some problems, you are instructed to lay the appropriate foundation, as if at trial, for the introduction of a "statement." You should in those cases prepare to ask precisely those questions which would warrant (provide the "foundation" for) the admissibility of the "statement." Be alert to authentication issues in phone conversations and to both authentication and best evidence problems with regard to documents.

132. Prosecution seeks to admit Quinn Washington's testimony that Leslie Mitchell appeared "frightened and nervous." Defense objects that the "non-verbal conduct" of Leslie is hearsay. Respond for the prosecution. [Mitchell]

133. Prosecution seeks to admit Slyviak's testimony that Joe was walking furtively toward the station house back door. Defense objects on hearsay grounds to the "non-verbal conduct" described. Respond for the prosecution. [Mitchell]

134. Jesse seeks to testify that Emerson rolled her eyes after Mrs. Easterfield asked Jesse to go look for the brooch (page 11). Defense objects on hearsay grounds. Argue the objection. [MacIntyre]

135. Kelly Emerson is asked to state her name for the court and the jury. Plaintiff objects on hearsay grounds and offers to conduct voir dire of the witness to show that she is relying on hearsay from her mother. Respond for the defense. [MacIntyre]

136. Reverend Taylor seeks to testify that Mrs. Easterfield never complained about Jesse's demeanor or work. Argue the hearsay objection. [MacIntyre]

137. Easterfield is testifying. He is describing the events of July 17 and says "I told her she could stay . . . " (page 26). Plaintiff objects and moves to strike as hearsay. For the defense, respond to the objection. [MacIntyre]

138. Easterfield then testifies that Jesse responded "No!" to his invitation for her to stay (pages 26–27). Plaintiff moves to strike on hearsay grounds. Respond for the defense. [MacIntyre]

139. Plaintiff in MacIntyre offers an edition of the Nita City Tribune containing the ad placed by the Nita Athletic Club (pages 59, 123). Defendant objects on hearsay grounds. For the plaintiff, respond.

140. Plaintiff in MacIntyre calls Gina Lordowicz who owns a pawn shop in Nita. She seeks to testify that she was approached by a small-time thug whose name she doesn't know who told her "this Easterfield woman I know wants to unload a piece of jewelry off the books." Argue the hearsay objection.

141. Taylor testifies consistently with his deposition as to Jesse's fine qualifications for the job at the club (page 46). Defendant seeks to introduce the letter he wrote to the Nita Transit Authority (page 99) to impeach his testimony. Argue the objection. [MacIntyre]

142. Defense in *MacIntyre* calls Holman. Holman testifies that he told Jesse about his plans to rob the gas station before the attempted robbery. After his testimony, he returns to San Diego to continue serving his prison term. In rebuttal, plaintiff seeks to introduce the statement on page 80. Argue the objection.

143. Emerson seeks to testify to the words the Easterfields exchanged in the argument recounted on page 54. Defendant objects on hearsay grounds. Argue the objection. [*MacIntyre*]

144. Marlow testifies for the defense. On cross-examination, the plaintiff seeks to inquire into the "rumor" that Marlow described on deposition about the firing of the previous executive director (page 63). Defendant objects on hearsay grounds. Argue the objection. [*MacIntyre*]

145. Plaintiff offers Reverend Taylor's letter on page 93. The only objection is hearsay. Respond to the objection for the plaintiff. [*MacIntyre*]

146. On redirect, Jesse is asked why she pled guilty. She answers she did that because her lawyer told her that if she didn't she would be found guilty anyway and sentenced to fifteen years (page 19). Defense objects and moves to strike on hearsay grounds. For the plaintiff, respond to the objection. [*MacIntyre*]

147. Jesse MacIntyre testifies that Marlow told her that she "is exceptionally well qualified for the job" (page 16). Defense objects and moves to strike on hearsay grounds. For the plaintiff, argue the objection. For the defense, respond. [*MacIntyre*]

148. Kelly Emerson is testifying for the plaintiff. She recounts her telephone call to Jesse after the brooch was found (page 53). She testifies that Jesse told her that "she [Jesse] couldn't get a job and that everywhere she turned Mr. Easterfield had ruined her chances for the job." Respond to the hearsay objection. [*MacIntyre*]

149. Reverend Taylor has testified. On cross, defense asks whether Jesse, on July 17, shouted out, "Do you think I took it [the brooch]?" and then started crying and said, "Oh, I'm sorry." Plaintiff objects on hearsay and relevancy grounds. For the defense, respond to the objection. [*MacIntyre*]

150. Ross Easterfield testifies for the defense. He seeks to testify to the conversation he had with Peter Zanoni on July 17 (page 28). Argue the hearsay objection. [*MacIntyre*]

151. Jesse testifies for the plaintiff. She seeks to testify that upon returning to the dining room on July 17, she said to Mrs. Easterfield, "You know it will turn up. It always does" (page 12). For the plaintiff, respond to the hearsay objection. [*MacIntyre*]

152. Plaintiff in *MacIntyre* calls Frank Holman. He proposes to testify that he did not tell Jesse about his plan to rob the grocery store. For the plaintiff, respond to the hearsay objection.

153. Plaintiff calls Kelly Emerson and questions her concerning Ross Easterfield's conversation with his wife concerning an earlier "missing" piece of jewelry. ("She looked down . . ." [pages 50–51].) Consider the admissibility of each of the sentences in Emerson's description of that exchange. [*MacIntyre*]

154. Ross Easterfield testifies for the defense. On cross-examination, the plaintiff asks him what Mrs. Easterfield said as Jesse left the library. ("That vulgar little tramp!" [page 26].) Argue the objection(s). [*MacIntyre*]

155.   Ross Easterfield testifies for the defendant. During his direct examination, he testifies that he mailed the original of the letter on page 113 to the insurance company on July 21. (The insurance company has no record of receiving the original.) Defendant offers the printout of the letter. Argue any objection. [*MacIntyre*]

156.   Marlow testifies for the defense. On cross-examination plaintiff seeks to inquire into Mrs. Easterfield's relationship with George Williams, the tennis coach (pages 62–63). She asks the following questions: [*MacIntyre*]

    1.   Was Mrs. Easterfield having an affair with your tennis coach?

    2.   Was there a rumor to the effect that Mrs. Easterfield was having an affair with your tennis coach?

    3 .   [After laying the foundation for the conversation with George Williams recounted on pages 62–63.] What did you say to him and he say to you?

Argue the appropriate objections to each question.

157.   Argue the admissibility of Jesse's statement, offered by her on direct, that Marlow's secretary called her on July 22 and: [*MacIntyre*]

    1.   asked her for her social security number,

    2.   described at length the employees' lounge at the club and told Jesse in detail how lavish it was, and

    3.   said, "I have already prepared your W-4 forms. They are here on my desk."

158.   Quinn Washington is testifying for the prosecution. She testifies that, on the night of September 10, she said to Mitchell, "Joe, what have you done to Leslie? Why don't you leave her alone? She's afraid of you, Joe" (page 42). Defense objects on hearsay grounds and moves to strike. Argue admissibility of each of those sentences, one at a time, for the prosecution. For the defense, respond to the prosecution's arguments. [*Mitchell*]

159.   Slyviak is testifying in the *Mitchell* case. On cross-examination defense asks whether Slyviak told Detective Bradley that Slyviak believed Mitchell didn't do it (page 6). The only objection is hearsay. For the defense, respond.

160.   Jesse MacIntyre testifies for the plaintiff. She seeks to recount her conversation with the cab driver who took her to Reverend Taylor's and in particular the cab driver's remarks to her (page 15). Argue the objection. She then seeks to testify to what she told Marlow, recounted on the last twelve lines of the second full paragraph of page 17, beginning with, "You have a good job . . . " Argue any objection. [*MacIntyre*]

161.   Reeve Winsor has been called by the plaintiff. During his testimony, he says that he negatively evaluated Jesse MacIntyre before he spoke with Ross Easterfield. Plaintiff seeks to confront him with his deposition testimony (page 55), "After I had spoken with Mr. Easterfield, I negatively evaluated her file . . ." Permissible? At the end of plaintiff's evidence, defense moves for a partial directed verdict, arguing that there is no evidence of causality between Easterfield's statements and the ABC Employment agency's negative evaluation. Ruling? [*MacIntyre*]

162. Marlow testifies that the club had a firm policy against the hiring of ex-convicts when Jesse applied. Reverend Taylor then seeks to testify that Marlow had previously offered to hire ex-convicts (pages 46–47). This alleged conversation had not been mentioned to Marlow on cross. Argue the objection. [*MacIntyre*]

163. Jesse testifies and is impeached under Rule 609 by her conviction in the Holman matter. On redirect, Jesse identifies her signature on her sworn statement (page 89) and offers the statement into evidence. Argue the objection. [*MacIntyre*]

164. Brooke Thompson testifies that she told the police officers who arrived at her home on September 10 that she had just seen Joe Mitchell kill her stepdaughter. Defense objects on hearsay grounds. Argue the objection. [*Mitchell*]

165. Pat Slyviak testifies that Brooke Thompson said when Slyviak arrived at the Thompson home that she had just seen Joe Mitchell kill her stepdaughter. Argue the objection. [*Mitchell*]

166. Defense in *MacIntyre* offers the (previously authenticated) loan application Jesse made to Fidelity (page 85). [See page 22 for Jesse's explanation.] Plaintiff objects on hearsay and relevancy grounds. Argue the objection.

167. Jesse has testified. On cross-examination, defense puts this question to Jesse: "Isn't it true that you testified at your deposition that Mr. Easterfield 'never seemed to take any of her [Mrs. Easterfield's] ravings seriously'?" Plaintiff objects on best evidence and hearsay grounds and on the grounds that the statement is improper lay witness opinion testimony. For the defense, respond. [*MacIntyre*]

168. Easterfield testifies that Jesse responded, "No!" to his invitation for her to stay (pages 26–27). Plaintiff moves to strike on hearsay grounds. Respond for the defense. [*MacIntyre*]

169. Jesse is testifying for the plaintiff. She testifies (page 15) that as she was leaving she said to Mr. Easterfield, "After all this time, now you're calling me a thief" and that they then said nothing. Argue the hearsay objection. [The defense knows that Mr. Easterfield would testify that he shook his head "No!" to Jesse's claim that he thought she was a thief (page 26). The defense also knows that Jesse would say that "Mr. Easterfield was shaking his head violently back and forth during this time." Should the court consider these two latter facts in ruling on admissibility? What procedure could the defense follow to allow the court to consider them?] [*MacIntyre*]

170. Jesse denies that she knew about Frank Holman's intention to rob the gas station. Defense calls the court reporter who took down the proceedings on page 80 and seeks to offer testimony to the "basis" there described. Plaintiff objects on hearsay grounds. Argue the objection. [*MacIntyre*]

171. Reverend Taylor is the witness. He seeks to testify that Kelly Emerson told him that breakfast was always served at the Easterfield house at 9 A.M. weekends and at 7 A.M. during the week. The only objection is hearsay. For the plaintiff, respond. [*MacIntyre*]

172. Joe has been charged with only one count, first degree murder. No conspiracy count is included. Prosecution offers testimony of the bartender at the Silver Dollar Bar that Ms. Porter's handyman, George Tomas, was in on September 13. The bartender would testify that Tomas mentioned that he had some extra cash to spend because he had been paid "a small bundle" to leave the ladder down on the fire escape at Porter's "a couple days ago. God knows why." Tomas died last winter. Argue the admissibility of Tomas's statement. [*Mitchell*]

Daniel Kiley is an old friend of Joe's with a long criminal record. Telephone records show he spoke with Joe on the phone two or three times after Joe was imprisoned. He would say only that he and Joe talked "small talk." Mrs. Porter would testify that Kiley telephoned her on September 26, identified himself, and said, "Joe wanted me to tell you that he had no intention of shooting Leslie, only 'the old lady.' You know why." Kiley denied calling Porter. Is Porter's proposed testimony admissible? [Mitchell]

173. The prosecution in Mitchell seeks to elicit from Chris Ravenna the following testimony (page 52): "I remembered I said to him [Joe] that he'd better be careful, because it was loaded, or something like that." Ravenna would testify to saying that immediately after noticing two bullets in the gun, something that surprised Ravenna (page 52).

174. Kelly Emerson has testified only that she found the brooch "in the library." There was no cross-examination on that point. In the defense case, Kerry Easterfield testifies that Kelly Emerson told her that she found the brooch "hidden behind a book in the study . . ." (page 37). Argue the hearsay objection. [MacIntyre]

175. Assume Kelly Emerson described finding the brooch as she did in her deposition (page 52). In the defense case, Kerry now seeks to testify to what Kelly told her (page 37). Argue the objection. [MacIntyre]

176. Jesse seeks to testify (page 18), "In early August, Kelly Emerson called me and told me that the missing brooch had turned up in the library of the Easterfield home. She called me fifteen minutes after she found it, she said. I think that Kelly told me that Mrs. Easterfield admitted leaving the brooch in the library." Objection is hearsay. Argue the objection. [MacIntyre]]

177. Brooke Thompson testifies that she told the police officers who arrived at her home on September 10 that she had just seen Joe Mitchell kill her stepdaughter. Defense objects on hearsay grounds. Argue the objection. [Mitchell]

178. Pat Slyviak testifies that Brooke Thompson said when Slyviak arrived at the Thompson home that she had just seen Joe Mitchell kill her stepdaughter. Argue the objection. [Mitchell]

179. Jesse MacIntyre is testifying on direct. She testifies that Mrs. Easterfield, on the morning of July 17, asked her to look for the diamond brooch. She is then asked what she said in response ["All right, but I'd rather not. I have to go to church"]. Defense objects on hearsay grounds. Argue the objection. [MacIntyre]

180. Kelly testifies that she had a telephone conversation with Jesse after the brooch was found. In the conversation, Jesse said, "I just feel so, so bad. There's nothing for me, just nothing." Argue the hearsay objection. [MacIntyre]

181. Jesse seeks to testify that she said to Mr. Easterfield in the library on the 17th: "What's going on here? You're making me feel very uncomfortable" (page 12). Argue the hearsay objection. [MacIntyre]

182. Kelly Emerson testifies for the plaintiff. She testifies that Jesse told her, on the morning of July 17, "that she didn't want to be late that day, since the opening hymn was one of her favorites and always gave her the courage to go on" (page 51). Argue the hearsay objection. [MacIntyre]

183. Jesse testifies for the plaintiff. She seeks to testify to Reverend Taylor's remarks upon her return to the rectory on July 17: "I've always thought that Easterfield was a self-centered bas—, person. He'd be better off if he hadn't gotten involved in this program at all. It's pure, thoughtless cruelty. A child pulling the wings off a butterfly. I'm just so sorry, Jesse" (page 17). Argue the objection. [MacIntyre]

184. Jesse is testifying for the plaintiff. She testifies that when she arrived at Reverend Taylor's on July 17, she said that she "had left the Easterfields' because Mr. Easterfield had accused her of stealing some of his wife's jewelry" (page 44–45). Argue the hearsay objection. [MacIntyre]

185. The objection is sustained. Jesse has now been cross-examined. The defense suggested on cross that Jesse left the house because she had been caught in the act of stealing and that the slander action was an idea hatched by a clever lawyer weeks later. On redirect, Jesse again seeks to recount her words to Reverend Taylor. Now argue the objection. Consider whether it would matter whether Reverend Taylor was the witness to Jesse's words, rather than Jesse. [MacIntyre]

186. Kelly Emerson has testified that she cannot remember how she felt when Easterfield asked her about the brooch on the 17th and cannot remember whether Mr. Easterfield asked her how she herself felt about his inquiries on the morning of the 17th (page 52). Her recollection cannot be refreshed. Easterfield then testifies that he did indeed speak to Kelly several days after the 17th and "said something like 'Kelly, I hope you know that I did not mean to imply anything by asking you if you had seen the brooch on the morning Jesse left'" (page 27). Argue the hearsay objection. [MacIntyre]

187. The objection is overruled. Easterfield then testifies that Kelly replied, "No, of course not, Mr. Easterfield. I didn't feel that you were accusing me at all" (page 27). Again, there is a hearsay objection and motion to strike. Argue the objection. [MacIntyre]

188. Kerry Easterfield testifies for the defendant. She seeks to testify that she told her husband on the morning of July 17 that she remembered "thinking about the brooch when I was in the library for a few moments the night before, and how he had given it to me for our wedding, and that I was almost positive I went upstairs to our bedroom, took it off and put it on my dresser" (page 35). Objection? [MacIntyre]

189. Assume that Brooke Thompson's neighbor, John Samaritan, rushed over to her house after he heard the gunshot. Brooke told him that Joe had shot her with a revolver. Samaritan accompanied Leslie to the hospital in the ambulance. When the paramedic asked him what happened, Samaritan said, "Her husband shot her with a revolver." Assume the paramedic is called to give other occurrence witness testimony and is asked what Samaritan told him. The objection is hearsay. Response? [Mitchell]

190. Defense in MacIntyre wants Ross Easterfield's desk calendar to be physically in evidence as an exhibit. For the defense, ask Easterfield precisely the questions that would serve as a foundation. For the plaintiff, be prepared to object based on the foundation laid.

191. Ross Easterfield's bank statement was obtained from him in discovery. He received it in the mail from the bank. Does the hearsay rule preclude its admission? [MacIntyre at 105–106.]

192. Argue the admissibility of the St. James Parish Schedule of Services. [MacIntyre at 77–78.]

193. Winsor testifies for the plaintiff. For the plaintiff, ask precisely the questions necessary to admit the document at pages 115–116. For the defendant, make any objections, requests, and/or argument based on that foundation. [MacIntyre]

194. Defense in MacIntyre offers the (previously authenticated) loan application Jesse made to Fidelity (page 85). (See page 22 for Jesse's explanation.) Plaintiff objects on hearsay and relevancy grounds. Argue the objection.

195. An investigator for the plaintiff has reviewed all of the Nita City Athletic Club personnel records for the last twenty years. Over that period the club has employed approximately 1,214 persons. The investigator has subpoenaed the criminal records of each of those persons from the Nita City police. Eighteen of those employees were found to have had non-traffic criminal convictions by the time they were hired. Consider what the plaintiff would have to do to present the above information in a summary exhibit. [MacIntyre]

196. Marlow has testified to calling Reverend Taylor the day Jesse applied for the job at the club. The Rectory has a phonogram system on which a secretary records incoming calls. The secretary would testify that, at the time of calls, she asks the name of each person who calls and records the call even if there is no message. The phonogram has no record of a call from Marlow on July 22. In rebuttal, plaintiff seeks to admit the phonogram records from July 22 showing no call from Marlow. Argue the objection. [MacIntyre]

197. Plaintiff offers the Nita Transit Authority Bus Schedule [MacIntyre at 75–76]. Respond to the hearsay objection.

198. Reverend Taylor is testifying. Plaintiff wishes to show that Jesse's attorney in the Holman matter was incompetent or worse. Taylor seeks to testify to reading the Memorandum Opinion of the Attorney Registration and Discipline Commission disbarring him for lack of zealous representation and that the Commission found that he had represented 600 criminal defendants between 1994 and 2001 and never tried a single one of their cases. All cases ended in plea bargains. Argue the objection. [MacIntyre]

199. Argue the admissibility of the certified copy of the Crime Lab Report. [Mitchell at 79–80.]

200. Argue the admissibility of the Coroner's Report. [Mitchell at 81.]

201. Argue the admissibility of the copy of the Section Map of Nita City containing annotations by the Deputy City Engineer. [Mitchell at 59–61.]

202. Defense in MacIntyre seeks to introduce a certified copy of Jesse's theft conviction to impeach her. Plaintiff objects on hearsay grounds. For the defense, respond.

203. Plaintiff in MacIntyre offers the certified copy of the Order of the Nita Prisoner Review Board (page 97). For the defense, state the objection. For the plaintiff, respond.

204. The cross-examination of Mrs. Easterfield suggested that she might have wanted to dispose of the brooch herself for cash. She indignantly protested that it was a beloved wedding gift and she would never part with it. She testifies further that she was married on June 7, 1982. Ross Easterfield has authenticated the Bill of Sale from Carol's as the Bill of Sale for the brooch. In rebuttal plaintiff seeks to introduce the Bill of Sale. Defense objects on hearsay grounds. Respond to the objection. [MacIntyre]

205. Peter Steinfels is on the stand. He has testified that Jesse MacIntyre suffers from Borderline Personality Disorder and that this mental illness makes it likely that she will misunderstand and misdescribe events occurring around her and that she will lie whenever it serves her interests. You know that you will call a psychiatrist, Greta Van Klimvitz, who will testify to the authoritativeness of Karl Kasper's text, General Psychopathology (1987). The latter contains the following sentences at page 40, "There is absolutely no evidence of any connection between diagnosed borderline personality disorder and misperception or prevarication. Indeed, borderlines are typically concrete and precise in their descriptions and honest even when social conventions would counsel some deception (socially acceptable 'white lies,' for example)." [MacIntyre]

On cross-examination, Steinfels is asked whether he considers Kasper's work authoritative in the field. Steinfels says it is an eccentric work and no reputable psychiatrist would rely on it. [*MacIntyre*]

For the cross-examiner, address the court in the manner that will allow you to invoke Kasper's opinion. Now do what you would do with the opinion?

Assume that you know that Steinfels will dismiss Kasper's work. Could you simply offer this segment of Kasper's text in your case in chief without bothering to ask Steinfels about it?

206. Mrs. Easterfield has testified. Plaintiff recalls Kelly Emerson to testify that Mrs. Easterfield's reputation for truthfulness is bad. For the plaintiff, respond to the hearsay objection. [*MacIntyre*]

207. The objection is sustained. Plaintiff wishes to call a law school classmate of Jesse's lawyer who will testify that Jesse's lawyer had a reputation at the local bar association for incompetence. Argue the objection. [*MacIntyre*]

208. Plaintiff calls his present cook, Vern Kosko, to testify that Jesse's general reputation in the community was not good: "She was viewed as a criminal type . . . you know what I mean." Argue the objection. [*MacIntyre*]

209. Consider the admissibility of Winsor's testimony concerning the rumors about Easterfield's business practices in the small Ohio city he worked in before he came to Nita (page 56). [*MacIntyre*]

210. Plaintiff in *MacIntyre* calls Frank Holman. He refuses to testify on the grounds that he might tend to incriminate himself. Plaintiff then seeks to introduce Holman's statement to the court (page 31). Argue the objection.

211. Plaintiff in *MacIntyre* reports to the court that Holman is in prison in San Diego and offers the statement on page 80. For the defense, respond.

212. Alice Adams lives in California. Defense seeks to offer the first question and the first answer from her deposition transcript (whose authenticity has been stipulated) recounted on page 82. Argue the hearsay objection. [*MacIntyre*]

213. The hearsay objection is overruled. For the plaintiff, urge the admission of the remaining questions and answers in the deposition. [*MacIntyre*]

214. Brooke Thompson testifies that her stepdaughter turned around on the porch of their home, looked out at the white car that had just pulled up, and then cried out, "'Oh no . . . oh no, Joe!' or something like that" (page 10). For the defense, argue admissibility. For the prosecution, respond. [*Mitchell*]

215. Plaintiff in *MacIntyre* has been unable to procure the attendance of Frank Holman at trial by subpoena. Plaintiff seeks to offer (through the court reporter) Holman's statement to the court (page 80). Argue the hearsay objection.

216. On the issue of damages, Jesse testifies that Marlow told her that tips at the club averaged $50 to $75 per week (page 15). Defense moves to strike on hearsay grounds. Argue the objection. [*MacIntyre*]

217. Marlow testifies for the defense. On cross-examination, Marlow is asked what the tips for hat check attendants averaged. Marlow says that they averaged $50 to $75 per week. Marlow is then asked how she knows that. She says that she knows it because previous hat check attendants told her that in the course of their negotiations on their base pay. She says that she always told them that it was only fair that she take into account their tips in determining their base pay. Defense now moves to strike the testimony. Argue the motion for the plaintiff. Oppose the motion for the defense. [*MacIntyre*]

218. Reverend Taylor is testifying for the plaintiff. Taylor seeks to testify that Jesse said that Marlow had said that a positive recommendation from Taylor would assure her the job at the club, regardless of anything else in her background (page 46). Argue the hearsay objection. [*MacIntyre*]

219. Kelly Emerson testifies for the plaintiff. On cross-examination the defense seeks to elicit the following testimony (page 49): [*MacIntyre*]

> I recall that a cook who worked at the Easterfields for a few months, Martha Washington, told me that when Jesse had first seen the brooch, she had exclaimed, "My God, that's beautiful. I wish I had something half that gorgeous."

> I myself recall that Jesse told me once how "high class" the brooch was.
> I think she had a bit of a fixation on it.

Argue the objections to each of the sentences above.

220. Reverend Taylor is testifying for the plaintiff. Taylor seeks to testify that Jesse said that she had learned from Marlow that Ross Easterfield accused her of stealing the brooch (page 47). Argue the hearsay objection. [*MacIntyre*]

221. Jesse testifies for plaintiff (page 17): "I told Marlow then that, if Mr. Easterfield had accused me of theft while I was employed by him this was a lie. I told her that I had never stolen anything from the Easterfields. When I said this, Marlow looked down at the floor and was just silent." Argue admissibility of each of the first two sentences. [*MacIntyre*]

222. Easterfield is permitted to testify to his alleged conversation with Mr. Zanoni (page 28). Plaintiff, in rebuttal, seeks to introduce the authenticated deposition transcript of Maria Zanoni (page 107). Argue the objection. [*MacIntyre*]

223. Plaintiff in *MacIntyre* wishes to introduce Mike Stiko's sworn statement on page 95. Argue the objection.

224. Marlow has testified for the defense. Marlow has testified that the club has always had a firm policy against the hiring of ex-convicts and that they never actually decided to hire Jesse before Marlow's conversation with Easterfield. In rebuttal, plaintiff offers to play the videotaped interview with Martha Van Kirk (page 125). Argue the objection. [*MacIntyre*]

PRIVILEGES

225. Ross Easterfield's real estate practices have led the local United States Attorney to prosecute him under the federal criminal RICO statute. Mr. Easterfield wants to prevent Mrs. Easterfield from testifying in the prosecution case, fearing that she is a "loose cannon." She is deeply offended at the prosecution of her husband and says she will not "take the Fifth." She wants to testify. The Easterfields cannot resolve their disagreement. May Ross Easterfield prevent his wife from testifying if the federal prosecutor calls her? [MacIntyre]

226. Easterfield and his attorneys have agreed that Mrs. Easterfield's testimony will, on balance, hurt Easterfield's cause. They wish to keep her from testifying if she is called as an adverse witness by the plaintiff and assert the marital testimonial incompetency by making a motion in limine. Assume this case is being tried in federal court and that the cause of action is a new federal statutory claim for civil penalties for defamation by employers. Consider whether the motion should be granted. Assume that this is a diversity action filed by Jesse after moving to California from Nita. Everyone agrees that the Nita law of defamation provides the rule of decision. What issues are implicated in deciding the motion? [MacIntyre]

227. The federal prosecution fails. The county prosecutor is embarrassed that the federal prosecutor filed his case before she did and files her own criminal case against Easterfield, based on a transaction not involved in the federal prosecution. Again, Easterfield does not want his wife to testify. If the state of Nita follows the rule in most state jurisdictions, what is the likely result? [MacIntyre]

228. The defense in *Mitchell* makes a motion in limine, seeking the exclusion of Leslie Thompson's exclamation, "Oh no . . . Oh no, Joe!" The defense does not at this point urge hearsay objections, but seeks to exclude the statement on grounds of the "marital testimonial incompetency." For the prosecution, respond to the motion.

229. The defense in *Mitchell* objects to the introduction of the letter on page 73 on the grounds of the privilege for marital communications. Argue the objection. Assume that Leslie and Joe were not separated, but that Leslie was merely staying with Brooke while her stepmother was recovering from surgery. Would the analysis be any different?

230. Assume that the plaintiff theory of the case relies in part on proving that the Easterfields' marriage was fragile. Argue the admissibility, if offered by the plaintiff through Kelly Emerson, of the heated exchange between the Easterfields on page 54. Now assume that the exchange took place at a time when the Easterfields reasonably believed that they were the only people in the house. Is the conversation admissible? [MacIntyre]

231. The plaintiff's theory of the case in *MacIntyre* is that, on July 17, the Easterfields were engaged in a knowing insurance fraud scheme to recover for the brooch which they themselves hid. The theory suggests that the Easterfields later decided that they did not want a thorough investigation and then placed the brooch where Emerson would find it. May the plaintiff question Mrs. Easterfield about conversations she may have had with her husband in which they allegedly planned the scheme? Argue the issue.

232. A month before her death Leslie was especially concerned about the threat of violence that Joe posed. She distrusted her judgment, however, about the seriousness of the danger. She asked her friend, Quinn Washington, to listen in on the other line of the telephone when she returned a call from Joe to her at the Thompson residence. During the phone conversation, Joe said these words: "I'm telling you straight out. I will kill you if you do not return to me." Argue the admissibility, through Washington, of the conversation. [Mitchell]

233. Jesse MacIntyre calls Mrs. Easterfield as an adverse witness. She wishes to ask Mrs. Easterfield the identical questions and get the identical answers contained in her deposition on pages 34–35. Argue the admissibility of the questions and answers put to Mrs. Easterfield before the first objection and instruction not to answer. Consider Federal Rule of Civil Procedure 32(b) and 32(d)(3) for purposes of making this argument. Consider Rule 104 issues based on the later deposition testimony concerning Emerson (page 80). [MacIntyre]

234. Joe Mitchell knows that Brooke Thompson sees a psychiatrist every two weeks. Mitchell recently received a phone call at the jail from the psychiatrist's office manager of many years, Joyce Bennington. She seemed very upset and said that she had seen the psychiatrist's notes for her last few sessions with Brooke Thompson. They seemed to indicate that the psychiatrist was helping Thompson "work through" her feelings of guilt for the killing of her stepdaughter. She said that she had always been loyal to her employer but that she couldn't "just idly stand by the blood of my neighbor." Argue the question of whether Mitchell may call the psychiatrist, subpoena the notes, or call the office manager to testify to the contents of the notes. [Mitchell]

235. The state is cross-examining Joe Mitchell. The State's Attorney asks Joe about the clothes he was wearing when he returned to his room on September 10. Joe's lawyer objects, "Objection, Your Honor, that topic was the subject of a confidential attorney-client communication from Mr. Mitchell to myself and I object on the basis of the attorney-client privilege." For the prosecution, respond. [Mitchell]

236. Joe Mitchell's lawyers received a call yesterday from Donald Weston. Weston is a semi-retired attorney at a major law firm. Weston said that he was consulted by a client last week and felt obliged to share with you the contents of that conversation. (He told you that he doesn't "give a damn" whether what he tells you is within the requirements of the attorney-client privilege or not.) His client is a prominent local psychiatrist who is treating Brooke Thompson. The psychiatrist told Weston that she was helping Brooke Thompson "work through" her feelings of guilt about her killing of her stepdaughter and wanted to know whether she had any legal exposure for failing to come forward with this information in order to save Mitchell. The psychiatrist told him that whether or not she had exposure she would never reveal what a patient told her, except, of course, within a conversation which was itself privileged such as his conversation with her attorney. Weston was unable to convince her to come forward. [Mitchell]

What issues are implicated in the question of whether Mitchell's attorneys may call and question the psychiatrist about what Brooke Thompson told her? May you call Weston himself (1) in lieu of calling the psychiatrist, or (2) in order to impeach the psychiatrist, should she be required to testify and deny that Thompson admitted the killing? [Mitchell]

237. Joe called his attorney at home at 10:15 P.M. on September 10. The attorney was out and his baby sitter took a message to call Joe at Mrs. Porter's. May the baby sitter be called simply to testify to Joe's attempt to talk with his lawyer? Argue the issue. [Mitchell]

238. You represent Joe Mitchell, who is currently out on bail. He left your office at 2:30 P.M. on March 23. At 2:40 P.M., there was a hit-and-run accident a block away by a driver who resembled Mitchell. You have been subpoenaed to appear at a grand jury to testify as to whether Joe came to your office that day and the time at which he left. Is that information privileged? [Mitchell]

239.   Easterfield tells his lawyer to tell Jesse MacIntyre that he is sorry that he accused her in front of his wife in the library, to the ABC Employment Agency, and to Marlow. The next morning he calls his lawyer and tells him to forget it. [MacIntyre]

   Easterfield's lawyer receives the following Interrogatory:

   "Identify the time, place, and contents of all statements not privileged made by Ross Easterfield in which he describes in any way any statements made to the ABC Employment Agency and/or to Lee Marlow."

   Must Easterfield's lawyer identify the statement described in the first paragraph?

240.   Joe and his lawyer from his first trial were literally at one another's throats, with Joe physically attacking his attorney in anger over his "incompetence." The attack took place in the hallway outside one of the courtrooms. [Mitchell]

   Assume that Joe introduced opinion evidence in his second trial as to his character for peacefulness. May his first lawyer voluntarily come forward and offer to testify to his opinion as to Joe's violent character? May the state cross-examine Joe's character witness as to whether he took account of Joe's attacking his lawyer? May the state subpoena Joe's former lawyer to testify to (1) the attack, or (2) his (understandably quite low) opinion of Joe's peacefulness? [Mitchell]

241.   Reverend Taylor accompanied Jesse on her first visit to Jesse's lawyer and sat in on the first interview. Jesse says that Taylor "gave her the strength" to pursue her rights and that she could not have given the interview without him. The federal common law interpreted in light of reason and experience recognizes both a religious counselor and an attorney-client privilege. Argue the issue of the privileged nature of Jesse's statements and her attorney's statements in the initial interview. [MacIntyre]

242.   Jo Peterson is a member of your firm. She is the wife of Easterfield's second cousin and a good social friend of Easterfield's. She has always done Easterfield's personal tax returns. Peterson tells you after a few drinks that Easterfield came to her three days before his wife's brooch disappeared and asked for advice. Easterfield wanted to know whether insurance benefits for a "stolen" piece of jewelry were taxable. He also wanted to know whether any money made from the black market sale of a piece of jewelry falsely claimed to be stolen would be taxable. (Easterfield said that he didn't want to "screw around with the Feds.") Peterson answered those questions and told him to choose a very reliable fence for the resale. [MacIntyre]

   What ethical and evidentiary considerations does Peterson's revelation present?

243.   Assume that the MacIntyre case is a bench trial. Jesse's lawyer asserts that she believes that Easterfield had, with his lawyer's help, engaged in a knowing insurance fraud involving the brooch, and seeks to call Easterfield's trial counsel as a witness to show that.

   Assume you are Easterfield's counsel. You know that, in fact, Easterfield did ask a member of your firm about fencing the brooch, but that this firm member told him that this was wrong, that in no circumstances would she provide any advice on how to go about doing that, and Easterfield was making a big mistake if he went forward.

   Jesse's lawyer asks to inquire into the conversation between Easterfield and your firm member in order to determine whether that conversation was outside the privilege.

   For Easterfield and your firm, respond.

244. Easterfield asks his lawyer to draw up leases of six months duration for one of his developments. You know that the local ordinance makes it a misdemeanor for a landlord to offer written leases of less than a year's duration. He does not seem to know that. Are Easterfield's communications with you on this subject privileged? [MacIntyre]

245. Assume that Officer Slyviak, when arriving at Joe Mitchell's room, saw on a table a half-written letter addressed to Mitchell's lawyer, which read: [Mitchell]

> Dear Attorney Pauline:
>
> I have done something terrible and I need your help. I shot and . . .

At this point the letter leaves off. Assume that as Slyviak moved toward the letter Joe said, (1) "That's not for your eyes!" (2) "Search anywhere you want. I have nothing to hide!" or (3) nothing. Under each of the three scenarios, is the letter privileged?

246. The prosecution wants to call the attorney who drew Leslie's will to testify to the virulence of Joe's hatred of Brooke Thompson exhibited by his statements in the interview he conducted with both Leslie and Joe present before she drafted the will. Argue the privilege question. [Mitchell]

247. Joe Mitchell's attorney received a telephone call three weeks ago. The person who called identified himself as Phil Jones and said that he was at the bar with Joe on the night of September 10. He said that he had read about Joe's situation in the paper and was sympathetic to Joe's plight. However, he told Joe's lawyer that he had some bad news. According to him, Joe said to him at the bar, "I have a problem and, by God, I am going to solve it tonight." Jones tells Mitchell's attorney that he intended to talk to the prosecutor about this. May Joe's attorney discourage Jones from speaking to the prosecutor? May or must Joe's attorney reveal the contents of the conversation to the prosecutor? [Mitchell]

A month later the prosecutor calls and tells Mitchell's lawyer that he received a phone call from a man who refused to identify himself who described the conversation recounted above. The prosecutor wishes to call the defense lawyer to testify to the identity of the person in the bar and to the contents of the conversation. Joe's statement is an admission of a party opponent and so not hearsay. If you can circumstantially authenticate the phone conversation and identify a hearsay exception for Jones' statement, may the prosecution call the defense attorney?

248. During the Easterfield trial Jesse's lawyer inquires into any conversations Marlow may have had with lawyers. Marlow responds that she had conversations with a lawyer at the same firm that represents Easterfield, and that she, Marlow, had gone to this lawyer for legal advice concerning her participation in this case. Marlow testifies that she had, in fact, received legal advice from this attorney. Jesse's lawyer asks her to tell the court the contents of the conversation. Any response to the privilege objections?

The judge overrules the objection. The testimony proves devastating to Easterfield's case. May Easterfield seek reversal based on an erroneous admission of the evidence?

249. You are Brooke Thompson's lawyer. Sadly, Brooke stepped in front of the 5:10 train three weeks ago in what the police thought was a suicide committed in grief over the death of her stepdaughter. You know different. She had confessed to you that she had killed Leslie herself but could not bear the anxiety over being discovered. The state intends to proceed with Joe's prosecution. (They have obtained a pretrial ruling admitting Brooke's identification of Joe as a statement of identification of a person.) [Mitchell]]

Assume that you resolved your own ethical question in favor of informing Joe's attorney what you knew. Joe calls you as a witness.

For the state, make any objection. For the defense, respond.

250. Joe Mitchell wishes to call Frank Cato, a prominent criminal defense lawyer, who successfully represented Jerry Young in his criminal trials, to question him about anything Young may have told Cato concerning his actions on September 10. Assume that no one has seen Young for six months and, given the level of violence among his "business" associates, police think that he is dead. Argue the privilege issue. [*Mitchell*]

251. Mitchell calls Cato. Cato testifies, "Yes, I did have a conversation with Young concerning his whereabouts on September 10, but that is all I will say about the matter." By saying that much, has Cato waived the privilege? The judge finds that the privilege does not apply after making a preliminary finding that Young is dead, saying on the record that "I can't find that it's more probably true than not that he's dead, but there is evidence of Young's death sufficient to support a finding." The court orders Cato to testify further. Cato is as certain as he can be that the judge is wrong on the law. May he testify to Young's conversation? Must he testify to Young's conversation? If he does, has he waived the attorney-client privilege? [*Mitchell*]

He refuses to testify. What should the judge do? What should the defense do? What should Cato do?

252. Reverend Taylor testifies to Marlow's prior inconsistent statement described in Problem 125. Instead of calling Mrs. Easterfield, defendant wishes to call the partner in the law firm that advises the club on its corporate matters who will testify to a conversation with Marlow well before the MacIntyre matter arose in which Marlow asked the lawyer about the legality of a policy that excluded the hiring of ex-convicts. The partner advised her that such a policy was legal. Marlow then told him that they would follow such a policy. They then discussed the fact that the club had no Jewish, Catholic, or Black members. The partner advised Marlow that any policy of exclusion on religious grounds would violate the Nita statute. The law firm that serves as the club's legal advisor is the same firm that is representing Easterfield in the defense of MacIntyre's slander case. What issues are implicated in this situation? [*MacIntyre*]

253. Jesse asserts religious counselor privilege to protect the letter on page 91. Argue the issue. [*MacIntyre*]

254. Jesse asks Reverend Taylor concerning the conversation with Ross Easterfield on page 47. Easterfield asserts religious counselor privilege. Argue the motion. [*MacIntyre*]

LAY OPINION TESTIMONY

You should be prepared to argue whether each of the following is permissible testimony under Rules 602 and 701.

255. Quinn Washington (page 42): "Joe seemed angry, especially when he spoke of Mrs. Thompson, and also nervous." [Mitchell]

256. Pat Slyviak (page 16): "He [Mitchell] got very excited and said that 1751 Madison was not her home . . ." [Mitchell]

257. Quinn Washington (page 42): "She [Leslie] said she had received a letter from him that day and that he made terrible threats against her and her mother in the letter. She seemed to be frightened of Joe." [Ignore, for the present, the hearsay problem of Quinn's reporting what Leslie said.] [Mitchell]

258. Pat Slyviak (page 16): "As I exited our room I saw Mitchell walking very fast toward the front door of the station. He was looking around furtively like he was trying to sneak out. This was before we had told him he was under arrest. I'm sure he was making a run for it: you have a sense about these things after being on the street as long as I have." [Mitchell]

259. Jesse MacIntyre (page 13): "From his words and appearance, I felt that he was accusing me of stealing the brooch. I couldn't believe what was happening and I was terribly hurt." [MacIntyre]

260. Jesse MacIntyre: "Mr. Easterfield's country club is posh and lavish. The club is exclusive. It is only for the rich. The Easterfields treated me coldly. They always looked down on me. Mr. Easterfield was stiff and aloof. Mrs. Easterfield was careless about her jewelry." [MacIntyre]

261. Brooke Thompson (page 8): "This man had a violent temper." [Mitchell]

262. Brooke Thompson (pages 8–9): "Then he said to me: 'You are an evil person. You turned Leslie against me. You broke up this marriage, and I'll see that you pay for this. You'll be to blame for whatever happens now.' I cannot swear to the exact words used that night, but I do remember the substance of what each said." [Mitchell]

263. Pat Slyviak (page 15): "I told him that we appreciated his cooperation. Mitchell acted voluntarily and on his own at all times. We never arrested him or demanded that he come to headquarters with us. He volunteered to do that." [Mitchell]

264. Pat Slyviak (pages 13–14): "I recognized the bullet on the porch as a .38. On examining the door and doorway, I found a mark on the door post where the bullet might have struck and then dropped to the step where I picked it up. It might have passed through the victim's body and then struck the door post. Or it might have been dislodged from the victim's body by the impact of the fall." [Mitchell]

265. Quinn Washington (page 41): "I'm sure if Mrs. Thompson objected to Leslie's marrying Joe, she did this out of a sense of conscience and duty to warn Leslie and to advise her for her own good." [Mitchell]

266. Chris Ravenna (page 53): "I think she [Brooke Thompson] had such a hatred of Joe that, in her highly emotional state, she wanted to see Joe kill his wife. Her identification springs from her emotional bias toward him. She saw what her emotions wanted her to see." [Mitchell]

267. Jesse MacIntyre (page 15): "His words were so cutting and made me feel like I was the scum of the earth. I'll never forget what he said—he hurt me terribly then, and he's continuing to do it by making sure that I can't get a good job. He took away my self-respect and then he wouldn't even let me make a living. His words made me feel lower than I ever have since I left prison. It made me feel like when I was paraded in front of ordinary people in handcuffs . . . or when I had to submit to strip searches when returning from court to the prison." [MacIntyre]

268. Jesse MacIntyre (page 16): "When I talked to Marlow that day in the club, it looked like I would get the job for sure." [MacIntyre]

269. Jesse MacIntyre (page 18): "I've tried to get other jobs, at least ten or twenty, and nobody will hire me with Mr. Easterfield's bad character reference." [MacIntyre]

270. Pat Slyviak (page 16): "Yes, I did tell Bradley that my gut told me that Mitchell didn't do it. Frankly, I suspected the old lady but that's not the way the momentum of the investigation went and Bradley was calling the shots by then. I just think Mitchell was sincere about his having nothing to hide." [Mitchell]

271. Jesse MacIntyre (page 17): "Reverend Taylor became very angry. He's such a mild fellow. I've never seen him that angry before. 'I've always thought that Easterfield was a self-centered bas—, person. We'd have been better off if he hadn't gotten involved in this program at all. It's pure, thoughtless cruelty. A child pulling the wings off a butterfly. I'm just so sorry, Jesse.'" [Ignore the hearsay problem for now and consider only the admissibility of the various opinions expressed by MacIntyre and Taylor.] [MacIntyre]

EXPERT TESTIMONY

272. Assume the bullet Slyviak recovered on the porch of the Thompson home was lost before it could be analyzed. Prosecution seeks to have Slyviak testify that the bullet was a .38 caliber bullet as on pages 13–14 of the file. Argue the issue. [Mitchell]

273. On the issue of damages, plaintiff seeks to elicit an opinion from Reverend Taylor that Easterfield's accusations were likely to be particularly painful for Jesse and were likely to make the process of her reintegration into society much more arduous. Plaintiff relies on Taylor's graduate degree in criminology and experience with former convicts. Argue the admissibility of the opinion. [MacIntyre]

274. Joe Mitchell seeks to call as an expert witness a psychologist who will (1) testify generally about the unreliability of eye witness testimony; will opine specifically that (2) Brooke Thompson's identification of Leslie's killer took place under circumstances that contained a particularly serious danger of error; and that (3) Brooke misidentified Leslie's killer. What would Joe have to establish in order to present the testimony? Which portions of the proposed testimony are most likely to be accepted? [Mitchell]

275. Joe Mitchell protested his innocence after he was arrested and offered to take a polygraph test. The detectives at the station obliged him and the test results were that he was telling the truth when he denied killing his wife. Joe wants to offer the results of the test. Whom should Joe call and how should he go about trying to admit the results? Is he likely to fare any better under the Daubert test than under the Frye test? [Mitchell]

276. The prosecution in Mitchell seeks to offer general evidence presented by a psychologist about a "stalker syndrome." The characteristics of the syndrome match Joe's behavior, but the psychologist would not draw any conclusions about this specific case. What would the proponent have to establish in order to admit the testimony? Would it matter that the psychologist testified further than Joe's behavior closely matched the characteristics of the syndrome? [Mitchell]

277. Taylor opines that Easterfield has done lasting psychological damage to Jesse and emphasizes the "devastating" effect of a "second" false accusation by someone in authority. Taylor is asked what he relied on in reaching this judgment. He testifies that he relied in part on the Order of the Prisoner Review Board (page 97), the Memorandum Opinion of the Attorney Registration and Discipline Commission disbarring Jesse's lawyer, and Mike Stiko's statement (page 95). The court has previously ruled that each of those is inadmissible under Rules 802 and 403 to show Jesse's actual innocence. For the plaintiff, lay the foundation to allow Taylor to describe that evidence. Argue admissibility. [MacIntyre]

278. Easterfield testifies that he was motivated by "pure Christian charity" in giving a job to Jesse and in all his dealings with her. After he describes his education and experience, Reverend Taylor is asked whether he has an opinion to the degree of certainty prevailing in the field of spiritual direction, as to (1) Easterfield's motivation in his dealings with Jesse, and (2) as to Easterfield's character for truthfulness. He seeks to share the opinion expressed on pages 43–44. Argue the objection. [MacIntyre]

279. Defense in MacIntyre calls Dr. Peter Steinfels (pages 117–118). After he testifies to his qualifications and the steps he took to form any opinion he has reached, the defense asks this question, "Doctor, were you able to reach a psychiatric diagnosis of Jesse MacIntyre?" Steinfels testifies that he has been able to reach a diagnosis. Defense then asks him what that diagnosis is. Argue the objections.

280.   Steinfels is permitted to explain the diagnosis described in the second paragraph of the letter (page 117). He is then asked whether he has an opinion, to the degree of certainty that prevails in the field of psychiatry, as to whether Jesse MacIntyre was lying when she was testifying in court. He replies that he has such an opinion and is asked to tell the jury his opinion. Argue the objection. [MacIntyre]

281.   Steinfels is then asked whether he has an opinion to the degree of certainty that prevails in the field of psychiatry as to whether Jesse accurately interpreted the events of July 17. He replies that he has such an opinion and is asked to tell the jury his opinion. Argue the objection. [MacIntyre]

282.   Steinfels is then asked whether he has an opinion to the degree of certainty that prevails in psychiatry as to whether Jesse attempted to steal the brooch. In fact, he believes that petty theft is a classic symptom of Borderline Personality Disorder and thus he has the opinion that Jesse tried to steal the brooch. He wishes so to testify. Argue the objection. [MacIntyre]

283.   After Steinfels gives his opinion as to Jesse's ability to interpret accurately the events of July 17, he is asked what he relied on in reaching his opinion. He replies that he relied on his observation of Jesse at her deposition and in court and on (1) the school record (page 121), (2) the uncharged shoplifting recounted by Jesse at page 18, and (3) the incident at the rectory in which the two twenty-dollar bills disappeared recounted at page 46. The court had previously ruled that those three pieces of evidence were inadmissible under, respectively, (1) Rule 802, (2) Rules 404, 403, and 609, and (3) Rule 104. For the defense, ask the foundation question(s) necessary to allow Steinfels to describe those three pieces of evidence. Argue the objection to Steinfels' describing the three pieces of evidence. [MacIntyre]

284.   Taylor testifies that he relied in part on the conversation he had with Easterfield, recounted on page 44, in reaching his opinion of Easterfield's character for truthfulness. He seeks to describe the conversation. Argue the objection. [MacIntyre]

JUDICIAL NOTICE

285. The court in *MacIntyre* takes judicial notice of the tightness of the job market for unskilled workers in Nita City, after the defendant presented the court with statistics from a current report of the Bureau of Labor Statistics showing the unemployment rate for unskilled workers to be 18 percent locally. The plaintiff objects that the numbers are not generally known and so are inappropriate to be judicially noticed. Ruling?

286. Assume that the plaintiff has a study conducted by two reputable economists at the University of Nita which criticized the methodology of the Bureau's study and concluded that the unemployment rate was only 8 percent. Assume further that the court has determined that the unemployment rate is relevant. What should the plaintiff do with the study? Under what conditions should the court take judicial notice of the unemployment rate? [*MacIntyre*]

287. Assume the court concludes that the Bureau's statistics are reliable and the study of the University economists is deeply flawed. It takes judicial notice. The plaintiff wishes to call the economists from the University to present their view of the unemployment rate. Should the court permit the contrary evidence? [*MacIntyre*]

288. The prosecution in *Mitchell* asks the court to take judicial notice that Marines receive training in firearms and that Joe Mitchell knew how to clean a gun quickly. Ruling?

289. Assume that the trial judge himself served in the Marines and knows that Marines receive training in the use of firearms. On that basis he is willing to take judicial notice. Permissible? [*Mitchell*]

290. Assume the trial judge is willing to take judicial notice that Marines receive training in the use of firearms. How should he instruct the jury on that question? [*Mitchell*]

291. Assume that it turns out to be necessary that the plaintiff in *MacIntyre* prove that the act of which Easterfield accused Jesse is a felony, something that requires that the brooch have a value of more than $1,000. Plaintiff rests without producing any evidence of the value of the brooch or of the criminal statute. The defense put on its case and moves for judgment as a matter of law at the end of all of the evidence, arguing that there is no evidence that the alleged act was a felony. What can the plaintiff do?

292. The court in *Mitchell* rules that Joe's aggravated assault incident is admissible under Rule 404(b) and that his acquittal does not preclude its admissibility in this case. The court takes judicial notice of the facts alleged in the indictment, concluding that he may notice "the contents of the documents in all the court files in this court system." Permissible?

CONCLUDING QUESTIONS

293.   Is the law of evidence sufficiently definite to control the trial judge's discretion in deciding evidentiary questions?

294.   Is the law of evidence sufficiently simple and clear that it can be used under the conditions that prevail in the trial courtroom?

295.   As it applied in the *Mitchell* case and in the *MacIntyre* case, did the law of evidence further "the end that the truth may be ascertained and proceedings justly determined" (Fed. R. Evid. 102) or would it have frustrated those goals?

Case One: Murder

State v. Mitchell

CONTENTS

STATE V. MITCHELL

INTRODUCTION

The Grand Jury has charged Joe Mitchell with first degree murder of his estranged wife, Leslie Thompson Mitchell, on September 10, 2002.

The State alleges that the defendant, Joe Mitchell, shot and killed his wife on the front porch of her stepmother's house at 1751 Madison in Nita City. An eyewitness, the deceased's stepmother, claims she saw the defendant drive up in his car along the curb in front of the house and fire a pistol shot that struck and killed Leslie Thompson Mitchell. The shooting occurred at approximately 10 P.M., and it was dark and raining.

The defendant Joe Mitchell has pleaded not guilty. He vigorously asserts his innocence and claims he was elsewhere at the time of his wife's death.

The case went to trial and ended in a hung jury. The State has elected to pursue the charges against Mr. Mitchell and to take the case to trial again. The testimony of the defendant, Joe Mitchell, from the first trial may not be used by the State during its case-in-chief, but may be used for impeachment if the defendant elects to take the stand at the second trial.

The applicable law is contained in the statutes and proposed jury instructions that are set forth at the end of the case file.

Grand Jury Indictment

IN THE CIRCUIT COURT
OF DARROW COUNTY, NITA

THE PEOPLE OF THE STATE OF NITA,	)	
	)	
Plaintiff,	)	
	)	
vs.	)	Case No. CR 2126
	)	INDICTMENT
JOE MITCHELL,	)	
	)	
Defendant.	)	

The Grand Jury in and for the County of Darrow, State of Nita, upon their oath and in the name and by the authority of the State of Nita, does hereby charge the following offense under the Criminal Code of the State of Nita:

That on September 10, 2002 at and within the County of Darrow in the State of Nita, Joe Mitchell committed the crime of

MURDER IN THE FIRST DEGREE

In violation of Section 18-3-102 of the Nita Criminal Code of 1974, as amended, in that he after deliberation and with the intent to cause the death of Leslie Thompson Mitchell or the death of another person with a deadly weapon, namely a gun, fired said gun and killed the deceased.

Contrary to the form of the Statute and against the peace and dignity of the people of the State of Nita.

A TRUE BILL:

George L. Pingree

Foreperson of the Grand Jury

Christopher Madden

Christopher Madden
District Attorney
Darrow County
State of Nita

SUMMARY OF BROOKE THOMPSON'S TESTIMONY AT FIRST TRIAL

BROOKE L. THOMPSON, called to testify as a witness for the State and having been duly sworn, testified as follows:

My name is Mrs. Brooke L. Thompson. I live at 1715 Madison Street, Nita City, Nita. I am forty-nine years old. I am a widow. My husband, Henry J. Thompson, died on October 1, 1990. We had no children. I married him in 1982. It was my first marriage and his second. His first wife died in 1980. They had one child, Leslie, who was six years old when I married him. Leslie was my stepdaughter. My husband had been a prominent lawyer in Nita City and then, during the first year we were married, he was appointed judge for the Circuit Court here in Nita City. He was a judge until he died.

When I married Mr. Thompson, he owned the house at 1751 Madison. I have lived there ever since. Of course, Leslie, my stepdaughter, lived there too until she married Joe Mitchell. In his will, my husband left all his property to me for my life, and then to Leslie when I die. The will provided that if Leslie were to die before me, I could dispose of the property as I see fit. The will also set up a trust fund for Leslie and me, with the Nita National Bank and Trust Company as trustee. I was also named Leslie's guardian until she was twenty-one. Her father's estate had given me an income of $25,000 a year on the average, mainly from stocks, bonds, and other investments. Because of poor investment decisions, my income sank to $18,000 per year in 2000. I had a life insurance policy on Leslie for $300,000. I was the beneficiary and the policy has paid off, double indemnity. So I received $600,000 on it, a couple months after she died. The double indemnity provision included homicides, unless, of course, the beneficiary was the killer.

I needed to supplement my income. So in 2001, on the recommendation of a real estate agent, I bought two apartment buildings in a rather unpleasant part of Nita City. All the residents were minorities: about twenty-four families, or what they call families. The real estate guy said I was in a good position to have a steady income because the judges knew I was a judge's widow and would be "attentive to my concerns" in any building court cases. Those cases are a big problem for landlords in those neighborhoods. I had a management company run the buildings, but I insisted on collecting the rents myself. You have to lay down the law to those people. The tenants I mean. So I went over there on the first of the month and collected the rents myself: no "ifs," "ands," or "buts." If they didn't have the rent right there in cash or money order I just phoned in the names and began eviction proceedings. Even if they came up with the money the day after, that was just too bad. It's important to maintain your credibility. I carried my .38 and it was a good thing, too. Once this guy came at me with a knife and I shot him right in the chest. Justifiable homicide, the police said. They also told me I was crazy to collect the rents in those buildings myself. But it hasn't stopped me.

Leslie and I lived comfortably on Madison Street. Although I never formally adopted her as my daughter, I always regarded her as mine. I loved her and took care of her upbringing as if she were my own child. She was so young, only four, when her own mother died that she could hardly remember her. She called me "mother," and our relations were always the intimate relations of mother and daughter. I was interested in her welfare and in her future happiness and always wanted to advise her as her mother.

I supported Leslie, sent her to school, and raised her. For high school, she went to Greenwood Academy, a private boarding school for girls in Jackson City, Nita. She graduated there in 1994. Then, because she didn't want to go to college, I sent her to the Katherine Gibbs Business School in New York in 1998. She came back to Nita City and got a job at the First State Bank. At the time of her death, she was private secretary to Mr. Robert Allen, the president, and making $1,500 a month. Of course, when she married she was also getting about $500 a month from the trust fund under the terms of the trust document. I receive that now. Leslie's trust contained the provision that I would maintain title to the principal until she was married for four continuous years. Thereafter she gained control of the principal to do with as she wished. She lived at home with me before her marriage and all the trust income came to me to use for our benefit as I saw fit. I charged her only market rates for room and board and for household expenses and never asked her to contribute to the maintenance of the house. I knew I could have charged more but I didn't want to—I loved her as my own child.

Late in 2000, she began to date Joe Mitchell. She brought him home one night and introduced him to me. When I asked him what he did for a living, he said he was a "writer" of short stories and TV scripts, especially detective stories and murder mysteries. He told me he hadn't sold or placed any of his writing yet. In fact, he hadn't made a cent out of it. But he said he was working as a part-time attendant at a gas station to support himself. He said he was then living at Mrs. Porter's Boarding House at 800 Fillmore Avenue in Nita City.

I didn't like this man, I admit. And as Leslie continued to date him, my dislike of him increased. I never approved of him. I didn't think he would make Leslie happy if she married him. I warned her against marrying him; I thought it was my duty to her as her mother. I told her I thought he was lazy and shiftless, and would ruin her life. I told her she should date other young men and that she would find she could do better than marrying this fellow. And as it has turned out, my judgment about him was right.

In the winter and spring of 2001, Mitchell came to our house many times. He dated Leslie three or four times a week. She told me that she had to pay for the gas for the car, and for the dinners and shows they went to, because "Joe was short of money." I guess she sort of pitied him.

In spite of all I did to prevent it, Leslie told me in the summer 2001 that she was going to marry Joe. I wondered how he expected to support a wife. From what I saw, he was going to live on her money. I told her many times I didn't think Joe was the man for her and that her own father and mother, if they were alive, wouldn't approve of this marriage. I disliked Joe the more I saw of him. From what I saw of him while he was dating Leslie, I thought he was a lazy good-for-nothing. (I admit I never had much use for "writers" anyway.) I was convinced that he'd break her heart. I thought it was my duty to warn her, as her own mother would have, that this man would never make her happy. I said he was lazy and was just after what little money she had or could expect. But she became defiant and said she was over twenty-one and they would be married, no matter what I or anyone else said. She said she loved Mitchell. This was the first disagreement we ever had. I was heartbroken. I would have done anything to prevent the marriage. If only I had, she would be alive today. But they went ahead and were married by a judge in Nita City on November 15, 2001. I wasn't present because I was ill. I did not want to do anything to suggest that I was approving of what they had done, so I sent no wedding gift.

After their marriage, Joe and Leslie lived in an apartment at 50 Jackson Street. Leslie continued to work at the Bank, but Joe quit his job at the gas station so he could stay home and devote all his time to his writing. Leslie was supporting them both. That's just what I expected would happen.

After they were married, they came to my house a couple of times a month, and I was always civil to Mitchell. He admitted he was not making a dime from his writing. They used to come in Mitchell's old white Pontiac. I don't know why Leslie didn't buy a new car. She could drive. She had money. And Mitchell would park the car at the curb right out in front of the house. I had seen it there many times before the night he shot Leslie.

Sometime in late July, 2002, Leslie came home one night in a taxi. She and Mitchell had separated after a bitter argument. She said she had tried to get Joe to give up his writing and take a job at the bank, but he had refused. I told her I was glad to have her back home without Joe and that she certainly could live with me.

After they separated, Leslie lived with me, and Mitchell went back to live at Porter's Boarding House on Fillmore Street. Mitchell would come to the house about twice a week and argue with Leslie to get her to come back to him. She always refused to unless he quit his writing and got a "real" job. I was always present during these arguments. I didn't trust him; I was also afraid that, with all his smooth talk, he would get her to go back. So, I insisted on being present. After all, it was my house and it was my duty to watch out for her welfare as her mother. I didn't want to see her heart broken any more than it was already. I told her not to go back to him and urged her to consider divorcing him.

Several times, I told Mitchell in very plain language what I, Leslie's mother, thought of it all. I told him he was lazy and a no-good to be living off his wife's income. We had bitter words in Leslie's presence, and a couple of time he threatened me. He said something about getting even with me because I had broken up his marriage to Leslie. (I am not sure of his exact words, but that's what he meant.) And several times, he threatened to hurt me or Leslie for ruining his marriage. This man had a violent temper. Sometimes he would try to coax Leslie to come back to him; other times he would fly into a rage.

One time in late August, 2002, he was at the house arguing with Leslie and got angry and rushed out of the house. He slammed the front door so hard I thought it was smashed. I ran to the door and opened it, and saw him run down the walk. I saw him get into his car at the curb across the street. I could see him clearly, even though it was about 9:30 P.M. and dark and raining. I watched him get into the car, and then, before he drove away, I saw him lean out of the car window and shake his fist at me. I was standing at the door, and I could easily see him and recognize his face—pale and sort of drawn.

As I said, he had an uncontrollable temper. When he came to see Leslie, he would shout and scream and say that she was "heartless" and "selfish," and he'd turn on me and accuse me of breaking up his marriage. A couple of times he swore and cursed at us. Then he'd storm out of house, but a few days later he'd be back, and the same things would happen again. Leslie would never leave the house with him. He would ask her to go with him "to talk things over" where I couldn't be around. She would never do it; she was afraid of him, she said. When she told me that, I told her never to leave the house with him. I was really afraid, then, that he would do some violence to her.

The last time he visited her before he killed her was on September 9, 2002. I was present. He didn't quarrel with her then, and he only stayed a little while between 9 and 10 P.M. He asked her to come back to him. He said: "Leslie, I'm asking you for the last time. You'd better listen to me now, if you know what's good for you." And she said: "Joe, I'm not coming back until you get a real job and quit this silly stuff about writing." He said: "You know I won't do that. I'm not giving up my work, even for you." She said: "Then this is the way it's got to be. I'm all through with you, Joe. I'm sorry it worked out like this." Then Joe said: "Well, I guess there's no use trying anymore, the way you feel. I won't bother you again. But don't forget this—I'm going to make you regret what you've done to me, if it's the last thing I ever do." Leslie then said, "Are you threatening me?" And he just looked at her real mean and angry. Then he said to me: "You are an evil person. You turned Leslie against me. You broke up this marriage, and I'll see that you pay for this. You'll be to blame for whatever happens now." I cannot swear to the exact words used that night, but I do remember the substance of what each said. Mitchell left the house at about 9:30 P.M. Just before he left the house, Joe went into the next room to get his jacket. While he was gone, I said to Leslie: "That man's a loser. I'd rather die than see you go back to him." At that moment he came back into the room and glowered at me. I think he heard me and it made me nervous.

Yes, I did own a Smith and Wesson .38 caliber revolver, which I bought a few years ago. It was registered. I kept it in the drawer of the night table next to my bed in my bedroom on the first floor of the house. I last saw it on the first or second day of September when I happened to be looking in the drawer. Joe had seen me put the gun in that drawer several times. I looked in the drawer a couple days after Leslie's death and it was empty. I didn't say anything to the police about its disappearance because I didn't think it was that important. I mentioned it only when the detective asked me if I owned a .38 and whether they could see it. That was about three weeks after Leslie's death. Frankly, I think Joe took it. The gun they recovered from Joe was not mine.

The next day, September 10, was Leslie's birthday. We had dinner at 6 P.M., and I gave her a ring for a present. At about 7 P.M., she left the house to go to a movie at the Palace Theater. She said she would be home around 10 P.M. She went alone. The theater is on Madison Street, about five blocks east, and she walked. It wasn't raining then, but she took an umbrella with her. It was a warm sort of fall evening. After she left, I went upstairs. I noticed that she had left the light on in her room—the front bedroom on the east side of the house. I went in to turn it off, and I noticed she had left her front door key on the night table. I also saw a piece of paper with some handwriting on it, but I didn't read it then. I decided to wait up for her, since she had forgotten her key.

At 7:30 P.M., the front doorbell rang. I went to answer and opened the door. It was raining then, but just a drizzle. I saw Mitchell standing on the porch. His car, that old white Pontiac, was parked at the south curb across the street—facing east. He asked for Leslie. I told him she had gone to the Palace Theater. He wanted to know when she'd be home, but I said I wasn't sure. I told him this because I didn't want him bothering her again after what he'd said last night—he had said that he wouldn't see her again. I was afraid for her. (I expect that he knew that Leslie almost always went to Heggarty's after seeing a show and almost always stayed until 12:30 A.M. or so. Heggarty's is one of those beer, burger, and ice cream places where neighborhood young people gather. Nice quiet place a couple blocks east of the Palace.) He spoke clearly and calmly. He had something under his right arm. It was wrapped in an old newspaper, and I couldn't tell what it was. He was wearing a sort of black or dark blue jacket.

Around 10 P.M., the doorbell rang again. I went and opened the door. (It opens in.) Leslie was there. She was standing on the porch about two or three feet from the step. The bracket lights at the door were on. I also had the lights on in the two front rooms on the first floor, and the window drapes were open.

Leslie had her back to the street. It was raining and dark—cloudy and no moonlight; there was no street light at the curb. But there was a street light at the south curb, across the street—thirty feet west of my front door.

Just then, I heard a car coming from the west and going east on Madison. There were no other cars on the street. I looked out and saw a white car—it was a Pontiac, same style and shape as Mitchell's. You see, I had the door open, and I looked out over Leslie's head as she stood down on the porch. The car came on fast, going east. All of a sudden, I heard the brakes squeal, and the car stopped out at the curb right in front of our house.

I suddenly realized this was Mitchell's car, and then Leslie cried out, "Oh no . . . oh no, Joe!" or something like that. It all happened in a matter of seconds. I saw a man lean out of the car window—put his head and shoulders out of the front window on the side facing us. He didn't have a hat on. I saw a small, dark object in his hand, like a gun or some kind of revolver. Then I heard a shot—only one shot—and I saw Leslie fall over backwards. She sort of spun around and fell on the porch, with her head towards the street and her feet in the direction of the door. The car sped away down the street, going east. I saw the taillights, but I couldn't see the license plate number. The motor or engine of this car was running through the whole thing—I could hear it all the time the car was stopped at the curb.

The first thought that flashed in my mind was that Joe had shot my daughter. I can positively swear that the face of the man who leaned out of the car was the face of Joe Mitchell and that it was his car. I saw his face. I saw the car. I know it was Joe Mitchell. As I told you, I had seen Mitchell hundreds of times before, right out there at the curb in that car—the white Pontiac. And I had seen him there only three hours before. I'm not identifying a stranger I had seen on the night of the murder for the first time; I had seen Mitchell hundreds of times. I knew him; he was no stranger. And I recognized the car, too.

Joe Mitchell is definitely the man I saw fire the shot from the car. I saw his face for a couple of seconds, but that was enough. Leslie was not blocking my view; she was only 5'2" and was standing down on the porch, while I was on the step at the door, about one foot up from the porch. Leslie had an umbrella and was just closing it, but she had it down when she turned and faced the street.

The two porch lights were on and there was light from the two front room windows. The car had its headlights on. No, there wasn't any moonlight. It was dark and raining—not hard, but there was rain splashing on the porch.

Some neighbors came running over right away and took me into the house. I was in shock. Some police came, but I don't know who called them. One of the police officers—I can't remember his name now—asked me some questions, and I told him pretty much what I've told you. I told him Leslie's husband was Joe Mitchell and he lived at Porter's Boarding House at 800 Fillmore Avenue. I said that Joe Mitchell had shot and killed his wife, Leslie, my stepdaughter. When the ambulance came to take Leslie to the hospital, I rode along, and a doctor there pronounced her dead on arrival. Then I had to identify Leslie's body to a man who said he was the coroner.

I'm sure it was 10 P.M. when Leslie came home from the Palace Theater, because just as she rang the doorbell, I heard my clock in the living room strike ten.

I only saw Mitchell out there in the car for a few seconds, but saw the car for a longer time. I saw it coming for about four to five seconds before it stopped. Then I saw Mitchell lean out of the window, take aim, and shoot Leslie.

September 10 was Leslie's birthday. When Mitchell came to the house earlier that night asking for Leslie, he didn't say anything to me about her birthday. The package he had under his arm was large enough to conceal a pistol or handgun. He didn't have a hat or an umbrella, and his jacket was soaked with rain.

One day while Mitchell and Leslie were dating, he came to the house to see Leslie, and he had a handgun with him. He said he had been out target shooting with the gun. He claimed he was an expert shot.

After Leslie's funeral, I was in her room, and I remembered the piece of paper I had seen on her night table the night she was shot. I looked at it then, and it was a letter to Leslie from Joe. I recognized the handwriting—it is Joe Mitchell's handwriting. I had seen him sign our guest book once, and I've seen his handwriting on his letters to Leslie. The handwriting on the letter is the same as the handwriting on the guest book and the letters.

I remember that on the morning of September 10, a letter came special delivery for Leslie. I recognized Mitchell's handwriting on the envelope. (No, I have never found this envelope.) I gave Leslie the letter when she came home. That night at dinner, she said the letter was from him. She never said what was in it, and we never discussed this.

There's one other thing maybe I should mention, although I'm sure there's no connection. My husband, Leslie's father, had been a judge for several years before his death. He handled some notorious criminal trials, and I'm sure along the way he made some enemies, particularly some of those he sentenced. I remember one case especially, because I read in the newspaper last August that the person my husband had sentenced had been paroled and was returning to Nita City. That case involved a fairly well-known businessman who was convicted for killing his business associate. There was a lot of publicity and talk of connections with gambling and organized crime. My husband was under a lot of pressure at the trial and sentencing. He said he had to do his duty and do what the law required. The jury found the man—I think his name is John

Bierman—guilty, and my husband sentenced him to something like twenty-five to thirty years in prison. This was all about fifteen years ago, just a couple of years before my husband died. At the sentencing, Bierman said he was innocent and had been framed by my husband and the prosecutor. My husband said in his remarks from the bench that he had talked the sentence over with "my wife" and was sure it was fair. I wish he had not said that. Bierman said he'd get revenge "on you and your god damn wife" for having his life ruined and losing his family in a frame-up if it was the last thing he did. My husband and I were concerned about this threat at the time, and I remember him talking about it for some time. I also remember that Bierman had a wife and three children, and that she divorced him and left town shortly after he went to prison. Naturally, he lost his business when he went to prison.

CERTIFICATION BY COURT REPORTER

The above is a true and accurate transcription of (Mrs.) Brooke Thompson's testimony at the trial of the case of *State vs. Mitchell*, which testimony was recorded stenographically by me at the time it was given.

Signed and Attested to by:

a Marie Lane

Certified Court Reporter

Summary of Officer Pat Slyviak's Testimony at First Trial

Pat Slyviak, called to testify on behalf of the State and having been duly sworn, testified as follows:

My name is Pat J. Slyviak. I am and have been for five years a member of the Nita City Police Department.

On the night of September 10, 2002, Officer Walter Johnson and I were on duty in Squad Car No. 15. We were on routine patrol, and at approximately 10:10 P.M., there was a radio call to investigate a shooting at 1751 Madison Street. We were in the area and radioed that we would cover the call. We proceeded directly to the Madison Street address with lights and sirens, arriving at about 10:15 P.M.

When we got there, I saw some people on the front porch of 1751 Madison Street. We found a young woman, in her mid-twenties, lying on the front porch in front of the door. Her feet were pointed toward the door, about six inches from the step; and her head was towards the street. There was a substantial amount of blood from a chest wound. I checked for signs of life. There was a slight pulse in the wrist and jugular vein; the victim was gurgling and gasping. Johnson went in the house to make sure the ambulance had been called and was on its way. We had a camera in the squad car, and I took several photographs.

Johnson came out on the porch and reported that the victim's mother, Mrs. Brooke Thompson, was inside and that she apparently had observed the shooting. Johnson stayed with the victim, and I went inside the house to talk with Mrs. Thompson. When I entered the house, Mrs. Thompson was being comforted by two other women; she was crying and half hysterical. I calmed her down, and she said that the woman who had been shot was her stepdaughter, Leslie. She said that the victim had been shot by a man who came up in a car out at the curb in front of the house. She said the man leaned out of the car window and fired a handgun at her daughter, who was standing on the porch. Mrs. Thompson said she recognized this man as her daughter's estranged husband, Joe Mitchell. She said that Mitchell and her daughter had separated about a month before, and that since then her daughter had been living with her at the Madison Street address. Mrs. Thompson gave me Mitchell's address at a boarding house run by a Mrs. Porter at 800 Fillmore Avenue.

As I was talking to Mrs. Thompson, the ambulance arrived. Johnson came in the house and informed me that the ambulance was taking the victim to Memorial Hospital. Mrs. Thompson went with the ambulance. I found out later that the victim was pronounced dead on arrival at the hospital. (I understand that the coroner, Dr. James Waddell, is now deceased.)

When I was leaving the house, I found a .38 bullet on the step in front of the door near where the victim's head had lain. I am familiar with .38 caliber bullets. In fact, my gun is a .38; I recognized the bullet on the porch as a .38. On examining the door and doorway, I found a mark on the door post where the bullet might have struck and then dropped to the step where I picked it up. It might have passed through the victim's body and then struck the door post. Or it might have been dislodged from the victim's body by the impact of the fall. I put my mark on the bullet and later that evening turned it over to the lab for analysis.

Johnson had radioed headquarters for instructions. We were advised to contact the victim's husband, Joe Mitchell, to inform him of the shooting and ask him to come to headquarters for further investigation. We then proceeded to the Fillmore address that Mrs. Thompson had given me for the victim's husband, Mr. Mitchell. We left 1751 Madison Street at about 10:30 P.M., and got to 800 Fillmore around 10:40 to 10:45 P.M. It was about a seven to ten-minute drive. 800 Fillmore is a boarding house. A woman came to the door and said she was Raleigh Porter, the owner of the house. We identified ourselves as police officers and asked to see Joe Mitchell. She said he was a boarder there and asked us in. When we arrived at the Fillmore address, I noticed a white, '92 Pontiac two-door sedan parked at the curb in front of the house. I asked Raleigh Porter if it was her car, and she said, no, that it was Joe Mitchell's.

Raleigh Porter told us that Mr. Mitchell had a room on the second floor, at the top of the stairs leading from the entrance hall. We went up and knocked at his door. A young man (twenty-five to thirty years old) opened the door. We were in uniform, and I identified myself by name and said we were Nita City Police officers. I asked him his name and he said he was Joe Mitchell. He asked what this was all about, and I told him that his wife had been shot that night around 10:00 P.M. I noticed that he turned pale. His face turned a chalky white, and I thought he was going to faint. He asked us to come into his room. He was shaken up, and I helped him to sit down in a chair. Right after he sat down in the chair, he said, "Leslie's been shot? Is she dead?" I told him that we did not know if she was dead or not, and that she had been taken to the hospital by ambulance.

I then asked Mitchell if he would come to headquarters with us to answer some questions, and he said he would, gladly. He said if we could give him some time to dress, he would go with us to headquarters and help us all he could. There was a very slight smell of beer on Joe's breath, but he certainly didn't seem impaired. After we arrested him we asked him to take a Breathalyzer test. We didn't have it analyzed for a month or so after the arrest, which is not ideal. It was found that Mitchell had a rather higher level of blood alcohol than we had anticipated, about 0.06, a little over half of the level (0.10) that would require a suspension of a driver's license.

We stayed in the room while Mitchell was getting ready. When we came, Mitchell was dressed in a bathrobe. There was a bed in the room. I noticed that it was made up. It had the bedspread and pillows on it and had not been slept in, as far as I could tell.

While he was dressing, and without any questions from us, Mitchell said that he had been reading when we came to the door. I did not observe any books, newspapers, or other reading material near any of the chairs or the bed. The room was not tidy when we entered—there was clothing thrown on the floor in a heap: trousers, socks, underwear, and a dark-colored jacket—dark blue or black. This jacket was soaking wet. It had been raining heavily off and on that night, and the jacket looked as if it had been just recently worn in a rainstorm. I don't think the radio was on, but I'm not sure.

Near this jacket I saw a revolver. I recognized it as a .38. I looked towards it and sort of moved towards it. But then Mitchell, who was putting a shirt on, suddenly jumped in front of me and grabbed the gun. After he held it for a minute or so, he looked at me and handed it to me. He said: "This is mine. I bought it when I was in the service—Marines. I use it for target practice." He also told us that he was a writer of short stories and TV scripts, mostly crime and murder mystery stories. He said that he had to know all about guns so that he could write his stories, which involved guns and other weapons. He told me he had nothing to hide when he handed the gun to me. I examined the gun, broke it, and found no cartridges in it. It looked as if it had been cleaned recently. I told Mitchell that I would have to take the gun with me to headquarters. He said, "Okay, take it; I've got nothing to hide." Then he picked up the wet jacket and handed it to me. I looked at it and told him that I would have to take the jacket also. And he said, "Sure, go ahead."

Mitchell then went back to finish dressing. Several times while he was dressing, he said: "I have nothing to hide. I want to cooperate with you all the way. I'll be glad to go with you to police headquarters and to help in any way I can." I told him that we appreciated his cooperation. Mitchell acted voluntarily and on his own at all times. We never arrested him or demanded that he come to headquarters with us. He volunteered to do that. And we never asked him any questions. He spoke to us while he was dressing, but it was always at his own initiative.

As Mitchell was dressing, I noticed that he did not use any of the clothing on the floor. He got dry clothing from a clothes closet. I saw that the trousers on the floor were soaking wet with rain and the shoes were muddy and wet. He did not put those shoes on, but got a dry pair from the closet.

After he had finished dressing, he said he was ready to go, and we left his room. We went out the front door of the boarding house. As we were approaching our police car, which was parked behind the white Pontiac, Mitchell said that he wanted to lock his car. He said that the car was in poor condition and pretty beat up, but it was all he had.

Mitchell got in the squad car with us, and we proceeded to headquarters. Johnson was driving; I had the jacket and gun with me in the front passenger seat, and Mitchell was in the back. On the way to headquarters, Mitchell was nervous and agitated. He kept talking to us. He asked: "What really happened to my wife?" I told him that a man had driven up in front of her home at around 10 P.M. and fired a shot at her and that she was taken to the hospital by ambulance. He got very excited and stated that 1751 Madison was <u>not</u> her home; that it was her stepmother's and something about she shouldn't have been there. He asked how his wife was. I told him that we didn't know and that she had been taken to Memorial Hospital. At no time that night, either in the car or in his room, did he ask to be taken to the hospital. On the ride downtown, Mitchell also talked a lot about his being a short story writer and said he liked to write mystery stories.

Allan J. Bradley, a homicide detective, was there when we got to headquarters. It was around 11:15 P.M. We put Mitchell in an interview room. Bradley took me into a side room. I showed him the gun and the jacket. I told him about our investigation at 1751 Madison and what Mrs. Thompson had told me. I also described what had happened in Mitchell's room. Bradley then told me they had word from the hospital that Mrs. Mitchell (Leslie Thompson Mitchell) had been pronounced dead on arrival. Bradley and I left the side room to return to the room where Mitchell was sitting. As I exited our room I saw Mitchell walking very fast toward the front door of the station. He was looking around furtively like he was trying to sneak out. This was before we had told him he was under arrest. I'm sure he was making a run for it; you have a sense about these things after being on the street as long as I have. The desk sergeant said something to him, he stopped, and then Bradley approached Mitchell and informed him that he was under arrest for murder and informed him of his constitutional right to remain silent and to assistance of counsel. Bradley also informed him that he could use the telephone for any purpose, right then and there. Mitchell signed the waiver form and made a statement.

Yes, I did tell Bradley that my gut told me that Mitchell didn't do it. Frankly, I suspected the old lady but that's not the way the momentum of the investigation went and Bradley was calling the shots by then. I just think Mitchell was sincere about his having nothing to hide.

One thing did turn up in the investigation that did give me pause. Word was on the street that someone had spoken with a guy named Jerry Young a few times in early September about a hit on a woman, one of whose names was "Thomas" or "Thompson." Young beat two murder raps for contract-type killings in Nita during the last five years. The State's Attorney was really on the guy's case the second time, but they just couldn't make it stick. The second time involved a shooting of a prominent restaurateur who the word was wouldn't pay protection. The State said Young drove up and fired one shot from the curb when the guy went out to get the morning paper: right through the heart. He drives an old white Chevy, 1994. The I.D. was weak and it shouldn't even have gone to trial, but the state hoped that something would turn up. Young is about Mitchell's height, build, and coloring and couldn't account for his whereabouts on the evening of September 10. He denied any connection with Mitchell, Brooke Thompson, or Leslie Thompson

Mitchell. Just another lead that went nowhere. Anyway, he may have displeased some of his employers because he hasn't been seen since last October. We have no idea where he is, or whether he's still alive.

When Mitchell had finished making his statement, I took him to the Crime lab for some tests. Lab Technician Weibel was on duty, and he administered a paraffin test on Mitchell. Then Mitchell was placed in a cell. I filed the recovered evidence (the gun, jacket, and bullet) with the Custodian's Office and submitted a request to the Crime lab for an analysis of the gun and bullet.

I understand that the lab analysis of the bullet and gun were inconclusive. The bullet was a .38 caliber, as I had observed, but it was too smashed for any comparison ballistics tests. Also, the lab reported that the gun had been cleaned and was wet, and that it was therefore impossible to determine if it had been fired one, two, or even three times after it was cleaned. I imagine it could have been cleaned right after the shooting if the person knew anything about guns.

I'm not surprised that the paraffin test on Mitchell's hands was inconclusive; they often are. There are many ways to prevent gunpowder particles from showing up on the hands when a paraffin test is performed. A person can wear gloves or clean his hands with a chemical agent, like gasoline or any strong "cutting" agent. Even fertilizer, urine, or tobacco will give a false reading. It is a lot like fingerprints. If a print is left and the comparison is positive, then you know without a doubt the person was there; but if there is no print, it doesn't mean anything, because there are so many ways to prevent prints form being left.

I understand that Mitchell was arraigned and pleaded not guilty.

Before we left 1751 Madison Street on the night of September 10, 2002, Officer Johnson and I measured the distance from the front door of the house on the porch to the curb on the street. It was thirty-five and one-half feet. We used a fifty-foot tape measure.

When Officer Johnson and I arrived at 1751 Madison the night of September 10, we parked our squad car at the curb directly in line with the front door of the house. Our car was pointed east. When I found the .38 caliber bullet on the porch, Officer Johnson was sitting in the driver's seat of the squad car, calling headquarters for further instructions. I shouted to him that I had found the bullet, and he leaned out of the car window, with his head and shoulders out, looking towards me. I am positive that when I looked at Johnson in the car, I could see him distinctly. I could recognize his face and features at that distance. It wasn't raining then, but it was dark. There was no street light at the curb there, but there was one on the other side of the street, about twenty feet west of where our car was parked.

No, we didn't give Mitchell any Miranda warnings at his room on Fillmore Street. We didn't arrest him, and we didn't ask him any questions. We had been instructed by headquarters to inform him of the shooting and to ask him to come to headquarters for questioning and further investigation. We did just that; we asked him to come, and he volunteered to do so. He spoke to us several times, but we did not ask him any questions.

No, Mrs. Thompson never said anything to me about having found a letter by Mitchell to his wife threatening her with violence. I know nothing of this. Mrs. Thompson left with the ambulance shortly after I arrived. I just talked to her for a few minutes.

Officer Johnson is deceased. He died of wounds received in a gun battle in a holdup attempt. I was not on duty then and was not with him.

We checked out Mitchell's story about the death of his first wife. It's substantially correct. We were not able to get any information about the knifing and shooting incidents he described.

We checked out Mitchell's acquittal on the aggravated assault charge in 1996. He was charged and acquitted. I read over the testimony of the victim. She told a very different story, but the jury must have believed Mitchell . . . or they didn't know who to believe. There's a transcript. Seems like this is a guy who gets very angry at women who don't do what he wants.

We went through Joe's mail at the boarding house after getting Joe's permission. In the mail was a letter from Wilson Studios dated September 9, 2002. It was also postmarked September 9. We picked up the mail from the boarding house on the Thirteenth and I vaguely remember it was near the bottom of the pile so I guess it probably arrived on the Tenth or Eleventh but I didn't think it was important and so didn't notice exactly where it was on the pile. Anyway, the letter was from an administrator at the studio saying that the letter sending him the $500 as an advance had not been authorized and that they were making no commitment to producing his script. It said that in light of the inevitable disappointment they were permitting him to retain the $500. Some of the letters in the pile were open and we opened others. I don't remember whether that letter was open or not. Anyway, we lost this letter. I just didn't see the connection with the case when I read it and just didn't take sufficient care. We subpoenaed the copy of the letter from the studio. It's Exhibit 12.

There was one very strange twist in the case. Three days after we arrested Mitchell we received an anonymous letter typed on a standard Royal typewriter. We were never able to trace the typewriter on which it was typed. The letter is marked as Exhibit 17. [See p. 25.] We questioned Mrs. Thompson about it somewhat delicately since we didn't want to upset her. She had no idea of what it was about. I don't even think she understood what it was implying. Maybe it was one of Joe's friends trying to help him out.

CERTIFICATION BY COURT REPORTER

The above is a true and accurate transcription of Officer Pat Slyviak's testimony at the trial of the case of *State v. Mitchell*, which testimony was recorded stenographically by me at the time it was given.

Signed and Attested to by:

a. Marie Lane

Certified Court Reporter

EXHIBIT 16

Testimony of Maria Pietro at The Trial of Joe Mitchell (6/9/96)

Q. Would you describe what happened then?

A. Well, Mitchell and I got back to my apartment. He wanted to get physical right away. I told him to relax and that I wanted to listen to some music and talk before I decided whether I wanted to go any farther. He got real angry and made some remark about being willing to pay for it if that's what I wanted. I started screaming at him, he started screaming back, and then he pushed me real hard. I picked up a kitchen knife just to defend myself and he laughed. He's over 6' tall and I'm only 5' 1". He came after me and hit me real hard across the jaw. It was broken.

WILSON **S**TUDIOS

123 Fortune Plaza   Nita City, Nita 45656

September 9, 2002

Mr. Joe Mitchell
800 Fillmore Street
Nita City, Nita 45656

Dear Mr. Mitchell,

I expect that you are now in receipt of a letter from these studios and a check in the amount of $500. I am afraid I must tell you that the letter was sent and the check issued without authorization from the officials at this company who are responsible for decisions of this sort. We can, therefore, not allow you to think that we are making any commitment to the production of your script or to any further payment therefor. I am sure this is a disappointment and therefore you may keep the $500 "advance" in consideration of any such feelings.

I am sorry. I am afraid that one of our junior officials overstepped his authority rather significantly here.

Sincerely,

F. Scott Jenkins

C-O-P-Y

Dear Police:

You don't know who I am and I'd like to keep it that way. The old witch paid me to knock off her little precious. I took the money and ran. I guess she made other plans—quite resourceful. I've got my dollars and I'm feeling a little sorry for the stiff she's stuck it to. She never knew my name and so I think I can afford this little noble gesture. I'm out of your sick little city. Use your heads for a change.

With all "DUE" respect,

A man who is telling the truth

SUMMARY OF DEFENDANT JOE MITCHELL'S TESTIMONY AT FIRST TRIAL

Joe Mitchell, having taken the stand to testify on his own behalf and having been duly sworn, testified as follows:

My name is Joseph R. Mitchell. I am twenty-eight years old. I live at 800 Fillmore Avenue here in Nita City.

Yes, I am the defendant in this case, and I know I've been charged with the murder of my wife, Leslie Mitchell, on the night of September 10, 2002. My attorney has advised me that I do not have to testify in my own defense under the Constitution, but I want to waive that right and testify here today. I have nothing to hide. I didn't kill my wife—I loved her.

I am a freelance writer of short stories and TV and radio scripts, mainly murder mysteries, crime stories, and detective fiction. I don't work for anybody. I am independent and work on my own. My parents died when I was four years old. I was raised by my grandfather and grandmother, my mother's parents, now deceased. When I was in high school, I worked on the school paper and I decided I'd like to be a writer. When I graduated from high school, I enlisted in the Marines. During my term of service, I took correspondence courses in writing. When I got out of the service, I returned to Nita City. I had a little money saved, and I wanted to devote all my time to writing. I got a part-time job in a gas station and lived in Mrs. Porter's boarding house, 800 Fillmore Avenue. I gave all the time I could to my writing, but I did not sell any of my writing until September 10, 2002.

I've never been convicted of any crimes. About four years ago I was in a bar with a girlfriend about whom I was pretty serious. Anyway, this guy kept hitting on her and I got angry. I picked up a steak knife and went after the guy. I cut him across the hand—just a shallow cut. He grabbed a beer bottle and hit me across the head. The other patrons separated us. For some reason he didn't want anything to do with the cops and neither of us pressed charges.

I was married once before. My wife died of a gunshot wound to the chest. We were in the country up in Wisconsin hiking through the woods during deer hunting season. I was resting and my wife walked over to a stream. All of a sudden I heard a muffled shot. When I looked for my wife she was down on the ground. The police told me that she died of bullet wound inflicted by a standard deer-hunting rifle. They questioned four of five guys who had been hunting in the area. Two of them owned rifles that could have inflicted the wound, but a positive match-up was impossible. They wanted to charge someone with negligent homicide but since it could have been either of these guys—or even someone else—they were stuck.

I once took a shot at someone. It was back in the big snowstorm in 1997. I was at home and I had had a few drinks. This guy parked right in front of my driveway, which I had just shoveled out. I guess he couldn't find another spot. Anyway, I stuck my head out the window and told him to move. Well, tempers were short and he let loose with this stream of four-letter words. My gun happened to be in the drawer real close to where I was standing and I pulled it out and pointed it at him. I expected that would be enough, but he just gave me the finger. I got so mad I fired at him. Thank God I had had those drinks: the bullet went into a tree. He took off. I spent the next week waiting for the cops to show up, but they never did. I was wilder back then.

Once in the Marines, back in 1996, I was charged with aggravated assault by the civil authorities. It concerned an off-base incident. I hit this woman I met in a bar pretty hard. See, she and I went back to her place and we had an argument. I don't even remember what it was about. She came at me with a knife and I hit her. It broke her jaw. Anyway, I had a real good P.D. and he got me off on self-defense.

I met Leslie Thompson in the fall of 2000. We dated, and in the summer of 2001, we decided to get married. Leslie lived with her stepmother at 1751 Madison Street. Her real mother died when she was four years old. Two years later, her father married again to Mrs. Brooke Thompson, Leslie's stepmother. Leslie's father died in 1990 and Mrs. Thompson raised her. When I met Leslie, she was working as a secretary to the president of the First State Bank. I visited the Thompson home many times. From the beginning, Mrs. Thompson was opposed to me. She didn't approve of me, and told me that she was against my marrying Leslie. We were married anyway, on November 15, 2001. Leslie was interested in my work as a writer; she thought I had a future in it. It was her idea that I quit my job at the gas station and stay home to give all my time to my writing. We lived in an apartment at 50 Jackson Street. Leslie went on with her job at the bank. She was making about $1,500 a month and had an income of about $500 from a trust fund that her father set up for her in his will.

I understand that the main witness against me will be Mrs. Thompson. I'm told that she says she saw me fire the shot that killed my wife. But she couldn't have, because I wasn't there. I understand that she claims that around 10 P.M. on September 10, 2002, I drove up in my car, and parked at the curb in front of 1751 Madison Street; that Leslie was standing on the porch; that I leaned out of the car, fired my revolver and shot Leslie; that she, Mrs. Thompson, was then standing at the door to let in Leslie. Mrs. Thompson is mistaken. For one thing, it was a dark and very rainy night that night. Her hatred of me, her emotional reaction to me, has made her think I was the man who fired the shot. Because of her hatred, she saw what she wanted to see.

When I was dating Leslie and coming to the house, Mrs. Thompson repeatedly opposed me. She said that I was not the man for Leslie and that she would do all she could to prevent the marriage.

We were married, in spite of her opposition, on November 15, 2001, by a judge. Mrs. Thompson refused to attend either the wedding or the wedding reception which followed.

After we were married, Leslie and I did visit Mrs. Thompson at her home. At that time, Leslie had insisted that I give up my gas station job and spend all my time writing at home. I told Mrs. Thompson about this. In Leslie's presence, she told me I was lazy and "no good" and trying to live off Leslie's money.

After a while, I stopped going with Leslie to Mrs. Thompson's, and Leslie would go alone. She would come back after these visits and tell me that Mrs. Thompson was trying to get her to leave me and come back to 1751 Madison Street. And after a while, Leslie lost interest in my writing. She began to talk to me about getting what she called a "real job" and said she could get me some kind of work in the bank. I refused to give up my writing.

Mrs. Thompson finally persuaded Leslie to leave me. One night in July 2002, Leslie said she was leaving me. She told me she was going back to Mrs. Thompson if I did not give up my writing. I refused, and we had a bitter quarrel. She left in a cab and went to Mrs. Thompson's.

After that, I'd go to Mrs. Thompson's several times a week to try to persuade Leslie to come back to me. Leslie refused, unless I quit my writing. During these conversations, Mrs. Thompson was always present; she insisted on being there while Leslie and I were talking. She told Leslie not to come back to me. She told Leslie to divorce me. And again she told me, in front of Leslie, that I was no good and lazy and living off Leslie's money. Whenever I tried to get Leslie to go out of the house somewhere so that we could talk things over, Mrs. Thompson would step in.

It is true that during these conversations I sometimes lost my temper. I accused Mrs. Thompson of breaking up my marriage. Mrs. Thompson had poisoned Leslie's mind against me and was bound and determined that we not get back together. She hated me. During this time I joined "Men Angry About Divorce." It's a men's rights group. One of the tenets of the organization is that women who initiate divorce proceedings should be required to participate in mandatory mediation aimed at working out differences with their husbands. It also holds that a wife's verbal abuse of her husband should give rise to a husband's right to physical "self-defense" at a reasonable level.

The last time I saw Leslie alive was on the night of September 9, 2002. I went to Mrs. Thompson's between 9 and 10 P.M. I only stayed a little while. Mrs. Thompson and Leslie were there. I don't remember the exact words anyone said, but the gist of it was that I asked Leslie "for the last time" to come back to me. She still refused, unless I gave up my writing. I would not do that, and I said "We're all through then. I'm sorry it didn't work out." I admit I was angry at Mrs. Thompson and Leslie. I do remember I said something about making them both sorry for what they had done to me, and that Mrs. Thompson had broken up my marriage and that I'd make her pay for it. I don't recall the exact words, but what I meant was that when I made it big with my writing, they would regret what they had done. I didn't mean I'd do physical violence to them. I don't recall anything that Mrs. Thompson may have said that night. I left the house at about 9:30 P.M.

After I left them I drove around the streets for awhile, trying to think things out. I was confused, hurt, and upset. I loved my wife, and I wanted us to be together. Mrs. Thompson was the cause of our problems. The more I thought of it, the angrier I got at her.

When I got back to the boarding house, where I had gone to live after Leslie left me, I was still upset. I wrote a letter to Leslie, making still another plea for her to come back to me. I went out right then and sent it special delivery. I don't recall exactly what I said, but I do remember saying something about making them regret what they had done to me. I suppose they will bring this letter up against me, but I didn't mean physical violence. I only meant that Mrs. Thompson would regret what she had done when I made it big with my writing. After I mailed the letter special delivery I returned to the boarding house to find that a check for $500 as an advance for a TV script, a murder mystery, had arrived. I hadn't seen it because of my preoccupation with Leslie. I decided to wait until the next day and then surprise Leslie about it. I did not see their "retraction" letter until after I was arrested and my lawyer showed me a copy.

September 10 was Leslie's birthday. I cashed my check and bought a five-pound box of candy. I wanted to see Leslie to tell her about my good luck and maybe get her to come back after all. The box of candy was for her birthday. I went back to the boarding house and paid Mrs. Porter some back rent and board.

That night I drove to 1751 Madison Street in my car, a used 1992 Pontiac Ventura I've had for a couple of years. I wanted to surprise Leslie. I got to 1751 Madison at about 7:30 P.M., but I'm not positive about the time.

I parked at the south curb across the street from 1751 Madison, with my car pointed east. There were two porch lights on brackets on either side of the door, about five feet up from the ground. Both lights were on. Mrs. Thompson came to the door, and I asked for Leslie. She told me that Leslie had gone to the Palace Theater, where Leslie and I had often gone. I asked when she would be back, and Mrs. Thompson said 10:10 P.M. I thought that was a strangely precise hour. I couldn't quite describe her manner. It was strange, like the witch in "Hansel and Gretel": trying to be sweet but kind of rubbing her hands together. Being nice doesn't become her. Anyway, she said that if I wanted to talk with Leslie I should come back at exactly 10:10 and come alone. I did not tell Mrs. Thompson about having sold the TV script. I only talked to her for a few minutes at the most. She did not ask me in, of course; it was raining, and she made me just stand there in the rain. I didn't have a hat or an umbrella, and I was getting pretty wet. I had the box of candy under my arm. I hadn't wanted the wrapping to get wet, so I wrapped it in a couple of newspapers.

I left Mrs. Thompson's at about 7:35 P.M. or so, and drove to the Palace Theater. I thought I would try to surprise Leslie there. Since I had just gotten my first check for my writing, I wanted to share it with her. While I was driving there, I was trying to think things out. The idea that I would lose Leslie because of Mrs. Thompson upset me. I couldn't see myself living without her. I was in love with my wife. It seemed so cruel and ironic really that I should lose out by one day after waiting so long. I did not want to go on without Leslie, so I decided to make one more attempt to talk to her. I hoped that with my writing success and without Mrs. Thompson present we could get back together.

I parked near the theater. I knew the ticket seller there, Quinn Washington. I had met her often when Leslie and I went there, because she was a friend of Leslie's. I think it was about 7:45 P.M. or so when I arrived. The ticket booth is in front of the theater. I went up to the booth and asked her if she had seen Leslie. I told her I had been to Mrs. Thompson's and that Mrs. Thompson had told me that Leslie had gone to the Palace Theater. She told me that Leslie had gone into the theater. I remember asking Quinn several times when the show would be over. I think she said the first show would be over at about 9:40 or 9:45 P.M. We talked for a while. I recall Quinn said something about Leslie being "afraid" of me, or something like that. I told Quinn that there was nothing wrong between Leslie and me, but that it was all Mrs. Thompson's fault. I said that Mrs. Thompson was the "evil" person who had broken up my marriage and that my marriage would be okay if Mrs. Thompson were not in the way.

I bought a ticket and went into the theater. I was going to wait for Leslie. I went into the foyer, waited a while and then went to the men's room. I was thinking about selling my writing that day and how, if it hadn't been for Mrs. Thompson, everything would be perfect and Leslie and I would be sharing the success. I got upset, smoked a couple of cigarettes, and then decided to leave. I went out of the theater and got into my car. I drove further east about four or five blocks. I think it was about

8:30 P.M.—I am sorry I can't be precise about the time—and I went into the Silver Dollar Bar there on the south side of Madison Street, about five blocks from the theater.

I had four glasses of beer at the bar. There were about thirty-five people in there. I talked to the bartender, but I don't know his name. As best as I can remember, I was there for about forty-five minutes.

I talked with the bartender, but he was busy serving all the other customers, so we didn't talk continuously. I did not tell him my name, but I do recall telling him I was a writer of short stories, murder mysteries, and crime stories for TV and radio. And I did say something about my mother-in-law having broken up my marriage and poisoning my wife's mind against me so much that she had left me. I recall I said that my mother-in-law hated me, and maybe I said I hated her too, for all she had done to me. I was pretty down and depressed at the time. I couldn't get the thought out of my head that we were separated, and now I'd made it with my writing.

After about an hour, I think, I left the Silver Dollar. I was certainly not drunk. I went to my car and sat in it a while before driving off. I can't say exactly how long it was, but I think that I left there at about 9:30 P.M. I was trying to decide whether to go back to the theater or go home. My favorite radio program was due to come on at 10 P.M. I turned around and drove west on Madison. I passed the theater, but didn't stop; I didn't even look over to the ticket booth as I passed. I went past the house at 1751 Madison Street, and the porch lights and the lights in the two front rooms were on. It was still drizzling rain.

I decided to go pick up my .38 caliber revolver at Ravenna's Gun Shop at 2165 Madison. I had left the gun there for cleaning and some minor repairs about a week before. I found the place still open, so I went in. Chris Ravenna, who is a clerk for his brother Sam who owns the shop, was there. Chris got the gun for me, and I paid the bill—$32.50—and left. I was only there for a few minutes. You can check that out with Chris.

I bought this gun when I was in the service, and kept it as a memento of service days. The only time I used it was to practice target shooting on the outskirts of Nita City. Since I was a writer of murder mysteries, and many of them involved guns, I thought I ought to be familiar with guns as part of my business. I used to practice a couple of times a week, shooting at paper targets on a tree. This was my only relaxation or sport. I became an expert shot. I once told Leslie I could hit a dime at 100 yards. And I probably told other people at some time or other in a bragging way that I could do this. Leslie knew I had the gun. I used to keep it in my closet in an old five-pound candy box. I kept it on a shelf of the closet in the boarding house.

At the beginning of September 2002, I had some trouble with the safety catch, so I took it to Ravenna's Gun Shop for repair and cleaning. Chris Ravenna returned it to me the night of September 10, as I said. When he gave me the gun, I did not notice that there were two shells or bullets in it. I guess I had left them there in the gun when I took it in for repair, and Ravenna must have taken them out while he was making the repairs and doing the cleaning and then replaced them later. Chris reminded me of them when he gave me the gun, and told me to be careful. I took the shells out of the gun and put them in my pants pocket. I put the gun in my jacket pocket. I got in my car and drove home to 800 Fillmore Avenue. I was never near 1751 Madison Street again that night. Each time I have had the gun repaired on previous occasions I have taken it to the Nita Gun Club for a test firing right away. I have had the gun repaired three times before. The firing range is open until midnight and is about ten minutes from Ravenna's. No particular reason why I didn't do it that night. My radio program, maybe.

When I got home, I went up to my room on the second floor of Mrs. Porter's boarding house. I took off my wet clothes and got into a bathrobe and pajamas. I sat down to read and listen to a rebroadcast of *The Shadow* on the radio. I listen to it every Saturday at 10 P.M. I've learned more about mystery writing by listening to those shows than any other way. I had a headache that wouldn't go away, and around 10:15 or 10:30 P.M. I went down to Mrs. Porter's to borrow some aspirin. I heard her TV and knocked. She was watching TV in her living room, which is on the first floor, facing the street. She gave me some aspirin, and I went back up to my room.

Around 10:45 P.M., I think it was, I heard a knock on my door. I opened the door, and there were two men there in police uniforms. One said that he was Officer Slyviak and he asked me my name. I told him "Joe Mitchell," and I said "What's this all about?" Slyviak said that my wife had been shot. That really shook me up. I asked, "Is she dead?" Officer Slyviak said that they did not know whether she was dead or not, but that she had been taken to the hospital by ambulance.

Officer Slyviak asked me if I would go to Police Headquar-ters with them, and I said I would gladly do so. I told them that, if they would let me dress, I would go with them and help all I could. I told them that I had been reading and listening to the radio. (I had been sitting in a chair reading, and so the bed was still made up.)

I went to get some dry clothing from my closet. When I came in earlier that night, I had thrown my wet clothing on the floor. As I went to get some clothes from the closet, I noticed my wet jacket on the floor and, right alongside it, my gun. I guess it had fallen out of my pocket when I dropped my jacket on the floor. I had taken the shells out of my pants pocket when I got in and had put them in the dresser drawer.

I saw Officer Slyviak sort of move over to pick up the gun, but I picked it up before he got it. I was afraid I was going to get into trouble because I didn't have the gun registered, so I picked it up. But then I handed it over to the officer. I said "I have nothing to hide, officer." I handed him the jacket too. I told him again, "I have nothing to hide. You take them."

The officers did not force me to go with them; they did not arrest me. They asked me to go downtown to headquarters, and I went with them voluntarily. I felt at all times that I was free to go with them or refuse to go with them. Neither of these officers at any time said anything to me about having a lawyer, remaining silent, or that anything I said might be used against me.

I told the officers I had bought the gun while in the service and that I used it for target shooting. I told them I wrote murder mysteries and had to know a lot about guns for my writing.

I finished dressing and went out with them. I went to the station in their police car. They did not force me to do this. A man at the station who said he was Detective Bradley, a homicide detective, told me my wife was dead—dead on arrival at the hospital. Bradley went into a room with Officer Slyviak. While Bradley and Slyviak were in the room together, I was left in an interview room. It got stuffy in there and I decided that I needed a little fresh air. I got up and walked toward the front door. The sergeant sitting at the front desk said to me, "Where the hell do you think you're going?" I said, "To get a little fresh air." At that point Bradley came out of the room where he had been with Slyviak. He told me that I was being arrested for the murder of my wife. He said that I had the right to remain silent, that anything I said might be used against me, and that I had the right to call a lawyer. I signed a form and made a statement. I told them I had absolutely nothing to do with my wife's murder, and I knew nothing about the shooting. I told them what I did that night and how I certainly wasn't near 1751 Madison Street at the time of shooting. I told them I was at Chris Ravenna's shop and then I went right home. I told them to check this with Chris Ravenna and Mrs. Porter. I went right home from Ravenna's shop; I wasn't near 1751 Madison at 10 P.M., and I certainly didn't shoot my wife.

After I made the statement, Officer Slyviak took me to the crime lab, and one of the technicians performed a test on my hands. At the lab, the technician put a plaster cast on my hands and performed a test. I think it's called a paraffin test.

I was arraigned in court and have been staying in jail, because the bond is too high for me to get out. I was permitted to visit the funeral parlor under police escort to see my wife's body.

I didn't kill my wife. I loved her.

Mrs. Porter has been a good friend to me. She was interested in my writing, and she has often loaned me money for room and board charges. I have paid her all I owed her.

Mrs. Porter's boarding house has a fire escape from the second floor outside my window, but I've never used it. I keep it locked from the inside, and I use the other two windows in the apartment for ventilation.

I belong to a club of amateur writers in Nita City called the Scribblers Club. Chris Ravenna is a member. He certainly knows my reputation.

Although I have never seen it, Leslie did explain to me several times her father's will. Under it, Leslie had a trust fund set up for her. Mr. Thompson's property went to Mrs. Thompson for her life, and, after that, to Leslie. As I understand it, if Leslie was dead when Mrs. Thompson died, then all the property goes to the one named in Leslie's will. Soon after we were married, Leslie insisted that she make a will which left everything to me.

CERTIFICATION BY COURT REPORTER

The above is a true and accurate transcription of the defendant Joe Mitchell's testimony at the trial of the case of *State v. Mitchell*, which testimony was recorded stenographically by me at the time it was given.

Signed and Attested to by:

A. Marie Lane

Certified Court Reporter

[Editor's Note: Defendant's testimony at the first trial may not be used during the prosecution's case in chief. It may be used for impeachment if the defendant elects to take the stand to testify on his own behalf at the second trial.]

STATEMENT GIVEN BY JOE MITCHELL TO POLICE

WARNING AND WAIVER / WARNING AS TO RIGHTS   **CASE NO. 275622**

Before we ask you any questions, it is our duty as police officers to advise you of your rights and to warn you of the consequences of waiving your rights.

You have the absolute right to remain silent.

Anything you say to us can be used against you in court.

You have the right to talk to an attorney before answering any questions and to have an attorney present with you during questioning.

You have this same right to the advice and presence of an attorney, whether you can afford to hire one or not. We have no way of furnishing you with an attorney, but one will be appointed for you, if you wish.

If you decide to answer questions now without an attorney present, you will still have the right to stop answering at any time. You also have the right to stop answering at any time until you talk to an attorney.

WAIVER

I have read the above statement of my rights, and it has been read to me. I understand what my rights are. I wish to make a voluntary statement, and I do not want an attorney. No force, threats, or promises of any kind or nature have been used by anyone in any way to influence me to waive my rights. I am signing this statement after having been advised of my rights, before any questions have been asked of me by the police.

Joe Mitchell

(Signature)

CERTIFICATION

I hereby certify that the foregoing warning and waiver were read by me to the person who has affixed his signature above, and that he also read it and signed it in my presence this 10th day of September, 2002, at 11:25 o'clock P.M. at Police Headquarters, Nita City.

Allen J. Bradley

(Signature - Police Officer)
Allen J. Bradley, Det.

Pat Slyviak

(Witness)
Officer Pat Slyviak

(Form #84)

VOLUNTARY STATEMENT

Page 1 of 2   Case # 275622

DATE: <u>September 10, 2002</u>   LOCATION: <u>Police Headquarters, Nita City, Nita</u>

Time Statement Started _____ A.M. <u>11:25</u> P.M. I, the undersigned <u>Joseph R. Mitchell</u> of <u>800 Fillmore Avenue Nita City, Nita</u> being <u>28</u> years of age, born at <u>Nita City Nita</u> on <u>October 16, 1974</u> did hereby make the following statement to <u>Allen J. Bradley</u>, he having first identified himself as a <u>Detective with the Nita City Police Department</u>.

This statement is voluntarily made by me without any threats, coercion or promises of any kind or nature. Before making any statement to the Police, I was advised that I had the absolute right to remain silent and that anything I might say could be used against me in a criminal proceeding. I was advised also of my right to have an attorney present before answering any questions and that, if I was unable to afford one, an attorney would be provided before questioning. I have freely and voluntarily waived my right to remain silent and my right to consult with an attorney before answering questions.

Q.   Have you had your rights read to you?
A.   YES
Q.   Do you understand your rights?
A.   YES
      Whereupon Mr. Mitchell gave the following statement:

> I don't know anything about my wife, Leslie, being shot. I had
> absolutely nothing to do with that terrible murder. I wasn't even near
> her stepmother's house at the time of the shooting. I had stopped
> to see Leslie earlier that night around 7:00 or 7:30 P.M., but she had
> gone to a movie. I stopped at the Palace Theater, but didn't see her. I
> had a couple of drinks at the Silver Dollar.

I have read this statement consisting of <u>2</u> page(s) and the facts contained therein are true and correct.

WITNESSES:

Allen J. Bradley

Allen J. Bradley, Det.

Pat Slyviak

Officer Pat Slyviak

Joe Mitchell

Signature of person giving
voluntary statement

TIME STATEMENT FINISHED _____ A.M. <u>11:40</u> P.M.   DATE <u>Sept. 10, 2002</u>

VOLUNTARY STATEMENT   **Page 2 of 2**   **Case #** <u>275622</u>

DATE: <u>September 10, 2002</u>   LOCATION: <u>Police Headquarters, Nita City, Nita</u>

I left the Silver Dollar Bar and then decided to go home. I thought I would see Leslie tomorrow. On the way home, I stopped at Chris Ravenna's shop on 21st and Madison. I picked up the gun I use for target practice. I had left it there to be cleaned. That is the gun Officer Slyviak saw in my room and brought here with him. After I picked up the gun, I went straight home. You can check this out with Mr. Chris Ravenna, and Mrs. Porter probably heard me come in. I wasn't near 1751 Madison Street at 10 P.M., and I certainly didn't shoot my wife. I loved her. I picked up the gun from Ravenna and went straight home to my place on Fillmore. The gun you have wasn't fired after I picked it up at Ravenna's.

I have read this statement consisting of <u>2</u> page(s) and the facts contained therein are true and correct.

WITNESSES: _Allen J. Bradley_   _Joe Mitchell_

Allen J. Bradley Det.   Signature of person giving voluntary statement

Pat Slyviak

Officer Pat Slyviak

TIME STATEMENT FINISHED _____ AM <u>11:40</u> P.M.   DATE <u>Sept. 10, 2002</u>

STATEMENT OF QUINN WASHINGTON

My name is Quinn Washington. I live at 50 King Street, Nita City. I am not married. I am employed at the Palace Theater as a ticket seller and work in a ticket booth—enclosed with a glass window—at the entrance to the theater. The theater is on the south side of Madison Street, five blocks east of Mrs. Brooke Thompson's residence at 1751 Madison Street. I was working there on September 10, 2002. I understand Joe Mitchell is charged with the murder of his wife, Leslie, on that day. I was not a witness to this terrible thing, but I knew Leslie and Joe, and I saw both of them that night.

Leslie and I were close friends. I went to grade school with her. Later, she went to school in New York City, but came back and got a job at the First State Bank. I often visited her home at 1751 Madison Street and met her stepmother, Mrs. Thompson. Leslie's mother died when Leslie was four. Two years later, her father married his second wife, Brooke Thompson. Leslie's stepmother raised her. There were no other children.

I first met Joe Mitchell in the winter of 2001 when he and Leslie came to the theater, and she introduced him to me. They came to the theater often after that. That summer, Leslie told me they were going to be married. They were married in November 2001. I attended their wedding, which was small and quiet, but pleasant. Mrs. Thompson did not attend.

Just before they were married, Leslie told me that Mrs. Thompson was bitterly opposed to her marrying this man, but she said they were going to be married anyway. I have the highest respect for Mrs. Thompson's character and reputation. Mrs. Thompson always treated Leslie as her own daughter, and Leslie's welfare came first with her. She raised Leslie as her own, and Leslie always referred to her as "mother." I'm sure if Mrs. Thompson objected to Leslie's marrying Joe, she did this out of a sense of conscience and duty to warn Leslie and to advise her for her own good. But I admit that from what I heard, the marriage did create a strain in the relations between Leslie and her mother and between Mrs. Thompson and Mitchell.

After they were married, Leslie and Joe did not come to the theater very often. But in August, 2002, Leslie came one night and told me she and Joe had separated and that she was back living with Mrs. Thompson. She said Joe was living in boarding house at 800 Fillmore Avenue. She also told me that Joe was seeing her at Mrs. Thompson's and trying to get her to come back to him. She said he would get angry and make threats against Mrs. Thompson, whom he hated for, as he said, "breaking up his marriage." Leslie said he had even turned against her for leaving him. He accused Mrs. Thompson of "poisoning" Leslie's mind against him and blamed Leslie for listening to Mrs. Thompson.

I remember that night in August quite well, because I hadn't seen Leslie very much since she and Joe got married. Also, I was surprised to hear that they had separated. Leslie and I had been friends since childhood, and naturally I was concerned for her happiness.

I next saw her on the night of September 10, 2002. She came up to the ticket window to buy a ticket at about 7 P.M. We talked for a few minutes. I noticed that she was frightened and nervous; she kept looking up and down the street as if she expected someone. I asked if she had seen Joe and she said he had come to the house the night before and threatened Mrs. Thompson again. She said this time he had also threatened her and she was afraid something terrible was going to happen to her and her mother. She said: "Joe has been making awful threats against us. He has a violent temper, and he might try to do something violent to us." She said that she had told Joe they were through and that Joe hated them both now.

I don't remember her exact words—only the substance of what she said. I recall that she said Joe was furious with her. He accused her of having her mind poisoned against him by that "evil person," her mother. She said she had received a letter from him that day and that he made terrible threats against her and her mother in the letter. She seemed to be frightened of Joe. Just then, some other people came up to the window, and Leslie got her ticket and went into the theater.

At about 7:45 P.M., Joe Mitchell came to the ticket window. (I can't be sure about the exact time.) He asked me if I had seen Leslie. He said he had been to Mrs. Thompson's and she told him that Leslie had gone to the Palace Theater. I told him she had gone into the show at about 7 P.M. I said: "Joe, what have you done to Leslie? Why don't you leave her alone? She's afraid of you, Joe." He told me: "There is nothing wrong between Leslie and me. It's that evil old wretch of a woman, her mother, who has broken up our marriage. She's not going to get away with it." And he said: "If it weren't for her, we'd be together now. She always hated me. Believe me, they will be sorry for all this, but I hope it isn't too late. I love my wife, and it would be all right between us if her mother weren't in our way." Again, I can only give you the substance of what he said, not the exact words. He asked me when the show would be over, and I told him about 9:40 P.M. I recall that Joe repeated the question: "Are you sure it will be over at 9:40?"

Joe seemed angry, especially when he spoke of Mrs. Thompson, and also nervous. He didn't have a hat on and wasn't carrying an umbrella, although it had been raining off and on during the evening. He wore a black or dark colored jacket, which was wet, and he had a package under his arm. From what I could see, it looked like a box about the size of a five-pound candy box wrapped in newspapers.

Joe bought a ticket and went into the theater. I saw him leave about 8:30 or 8:45 P.M.

Leslie came out when the show ended at about 9:40, and I talked to her for a few minutes. She asked me if Joe had been there. I told her he had; that he had bought a ticket and gone into the show, and then left about 8:30–8:45 P.M. She asked me whether he had asked for her, and I said he had and told her all that he had said to me. She looked terribly frightened. I remember she asked me if I was sure he had left. Then she asked, "Did he have a gun with him?" I was shocked at a question like that; I didn't know what she was talking about. I told her, "Of course, he had no gun." I said if she were frightened, we could call the police and that they would see to it that she got home safely. And I said, if she didn't want to do this, she could stay with me in the booth until the second show was over, and I'd walk home with her or we could take a cab. But she said she would go home then, and wouldn't call a cab or let me call one. She said good night and walked west on the south side of Madison Street, and I never saw her alive again.

I think the box Joe had under his arm was big enough to have held a pistol or revolver.

When Joe was at the theater that night Leslie was killed, he didn't say anything to me about his writing. From what I understand, Joe writes short stories and TV scripts—mainly murder and crime stories.

Leslie left the theater at about 9:45 P.M. It's five blocks to her house.

I remember that when Joe and Leslie were at the theater in the spring of 2001, they stood at the ticket booth talking with me for a few minutes. There was a western film that night, and Joe was joking about the film. He told me: "I can shoot as well as anyone. I can hit a dime at 100 yards." And Leslie said, "I keep telling him he should give up his target shooting. He's always out with his pistol, shooting targets."

One time before Leslie and Joe ever met—I think it was in the spring of 2000—I drove to 1751 Madison to see Leslie. I parked the car at the curb in front of the house, and before I got out of the car, I looked up at the front porch. I could easily see Mrs. Thompson from where I was; she was standing on the porch there in front of her front door, and I was leaning out of the window of the car. The front door is about thirty-five feet from the curb. Mrs. Thompson called out: "Hello, Quinn. Leslie is waiting for you." This was before I got out of the car. It was about 9:30 P.M., and it wasn't raining. On either side of the front door were these bracket lights, about five feet up from the floor. They made it easy for me to see Mrs. Thompson. Of course, we had seen each other many times before this. As I recall, it was a bright, moonlit night, and there were no street lights at the curb where I was parked. There was a street light at the opposite curb, on the other side of the street, but that was twenty-five feet west of where I was parked. I only mention this because I understand there is some question about Mrs. Thompson's seeing Joe fire the shot at Leslie. (I understand that Joe supposedly drove up in his car, parked in front of the house, and leaned out of the car and shot Leslie, who was up on the porch with Mrs. Thompson.)

I saw Mrs. Thompson at the movie theater about five days after Leslie was killed. She was with a couple of her friends. I was sort of surprised to see her there. She was smiling and laughing, like nothing had happened.

About ten days after Leslie's death, Mrs. Thompson had a garage sale and sold off all the stuff in Leslie's bedroom. I was there, but I don't think she recognized me. What a hard bargainer! She wouldn't give an inch on the prices.

I have read the above statement and it is true and correct.

Date: 9-28-02   Quinn Washington

Date: 9-28-02   Witness: Detective Paul Jones
                     Nita City Police Department

Statement of Raleigh Porter

My name is Raleigh Porter. I live at 800 Fillmore Avenue, Nita City. I operate a boarding house licensed by the city. I am thirty-two years old and divorced, with one child, a boy, nine years old. The boarding house I operate is the house I grew up in. It was left to me by my parents when they died in an automobile accident five years ago. My husband left several years ago—almost seven years now. He drank a lot and had trouble keeping a job. I never hear from him. I support us from my part-time job in a department store and with the income from renting rooms in our house.

I understand that Joe Mitchell is charged with shooting and killing his wife, Leslie, on September 10, 2002. I did not know Leslie Mitchell; I never met her.

I first met Joe Mitchell in the fall of 1999, when he rented a room at my boarding house. He grew up in Nita City, graduated from Nita City High School, and had just finished serving in the Marine Corps. He said that he was very interested in writing and wanted to build a career as a writer of short stories and TV and radio scripts. He told me that he was working part-time in a gas station, just until he made it as a writer.

When he lived at the boarding house, before his marriage, he worked nights at the gas station and spent his days writing. He would often read his stories to me, and I enjoyed them very much. I thought he had real talent. He was a most satisfactory boarder; he never caused any trouble. He was not a drinker and rarely, if ever, touched liquor. He was quiet and orderly. I wish all my boarders were like him.

When Joe was at the boarding house before his marriage, he had it pretty hard financially. At various times, I would give him credit or a loan for the room and board charges. He was a nice, reliable person, and I thought he had a real future as a writer. He always paid me back what he owed. The loans or credit were usually for board, and he took most of his meals at my boarding house.

He left my place in November 2001, when he married Leslie Thompson. He owed me $150, which he paid back a couple of weeks after he was married. I guess he got it from his wife, who he said was continuing to work at her job at a bank in Nita City. He told me that he had quit his job at the gas station and was devoting all his time to his writing. He and his wife lived in an apartment on Jackson Street. I recall that before he was married, he told me that Mrs. Thompson, the girl's stepmother, was opposed to the marriage and had tried to prevent it. He said Mrs. Thompson hated him. Joe and Leslie were married before a judge. I attended the wedding, and it was a pleasant affair. I didn't meet Leslie's mother, Mrs. Thompson. I guess she didn't go to the wedding.

I did not see him for a long time after that—not until July 2002, in fact. At that time, he asked to have his old room again. Since it was vacant, I let him have the room. He said he and his wife, Leslie, had separated and that she was living with her stepmother at 1751 Madison Street, Nita City. He blamed Mrs. Thompson for breaking up his marriage. He said that she had worked on Leslie and influenced her to leave him and that he would never forgive that woman for what she'd done to their marriage.

He also mentioned that maybe a separation was best until he got on his feet as a writer and could make some money. Joe was very mature for his age. He also said that he had not given up hope that Leslie would come back. He thought she would, if Mrs. Thompson would leave them alone and stop interfering with their relationship. I remember him saying that she couldn't live forever and so there was hope that it would turn out all right for Leslie and him. He told me sometime—not when he first came back after the separation—that Leslie would inherit all her father's property when Mrs. Thompson died, because under the will Mrs. Thompson only had it for her life. He said something about how Mrs. Thompson had robbed Leslie of her inheritance and her happiness. He had been thinking about Leslie and was kind of down and depressed when he mentioned that.

When he first came back to the boarding house, he said that he was going to devote all his time to writing so he would make it to show Mrs. Thompson and Leslie that he could be a successful writer. He said that he had a little money saved, but I don't know where he got it. I didn't ask him about it.

Joe had an old, beat-up, white, 1992, Pontiac Ventura. He used to park it at the curb in front of my place. He lived at my place from July to September, 2002, and during this time, I know he frequently went to the Thompson house to try to get his wife to come back to him. I often saw him leave for there in his car. He told me that he went there about two or three times a week, but that Mrs. Thompson was doing her best to prevent any reconciliation between Leslie and him. He would come back from these visits very depressed and melancholy, but he wouldn't talk much about what had happened, even though we were good friends and talked a lot.

Early in the evening of September 9, 2002—I can't recall the precise time, but it was after 6 PM—Joe said he was going to see Leslie again and make one final effort to get her back. He said: "This is it. This is the last chance I'll give her." I saw him leave. He came back about 10:30 P.M. I heard him come in. My apartment is on the first floor, and I was in bed. I heard him go up the stairs to his room. The stairs go right up to the second floor, and his room is at the head of the stairs.

I distinctly recall September 10, 2002. That morning Joe came down and talked to me at about 8:30 A.M. He said that, the night before, Leslie had refused finally and positively to return to him unless he gave up his writing and got another job. He said he would not do this and that he and Leslie were through. He said that he would make them sorry for what they both had done to him, especially that evil old woman who had succeeded in breaking up his marriage. Without her interference, he said they could have worked things out. Then he said something about hoping the old lady died soon, because maybe then Leslie would come back and they could be happy again.

Later that morning, he showed me a check for $500 he had received in the mail, and said it was an advance for one of his TV scripts. He said: "I'm on my way at last. They are going to be sorry for what they did to me and for the way they treated me. I've finally made it." He went out to cash the check, and then he came back and paid me $100 he owed me for room and board. He said he was going to go over that night to see Leslie and tell her about his good luck. He mentioned that September 10 was Leslie's birthday.

As I said, his room was on the second floor, at the head of the stairs from the entrance hall. My living room is on the first floor at the foot of the stairs, and my bedroom is right behind it. The door of my living room is at the bottom of the stairs, and anybody going out from the second floor to the street has to come down the stairs and go by my door to go out the front door.

On the evening of September 10, 2002, I met him at the front door when I was coming in from shopping. It was about 7:15 P.M. He had a box—about as big as a five-pound candy box—wrapped in newspaper. It looked like a box of candy for Leslie for her birthday.

He seemed quiet and down when I saw him leave at about 7:15 P.M. I was surprised at this, because he had been so cheerful when the check for his story came earlier in the day. And he was usually a cheerful, joking, and talkative person. He sure didn't look like a happy husband on the way to celebrate his wife's birthday, but then again with the separation and the problems with Mrs. Thompson, he had cause to be down, even though it had been a big day for him as a writer. I felt sorry for him, and I hoped that things would turn out all right for him and Leslie.

I looked out and saw him get in his car at the curb. As he drove off, he waved to me. He left at about 7:15 P.M. or a little later. I am not positive now, and I can't fix the time more precisely.

That night I was watching TV in my living room. The door leading to the hall was open. While I was watching TV, I heard a car pull up at the curb outside my front window and the brakes sort of grind or screech. I didn't think much of it: there's a stop sign outside the place that's partly hidden behind some bushes and cars are always screeching to a halt there. I said to myself that Joe is certainly in a hurry tonight. I looked out my front window and I saw his car at the curb and Joe running up the walk. It was still raining. I heard him unlock the front door and saw him go past my living room door, which was open. He was in a hurry; he ran up the steps and didn't look into my living room. I didn't notice whether he was carrying anything or not. He may have had something under his arm, for all I could see.

I'd say that he came in somewhere between 9:40 and 9:55 P.M. I can fix the time because I remember I was watching a TV program, which always comes on at nine and ends at ten. After the first half hour, there is always a series of commercials and a station break, and that had already been on when I heard Joe's car and saw him go past my door. That program also always has a preview of the next week's program at 9:55 P.M., and that hadn't come on yet when Joe got home. I clearly remember that the program hadn't ended yet. I was watching the program and not my watch or the time, and so I can't say exactly what time Joe got home that night, but I can fix the time as being somewhere between 9:40 and 9:55. It had to be at least 9:40, because the station break had been over for some time, and it was into the second part of the program before Joe got home. The old radio classic, *The Shadow*, is broadcast at 10 P.M. every Saturday and Joe used to tell me how he never missed it. He thought they were just wonderfully written and thought he learned a lot about mystery writing by listening to them. He was careful always to be there on Saturday nights by ten—almost a religion. I heard two more screeching of tires outside between then and the time the police officers arrived but, again, I didn't think much of it and didn't look outside either time to see what the cause was.

I did not see him again until around 10:30 P.M., when he came down to my living room. I was still watching TV. He was dressed in pajamas and bathrobe and slippers. He told me he had a bad cold coming on from being out in the rain so much that night. He was feeling down, and he was coughing. I gave him some aspirin tablets. He did not say much of anything else and he went back upstairs.

At about 10:45 P.M., police officers came and introduced themselves as Officers Johnson and Slyviak. They said they were from the Nita City Police Department and wanted to talk to Joe Mitchell. I told them his room was at the top of the stairs at the second floor, and they went up. I did not go with them.

A little while later, I saw the police officers and Joe leave. I stayed in my living room. I didn't say anything to them, and none of them said anything to me.

I did not hear Joe's car being used again that night after I had heard him come in while I was watching TV, around 9:45 P.M. After the police left with him, I looked out and saw Joe's car at the curb. It was parked right where I had seen it before when I looked out. After Joe had come in earlier, I had drawn the drapes of my front window, and I did not look out the window again until after the police and Joe left.

There is a fire escape on the side of my building, and it leads to an alley back of my place, with a landing just outside the window of Joe's room. Of course, it would be impossible for me sitting in my living room on the first floor to hear any person using the fire escape.

Yes, it rained that night, pretty hard from 7:00 P.M. to around 10:30 P.M., I think. But whether the rain had stopped any time in between and then started up again, I simply do not know.

In all the time I knew him, Joe impressed me as an honest, truthful, and industrious person. I never heard a single thing against his character or reputation. I didn't know many of his friends or acquaintances. It is perfectly incredible to me, knowing him as I did and having observed his conduct so often, that he could be guilty of the terrible crime they've charged him with. He's not the kind of person who would do that.

I don't know anything about Joe owning a pistol or a gun. I never saw one in his room or in his possession. Also, I don't know anything about his being an expert shot or shooting for target practice.

I suppose that if I testify in this case, they will try to mention that I pleaded guilty to a charge of receiving stolen property in June 1998. That happened when a man named Dick Schwendler was a boarder in my place for a short time in the spring of 1998. In May 1998, he showed me a diamond ring and offered to sell it to me for $200. At this time, he owed me $150 in rent and board, and he didn't have any money, so he offered me the ring to pay his bill. He left the boarding house right after I took the ring in payment of his bill. A few weeks later, the police came to see me and told me the ring had been stolen by Schwendler. I had sold it to a jeweler shortly after I got it, and I was charged with "receiving stolen property." I employed a lawyer (Mr. Henry L. Stetson) to defend me. He is dead now. I told him that I didn't know the ring had been stolen when Dick gave it to me. Mr. Stenson arranged a deal with the prosecutor, where I pled guilty and was given a suspended sentence of one year. There is absolutely nothing else against me on my record.

I have read the above statement and it is true and correct.

Date: 10-12-02   Raleigh Porter

Date: 10-12-02   Witness: Jack Peters

This statement was taken at Mrs. Porter's boarding house by Jack Peters, an investigator for the defense.

STATEMENT OF CHRIS RAVENNA

My name is Chris Ravenna and I live at 500 Pine Street, Nita City, Nita. I am forty-six years old, and I am not married. I live with my brother, Sam Ravenna, who owns Ravenna's Gun Shop at 2141 Madison Street. I work for him there. We sell, repair, and clean guns. Most of our customers are Nita City residents who bring us their guns for cleaning and repairing. My brother also sells hunting rifles. He is a gunsmith. I work for him only as a clerk or salesman and keep the books. I am not, myself, a gunsmith, and I do not do any work on the guns. Our shop is on the north side of the street at 2141 Madison Street, west of the Thompson residence at 1751 Madison Street.

I understand that Joe R. Mitchell is charged with the murder of his wife, Leslie, on the night of September 10, 2002, and that they say he shot her while she was standing on the porch there. I was at the shop that night, and I didn't see Leslie Thompson get shot.

Joe Mitchell has been one of our customers for a couple of years. I first met him at the shop. He now lives at 800 Fillmore Avenue, but he formerly lived with his wife in an apartment at 50 Jackson Street. At the time she was shot, they had separated. She had left him and gone back to live with her stepmother at 1751 Madison Street, and he had gone back to live at 800 Fillmore, where he had lived before his marriage in 2001.

I know Joe Mitchell quite well, both as a customer and socially. I first became acquainted with him in a business way, when he came to our shop to have a gun repaired or cleaned, or to look over our stock of hunting rifles or other guns.

Yes, I saw Joe Mitchell on the night of September 10, 2002. At about 9:30–9:35 P.M. that night, he came into our shop. I was alone there; my brother had gone home. We keep the shop open until 10 P.M. I cannot fix the exact time when Mitchell came into our shop, but my best recollection is that he came in at about 9:30 to 9:35 P.M. We talked together for a few minutes, and I guess he was there for about ten minutes or so. I cannot give you the exact time he was in the shop. I closed up the shop at 10 P.M., our usual closing time. He had been gone about fifteen to twenty minutes before I closed up. I remember waiting for closing time with no one in the shop, and then getting everything ready for closing before 10 P.M., so it had to be fifteen or twenty minutes before 10 P.M. when he left. There was nothing special about that night, other than seeing my friend Mitchell in the shop. Although I don't have any special recollection of closing the shop at 10 P.M. that night, that is our usual practice, and I'm sure I followed it.

We talked when he came in the shop that night. He asked if his gun was ready and said that he had left it with my brother for repair and cleaning about a week ago. I checked the shelves and found a .38 caliber revolver with a tag on it which said "Joe Mitchell—Repair and Cleaning—$62.50." The tag had my brother's initials on it. I handed this gun to him,and he paid the bill. When I handed the gun to him, I saw him look at it and open or "break" it. I noticed that it had two shells or bullets in it. They must have been in it when he left it with my brother for repair and cleaning. I remember I said to him that he'd better be careful, because it was loaded, or something like that. I was surprised—my brother must have removed the shells when cleaning the gun and then replaced them but never said anything to me about them. Mitchell did not remove them when I gave him the gun. He put the gun in his jacket pocket. The jacket was dark blue or black in color, sort of wet, as if he had worn it out in the rain that night. It had been raining off and on all evening. I did not notice anything particularly unusual or strange about his manner or his appearance. He seemed quite calm, not nervous or agitated.

When he left the shop, I went to the door and looked out. It was raining and dark; there was no moonlight. I saw him walk from our front door down the walk to the curb in front of our shop and get in a car which was parked there at the curb. It was so dark and rainy that I could not see what kind or make of car he had. I had seen him on other occasions drive up in a white, 1992 Pontiac Ventura, but this time when I looked out, it was so dark and rainy that I could not tell what kind of car it was. I couldn't even make out the color of the car. All I could see out there at the curb was the dark outline or shadow of the car he got into.

After he got into the car, I could not make out his face or features. The distance from the front door of our shop out to the curb is thirty-five feet—I've measured it myself. It was too dark for me to see his face or features. Of course, from having been talking to him in the shop, I knew it was Joe Mitchell. With the darkness, the rain, and this distance of 35 feet, you could need cat's eyes to see out to the man in the car at the curb. I don't have that kind of eyesight; nobody does.

But even though I knew from previous experience that he usually drove this old '92 Pontiac, I could not swear that he had the same car out there that night. I can swear that, as I looked out the glass door to the curb that night, I could not see what kind of car he had, nor even make out the color of it. It was too dark, and the distance was too great.

I belong to a group in Nita City called the "Scribblers," and Joe is also a member. We have about fifteen men and women interested as amateurs in writing stories and we meet every month. I have heard these people speak very highly of Joe Mitchell; they know of his ability as a writer of short stories and TV scripts. His special interest is writing murder mystery stories and general detective stories. He used to read some of his stories to our group. He wanted to become a professional writer of short stories and TV scripts, but I've never heard of him selling any of his works or making any money from writing. When I first met him in this group in 1999, he had a part-time job as an attendant at a gas station and gave as much time as he could to his writing.

From all the conversations I had with the members of the group about Joe Mitchell, I would say he had the reputation of being a man of honesty, integrity, and decency, and a quiet, decent peaceable member of the Nita City community. Any faults? Well, I've driven with him once or twice and he drives very, very fast. He's real proud of his driving skill and he is able to maintain control, like a race driver. He does have a reputation as being a fast, though skillful driver.

I heard from other members of the group that in July, 2002, he had a row with his wife, and that she had gone back to live with her mother at 1751 Madison Street and he was living in a boarding house at 800 Fillmore Avenue. They said that she had deserted him, and he was pretty down about it. I'd never met her myself. They said that the cause of the separation was the mother-in-law, Mrs. Thompson, who had bitterly opposed the marriage of Joe and her daughter, Leslie. They said Mrs. Thompson had done her best to get the girl to leave Mitchell, breaking up the marriage, and it wasn't any fault of Joe's, but was solely the mother's fault. Actually, Mrs. Thompson was not Leslie's real mother, but was her stepmother.

I certainly regard Joe as an honest man. As far as I know, he was always prompt in paying his bill at our place. I would certainly believe anything he said, even if he weren't under oath. From my own knowledge of him and from the reputation he had among the other members of our group, I would say that he was not the kind of man who would injure any person, least of all his wife. I never knew him to lose his temper.

I do not believe he killed his wife. He is the victim of circumstances and of a mistaken identification made by Mrs. Thompson, the stepmother. I understand she will claim she saw him fire the gun that night, out at a curb in front of the house at 1751 Madison in the dark with no lights, while it was raining. The whole thing is incredible. I think she had such a hatred of Joe that, in her highly emotional state, she wanted to see Joe kill his wife. Her identification springs from her emotional bias toward him; she saw what her emotions wanted her to see.

I'll tell you who I think might have done it. I used to be bailiff for old Judge Thompson, Leslie's father. He sent a lot of guys away for a long time, and some of them wanted to get even. There was this one fellow, John Bierman, who thought Judge Thompson had ruined his life; Bierman threatened to get him for it. In 1989, Bierman was convicted of murdering his business partner, who was very well known in town. It was a real "headlines" case. Bierman claimed the Judge and the prosecutor rigged the trial. Bierman's whole life was wrecked; he lost a good business, his family, everything, and got twenty-five to thirty years from the Judge.

Last summer, I read in the newspaper that Bierman was getting out of prison and was returning to Nita City. In early September of last year, I saw Bierman in the Silver Dollar Bar. I recognized him right away, even though the trial was fourteen or fifteen years ago, because he had a very distinctive face, and he hadn't changed much. I was sitting at the bar fairly close to Bierman, but I'm sure he didn't recognize me. I heard him tell the bartender that "the Judge and the old lady" had railroaded him. He said he was glad Thompson was dead, but that it sure didn't even come close to making up for everything he had lost: family, business, everything.

I haven't seen Bierman since that night, but I know Joe Mitchell, and I don't believe he could have done this. I think the police ought to get hold of this Bierman.

It is true that on a number of occasions when he was in our shop, Joe Mitchell bragged that he was an excellent shot with his revolver. He said that he practiced target shooting regularly. I remember once he told me that he could hit a dime at 100 yards. Joe never discussed his private affairs with me, and I didn't know about his troubles with his wife or with Mrs. Thompson from anything he said to me. If he had troubles, he always kept them to himself. I have read the above statement and it is true and correct.

Date: 10-16-02

Chris Ravenna
_____
Chris Ravenna

Date: 10-16-02

Jack Peters
_____
Witness: Jack Peters

This statement was taken at Ravenna's Gun Shop by Jack Peters, an investigator for the defense.

EXHIBIT—STREET DIAGRAM

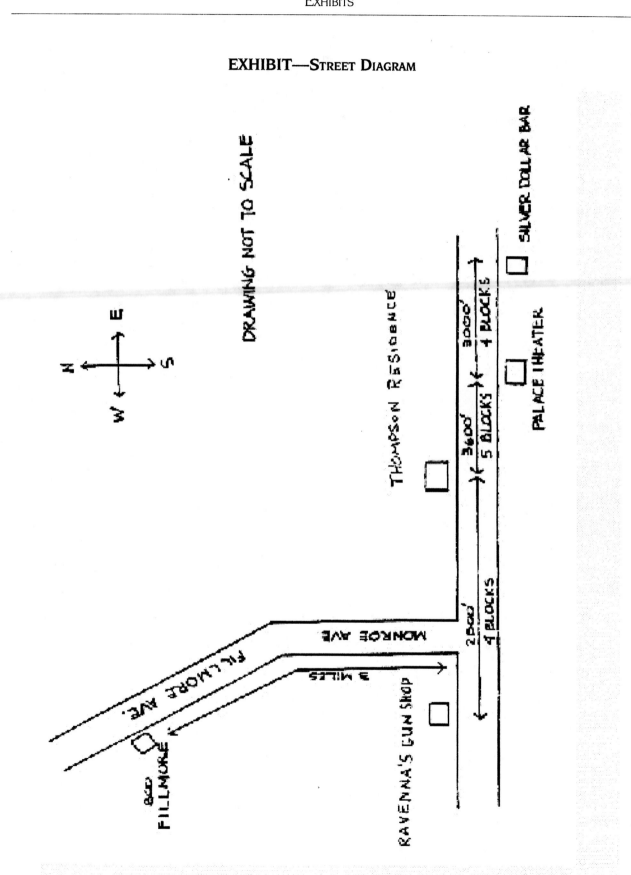

EXHIBIT—Diagram of Portion of Premises at 1751 Madison

Nita City, Nita

"The 43rd __Best__ Place to Live in the Nation . . . ." —Harold *Magazine*

**Office of the City Engineer,
John F. Baker, Deputy City Engineer**

I, John F. Baker, hereby certify that:

1. I am Deputy City Engineer of Nita City, Nita and in that capacity have custody and control of all maps, diagrams, charts, and documents filed in the City Engineer's Office.

2. On October 13, 2002, I made the attached copy of the original map of Section 100 of Nita City, Nita, as prepared by N. Allen Crow and filed in City Engineer's Office on September 25, 2001.

3. The attached copy of the original map was made by utilizing a standard photocopying machine in City Engineer's Office. The scale upon which the original map was drawn, as indicated thereon, is correctly shown on the attached copy. I have examined the attached copy and found it to be a correct and accurate representation of the original map.

4. Since the filing of the above-mentioned map on September 25, 2001, no amendments with respect to that map have been filed in the City Engineer's Office.

5. At the request of the District Attorney's Office of Darrow County, Nita, I have indicated on the attached copy the following data as ascertained by me from records on file in the City Engineer's Office:

   "A" —residence of Mrs. Brooke Thompson (north side of Madison St.);
   "B"—Palace Theater (south side of Madison St.);

   "C"—Silver Dollar Bar (south side of Madison St.);

   "D"—Ravenna Gun Shop (north side of Madison St.);

   "E"—Boarding House of Mrs. Raleigh Porter (800 Fillmore Avenue).

Dated: October 13, 2002

John F. Baker, Deputy City Engineer

I, Mary L. Johnson, Clerk of the Circuit Court, Darrow County, Nita City, Nita, do hereby certify that John F. Baker is a Deputy City Engineer and that he signed the above document in my presence.

Mary L. Johnson, Clerk

SEAL

EXHIBIT—Section Map of Nita City, Nita

PHOTOGRAPHS

Photographs 1 and 2 were taken by Officer Pat Slyviak of the victim, Leslie Thompson Mitchell, at the scene, 1751 Madison Street, at 10:15 P.M., September 10, 2002.

Photographs 3 and 4 were taken by the Crime lab of the porch and house at 1751 Madison Street, at 11:30 A.M., November 11, 2002.

PHOTO—FULL BODY PHOTO OF LESLIE MITCHELL

PHOTO—Close-up Photo of Leslie Mitchell

PHOTO—Photo of Front Door

PHOTO—FRONT OF HOUSE

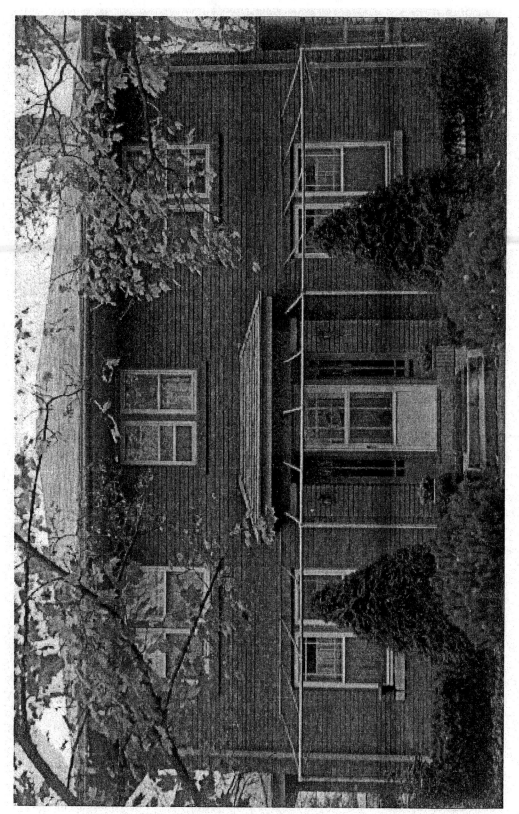

9-9-02

Leslie—

After what went on Tonight at your Stepmother's, I guess were finished. Life is intolerable without you + I'm going crazy at the Thought of this. You let your mind be Poisoned against me. You never gave me a real chance. That Evil OLD woman is to blame for all this. If it hadn't been for her, you wouldn't have walked out on me, as you did. She broke up our marriage, and believe me, I hate her for what she has done to us. You hurt me more than I can bear by taking her side against me. It would have been better for me if I had never met Either of you.

I'm going to make both of you regret what you did to me if its the last thing I do. I tried writing tonight, but I can't get you off my mind. I won't give you up as easily as you ran out on me. (over)

JOE'S HANDWRITTEN NOTE TO LESLIE   PAGE 2 OF 2

I suppose I ought to say I don't
love you anymore, but I do. From
all you said and did tonight,
especially your total agreement
with your stepmother, it looks like
were finished. But remember,
youre still my wife and always
will be. Nobody will take you away
from me, not your stepmother
or anyone else.

Joe

Police Custodian's Property Log

Owners Name _____ Joe Mitchell _____

Address_____ 800 Fillmore Ave., Nita City, Nita _____

Description___ #1 ___ .38 Caliber Revolver Serial No. 68717678 _____

_____ #2 ___ One dark-colored jacket recovered at Mitchell's Apt. 800 Fillmore

_____ #3 ___ One .38 caliber slug (found at scene of shooting,

_____ 1751 Madison St., Nita City) _____

_____ #4 ___ One movie ticket—torn (obtained from Mitchell) _____

_____

Inv. Officers_____ Time_____ Date_____

Received by_____

Received by_____

Received by _____

_____

_____

Received by _____

Received by_____

_____

_____

All property taken in charge by any member of this department to be described in detail on this form and receipted for by officer receiving such property from office and by each subsequent officer receiving property in order of receipt.

John Pierce

John Pierce is a sergeant with the Nita City Police Department. Sgt. Pierce is presently in charge of the Nita City Police Department Crime lab. He has been working in the Crime lab for seventeen years, serving as its head for the last five. Sgt. Pierce is a firearms expert and expert forensic technician and has been qualified as such in court on several occasions.

Sgt. Pierce filed a report on his examination of the .38 caliber revolver recovered from Joseph Mitchell's apartment at 800 Fillmore and the .38 caliber slug recovered at the scene—1751 Madison Street.

Additional Information Regarding Sgt. Pierce

Sgt. Pierce had many years of experience with the assembly, disassembly, and cleaning of firearms.

Sgt. Pierce would testify to the following with respect to the cleaning of a handgun:

1. That the time required to thoroughly clean a handgun depends on the number of times the weapon has been fired and also, to some extent, the particular type of handgun.

2. That a .38 caliber revolver is not a difficult weapon to clean.

3. That a .38 caliber revolver that is quite dirty (substantial powder residue from a number of firings) can be thoroughly cleaned in from twenty to thirty minutes.

4. That a .38 caliber revolver that is moderately dirty can be thoroughly cleaned in from ten to twenty minutes.

5. That a .38 caliber revolver that has been fired fewer than ten times after a thorough cleaning can be cleaned in five minutes or less.

6. That a .38 caliber revolver that has been fired once or twice after a thorough cleaning can be cleaned in one minute or less.

NITA CITY POLICE DEPARTMENT CRIME LAB REPORT

Lab File No.:   4011

Re: Paraffin Test, Ballistics Test, and Examination of .38 Caliber Revolver

Case: Leslie Mitchell Homicide

Date of report: September 11, 2002

Submitted By: Sergeant John Pierce

On Sept. 11, 2002, I was requested by Detective Allen J. Bradley of the Homicide Division to conduct an analysis of the evidence recovered in the Mitchell homicide. At approximately 8:50 A.M., I obtained a. 38 caliber revolver and a. 38 caliber slug from the Custodian's Office for analysis. These items were recovered by Officer Pat Slyviak and his initials appeared thereon. I also obtained the crime lab Report prepared by Technician Thomas Weibel on the paraffin test administered to Joe Mitchell on September 10, 2002.

Skid Mark Test. Measurements were made of skid marks found on the pavement from the street immediately in front of the Thompson house. Such marks could have been made from the tires of a car accelerating quickly from a stationary position. They could also have been made from a car applying the brakes hard. They could have been made on the night of September 10 or as much as two weeks before. The marks were made by a tire with a width of 16.35 centimeters. Mitchell's car has tires of that width. All full-size American cars do, as do 60 percent of all cars on the road.

Paraffin Test. Technician Weibel administered a paraffin test to the defendant Joe Mitchell at approximately midnight, Sept. 10, 2002. Technician Weibel's analysis of the test results indicated that the test was negative.

I examined the test data and my findings concur with that of Technician Weibel. The test was negative for the firing of a gun.

The negative finding can mean any one of several things:

(a)   The individual did not fire a gun,

(b) The individual did fire a gun, but no gunpowder particles were left on the individual's hand for any one of several reasons, such as:

(1)   Individual wearing gloves, or

(2)   The individual cleaned hands.

Ballistics Test. The .38 caliber revolver was test-fired. It is operable. The test-fired slug was obtained, and comparison was attempted with the slug found at the scene. No comparison could be made, as the slug found at the scene was too smashed to obtain any points of comparison.

Examination of the slug found at the scene indicates it is a .38 caliber bullet. The scarring on the sides of the bullet indicate that it was fired by a Smith and Wesson .38 caliber revolver. Approximately 40 per cent of revolvers in the United States are Smith and Wessons. Local market percentages differ markedly and there are no statistics for the percentages of the Nita City market held by Smith and Wesson.

Examination of a .38 Caliber Smith and Wesson Revolver. Visual (including microscopic) examination and physical tests were performed on the gun recovered from Joe Mitchell.

Examination and tests revealed:

(1)   The gun was remarkably clean.

(2)   Traces of oil in the mechanism.

(3)   It had been recently exposed to water.

The examination revealed no powder residue or stains. The traces of oil found in the mechanism and the absence of a buildup of powder residue clearly indicate a recent thorough cleaning. Examination also revealed traces of water in the mechanism, and Officer Slyviak's report indicated that the gun was wet when recovered.

Conclusion. The gun had been recently cleaned. No evidence of firing since the last cleaning was detected.

Certified By: _____

John Pierce
Badge #674

CORONER'S REPORT

STATE OF NITA   )

)   SS:

COUNTY OF DARROW   )

I, Allen J. Waddell, M.D. , Corner of said County, having examined the body of Leslie Thompson Mitchell at Memorial Hospital, September 10, 2002, same having there and then been identified in my presence by Mrs. Brooke Thompson as the body of her stepdaughter Leslie Thompson Mitchell do hereby find that the said Leslie Thompson Mitchell, deceased, came to her death on September 10, 2002 by reason of a gunshot wound. Said deceased being a female of the age of 25 years; weight 125; height 5' 2"; hair black; eyes blue ; complexion fair; race Caucasian.

REMARKS: Decedent brought to hospital in Police Ambulance at about 10:35 P.M., September 10, 2002, Decedent D.O.A. Examination of body disclosed bullet wound from firearm—bullet entered upper chest in front in area of heart and was ejected from body in back. Massive hemorrhages resulted, causing death. No powder burns; no physical deformities found on examination. Firearm apparently discharged at least two feet from body of deceased. No autopsy. Bullet discharged from revolver or pistol of some kind.

In Testimony Whereof I have hereunto set my hand and seal of my office this 11th day of Sept., 2002.

Allen J. Waddell M.D.
Coroner of Darrow County
State of Nita

JURY INSTRUCTIONS

1. The Court will now instruct you on the law governing this case. You must arrive at your verdict by unanimous vote, applying the law, as you are now instructed, to the facts as you find them to be.

2. The State of Nita has charged the defendant, Joe Mitchell, with the crime of First Degree Murder, which includes the crime of Second Degree Murder. The defendant has pleaded Not Guilty.

3. Under the criminal code of the State of Nita, a person commits the crime of First Degree Murder if, after deliberation and with the intent to cause the death of a person other than himself, he causes the death of that person or of another persons.

After deliberation" means not only intentionally, but also that the decision to commit the act has been made after the exercise of reflection and judgment concerning the act. An act committed after deliberation is never one which has been committed in a hasty or impulsive manner.

4. Under the criminal code of the State of Nita, a person commits the crime of Second Degree Murder if

   (a) He intentionally, but not after deliberation causes the death of a person <u>or</u>

   (b) With intent to cause serious bodily injury to a person other than himself, he causes the death of that person or of another person.

"Intentionally." A person acts intentionally with respect to a result or to conduct described by a statute defining a crime when his conscious objective is to cause such result or to engage in such conduct.

5. To sustain the charge of First Degree Murder, the State must prove the following propositions:

   (a) That defendant performed the acts which caused the death of Leslie Thompson Mitchell, a human being; <u>and</u>

   (b) That defendant acted after deliberation and with the intent to cause the death of Leslie Thompson Mitchell or any other person.

If you find from your consideration of all the evidence that each of these propositions has been proved beyond a reasonable doubt, then you should find the defendant guilty of First Degree Murder.

If, on the other hand, you find from your consideration of all the evidence that any of these propositions has not been proved beyond a reasonable doubt, then you should find the defendant Not Guilty of First Degree Murder.

6. To sustain the charge of Second Degree Murder, the State must prove the following propositions:

    (a) That defendant performed the acts which caused the death of Leslie Thompson Mitchell, a human being; <u>and</u>

    (b) That defendant intended to kill or cause serious bodily injury to Leslie Thompson propositions has not been proved beyond a reasonable doubt, then you should find the defendant Not Guilty of First Degree Murder.

If you find from your consideration or all the evidence that each of these propositions has been proved beyond a reasonable doubt, then you should find the defendant guilty of Second Degree Murder.

If on the other hand, you find from your consideration of all the evidence that any of these propositions has not been proved beyond a reasonable doubt, then you should find the defendant not guilty of Second Degree Murder.

7. It is your duty to determine the facts, and to determine them only from the evidence in this case. You are to apply the law to the facts and in this way decide the case. You must not be governed or influenced by sympathy or prejudice for or against any party in this case. Your verdict must be based on evidence and not upon speculation, guess, or conjecture.

From time to time the court has ruled on the admissibility of evidence. You must not concern yourselves with the reasons for these rulings. You should disregard questions and exhibits that were withdrawn or to which objections were sustained.

You should also disregard testimony and exhibits that the court has refused or stricken.

The evidence that you should consider consists only of the witnesses' testimony and the exhibits the court has received.

Any evidence that was received for a limited purpose should not be considered by you for any other purpose.

You should consider all the evidence in the light of your own observations and experiences in life.

Neither by these instructions nor by any ruling or remark that I have made do I mean to indicate any opinion as to the facts or as to what your verdict should be.

8. You are the sole judges of the credibility of the witnesses and of the weight to be given to the testimony of each witness. In determining what credit is to be given any witness, you may take into account his or her ability and opportunity to observe; his or her manner and appearance while testifying; any interest, bias, or prejudice he or she may have; the reasonableness of his or her testimony considered in the light of all the evidence; and any other factors that bear on the believability and weight of the witness's testimony.

9. The law recognizes two kinds of evidence: direct and circumstantial. Direct evidence proves a fact directly; that is, the evidence by itself, if true, establishes the fact. Circumstantial evidence is the proof of facts or circumstances that give rise to a reasonable inference of other facts; that is, circumstantial evidence proves a fact indirectly in that it follows from other facts or circumstances according to common experience and observations in life. An eyewitness is a common example of direct evidence, while human footprints are circumstantial evidence that a person was present.

The law makes no distinction between direct and circumstantial evidence as to the degree or amount of proof required, and each should be considered according to whatever weight or value it may have. All of the evidence should be considered and valuated by you in arriving at your verdict.

10. The State has the burden of proving the guilt of the defendant beyond a reasonable doubt, and this burden remains on the State throughout the case. The defendant is not required to prove his innocence.

11. Reasonable doubt means a doubt based upon reason and common sense that arises form a fair and rational consideration of all the evidence or lack of evidence in the case. It is a doubt that is not a vague, speculative, or imaginary doubt, but such a doubt as would cause reasonable persons to hesitate to act in matters of importance to themselves.

12. The defendant is presumed to be innocent of the charges against him. This presumption remains with him throughout every stage of the trial and during your deliberations on the verdict. The presumption is not overcome until, from all the evidence in the case, you are convinced beyond a reasonable doubt that the defendant is guilty.

VERDICT FORM

IN THE CIRCUIT COURT
DARROW COUNTY, NITA

THE PEOPLE OF THE STATE OF NITA,	)	
	)	
vs.	)	Case No. CR 2126
	)	JURY VERDICT
JOE MITCHELL	)	
Defendant.	)	

We, the Jury, return the following verdict, and each of us concurs in this verdict:

[Choose the appropriate verdict]

I. NOT GUILTY

We, the Jury, find the defendant, Joe Mitchell, NOT GUILTY.

———————————————
Foreperson

II. FIRST DEGREE MURDER

We, the Jury, find the defendant, Joe Mitchell, GUILTY of Murder in the First Degree.

———————————————
Foreperson

III. SECOND DEGREE MURDER

We, the Jury, find the defendant, Joe Mitchell, GUILTY of Murder in the Second Degree.

———————————————
Foreperson

CASE TWO: DEFAMATION

MacIntyre v. Easterfield

CONTENTS

INTRODUCTION

This is a libel/slander action brought in the Nita state court by Jesse MacIntyre against Ross Easterfield. Ms. MacIntyre was employed as a housekeeper in the Easterfields' home, and she claims that Mr. Easterfield falsely accused her of stealing Mrs. Easterfield's diamond brooch.

Ms. MacIntyre left her employment with the Easterfields after Mr. Easterfield allegedly accused her of theft. She attempted to obtain employment at the Nita City Athletic Club and through the ABC Employment Agency, and in both instances was unable to do so. Ms. MacIntyre claims that she was denied employment and has suffered emotional and economic injury because of Mr. Easterfield's libelous and slanderous statements against her.

The applicable law is contained in the memorandum of law.

SPECIAL INSTRUCTIONS FOR USE AS A FULL TRIAL

When this case file is used as a basis for a full trial, the following witnesses may be called by the parties:

Plaintiff	**Defendant**
Jesse MacIntyre	Reeve Winsor
Kelly Emerson	Ross Easterfield
Reverend MacKenzie Taylor	Kerry Easterfield
	Lee Marlow

Note: Ross Easterfield is a man; Jesse MacIntyre and Kerry Easterfield are women. The remaining witnesses may be portrayed by either gender.

A party need not call all of the witnesses listed as their witnesses. Any or all of the witnesses can be called by either party. However, if a witness is to be called by a party other than the one for whom he or she is listed, the party for whom the witness is listed will select and prepare the witness.

REQUIRED STIPULATIONS FOR FULL TRIAL

The parties must stipulate that the following exhibits are authentic and admissible, subject only to relevance objections:

1. Diagram of Easterfield's Home (p. 67)
2. Photographs of Easterfield's Home (pp. 69, 71, 73)
3. Bus Schedule (p. 75)
4. Mass Schedule (p. 77)

5. Loan Application (p. 85)

6. ABC Employment Agency Record (p. 115)

7. *Nita City Tribune* Ad (p. 123)

8. Easterfield Bank Statement (p. 105)

The following exhibits are all authentic. In the absence of stipulation by the parties, any objection other than authenticity may be raised to these exhibits:

1. Transcript of MacIntyre Guilty Plea (p. 79)

2. Transcript of Alice Adams (p. 82)

3. Nita Statutes (p. 87)

4. Statement of Jesse MacIntyre (p. 89)

5. Letter from Rev. Taylor to Easterfield (p. 93)

6. Statement of Stiko (p. 95)

7. Prison Board Order (p. 97)

8. Letter from Rev. Taylor to Nita Transit (p. 99)

9. Statement of Winsor (p. 103)

10. Zanori Transcript (p. 107)

11. Bill of Sale (p. 109)

12. Desk Calendar (p. 111)

13. Insurance Letter (p.113)

14. School Record (p. 121)

15. Van Kirk Interview (p. 125)

16. Marlow Letter (p. 127)

The letter from Peter Steinfel may not be used in full trials.

The purported letter from Jesse to Reverend Taylor (p. 91) is "authentic" only in the sense that it is the actual piece of paper received by Taylor. There is *no* stipulation that it actually was authored or sent by Jesse.

IN THE CIRCUIT COURT OF DARROW COUNTY,
NITA CIVIL DIVISION

JESSE S. MacINTYRE,	)	
	)	
Plaintiff,	)	
	)	COMPLAINT
v.	)	
	)	
ROSS J. EASTERFIELD,	)	
	)	
Defendant.	)	

Plaintiff, for her Complaint against the Defendant, alleges:

FIRST CLAIM FOR RELIEF-SLANDER

1. That at all times hereinafter mentioned, Plaintiff and Defendant were, and still are, residents of Darrow County, Nita.

2. That Plaintiff was employed by Defendant as a housekeeper from August, 2000, to July, 2002.

3. That on July 17, 2002, Defendant falsely accused plaintiff of theft, and the employment relationship was terminated.

4. That Plaintiff applied for a position with the Nita City Athletic Club by making an application to Lee Marlow, General Manager of the Club.

5. That on or about July 23, 2002, at the Nita City Athletic Club, Nita City, Defendant, in the presence and hearing of Lee Marlow and several other persons unknown to Plaintiff, spoke false and defamatory words concerning Plaintiff, the substance of which was that "Miss MacIntyre has slipped into her old ways and has stolen the diamond brooch."

6. That Defendant's statement was not protected by a qualified privilege, or, in the alternative, that, if it was so protected, Defendant abused that privilege and lost its protection by making the statement with malice toward Plaintiff or with a reckless disregard for her interests.

7. That prior to Defendant's speaking the false and defamatory words concerning Plaintiff, she was about to enter into an agreement with Lee Marlow, General Manager of the Nita City Athletic Club, whereby the Club would have employed Plaintiff at a salary of $125 per week plus tips averaging $50 to $75 per week, with meals provided by the Club. That as a result of Defendant's speaking such false and defamatory words, the Nita City Athletic Club refused to employ Plaintiff and to the present time Plaintiff has been unable to obtain comparable employment.

8. That by reason of such slanderous publication, Plaintiff was denied employment and incurred a substantial loss of earnings, was subject to contempt and ridicule, was injured in her reputation, and has suffered great pain and mental anguish, all to Plaintiff's damage.

SECOND CLAIM FOR RELIEF-SLANDER

9. Plaintiff realleges paragraphs 1 through 3.

10. That on or about July 21, 2002, Defendant spoke false and defamatory words concerning Plaintiff to the ABC Employment Agency, the substance of which was that "Miss MacIntyre was dishonest and had stolen a diamond brooch."

11. That Defendant's statement was not protected by a qualified privilege, or, in the alternative, that, if it was so protected, Defendant abused that privilege and lost its protection by making the statement with malice toward Plaintiff or with a reckless disregard for her interests.

12. That as a result of Defendant's publication of such false and defamatory words, the ABC Employment Agency refused to assist Plaintiff in seeking employment and to the present time Plaintiff has been unable to obtain employment commensurate with her skills and abilities. That as a result of Defendant's false and defamatory statements to the ABC Employment Agency, Plaintiff has been denied access to a substantial portion of the job market.

13. That by reason of such publication, Plaintiff was denied employment and incurred a substantial loss of earnings, was subject to contempt and ridicule, was injured in her reputation, and has suffered great pain and mental anguish, all to Plaintiff's damage.

THIRD CLAIM FOR RELIEF-SLANDER

14. Plaintiff realleges paragraphs 1 through 3.

15. That on Sunday, July 17, 2002, Defendant, in the presence of Kerry Easterfield and within the hearing of Kelly Emerson, spoke false and defamatory words concerning Plaintiff, the substance of which was that "Miss MacIntyre had stolen a diamond brooch."

16. That Defendant's statement was not protected by a qualified privilege, or, in the alternative, that, if it was so protected, Defendant abused that privilege and lost its protection by making the statement with malice toward Plaintiff or with a reckless disregard for her interests.

17. That by reason of such publication, Plaintiff was subject to contempt and ridicule, was injured in her reputation, had suffered great pain and mental anguish, and was forced to leave her employment, all to Plaintiff's damage.

WHEREFORE, Plaintiff demands judgment against Defendant in an amount that will fairly and adequately compensate her for her injuries and losses, together with interest thereon and her costs of this action, and for such other relief as the Court deems just and proper.

FOURTH CLAIM FOR RELIEF-PUNITIVE DAMAGES

18. Plaintiff realleges paragraphs 1 through 17.

19. That Defendant made the statements with malice toward the Plaintiff, or with a reckless disregard for the interests of Plaintiff.

20. That Defendant should be punished for such malicious statements.

WHEREFORE, Plaintiff demands judgment against Defendant for punitive damages, and for such other relief as the Court deems just and proper.

JURY DEMAND

Plaintiff demands a trial by jury in this action.

ARMSTRONG & DEMETRAL
by

Marianne Demetral

_____
Marianne Demetral
Attorneys for Plaintiff
Suite 720, Nita Bank Plaza
Nita City, Nita

RETURN ON SUMMONS

I hereby certify that the above Complaint was personally served on Ross J. Easterfield at his residence, 221 Rolling Hills Lane, Nita City, Nita.

Jane Bell

Jane Bell
Speedy Subpoena & Process, Inc.

IN THE CIRCUIT COURT OF
DARROW COUNTY, NITA
CIVIL DIVISION

JESSE S. MacINTYRE,	)	
	)	
Plaintiff,	)	
	)	
	)	
v.	)	ANSWER
	)	
ROSS J. EASTERFIELD,	)	
	)	
Defendant.	)	

Defendant, for his Answer to Plaintiff's Complaint, states:

1. Admits the allegations contained in paragraphs 1, 2, 4.

2. Denies the allegations contained in paragraphs 6, 7, 8, 11, 12, 13, 16, 17, 19, 20.

3. Admits that the employment relationship between Plaintiff and Defendant was terminated on July 17, 2002, and denies the remaining allegations in paragraph 3.

4. Admits that on July 23, 2002, Defendant spoke to Lee Marlow at the Nita City Athletic Club, and denies the remaining allegations in paragraph 5.

5. Admits that on July 21, 2002, Defendant received a phone call from the ABC Employment Agency and in response to said phone call spoke to said Agency, and denies the remaining allegations in paragraph 10.

6. Admits that on Sunday, July 17, 2002, Defendant spoke to Plaintiff in his home in the presence of his wife, Kerry Easterfield; states that Defendant is without sufficient information to admit or deny that Kelly Emerson was within hearing; and denies the remaining allegations in paragraph 15.

FIRST DEFENSE

7. That Plaintiff's Complaint fails to state a claim upon which relief can be granted.

SECOND DEFENSE-PRIVILEGE

8. That Defendant is a former President of the Nita City Athletic Club and is presently, and at all times material herein was, a member of the Board of Directors of the Nita City Athletic Club.

9. That the Nita City Athletic Club is a not-for-profit corporation duly organized and incorporated under the laws of the State of Nita.

10. That Lee Marlow is, and at all times material herein was, the General Manager of the Nita City Athletic Club and has responsibility for hiring all employees at the Club.

11. That in July, 2002, the Nita City Athletic Club, through its General Manager, Lee Marlow, was accepting applications for the position of hatcheck and coat room attendant at the Club.

12. That in late July, 2002, Plaintiff applied for the above-mentioned position at the Nita City Athletic Club.

13. That any statements alleged by Plaintiff in her first claim for relief were made by Defendant to Lee Marlow as General Manager of the Nita City Athletic Club, and were made solely in the interests of the Club and concerned the management and operation of the Club.

14. That Defendant, as Plaintiff's former employer, had the duty and responsibility to inform the Nita City Athletic Club through its General Manager, Lee Marlow, of the honesty and fitness of Plaintiff for employment.

15. That Defendant's statements were privileged business and community of interest statements.

16. That Defendant's statements were made in good faith, without any malice or intent to injure the Plaintiff.

THIRD DEFENSE-PRIVILEGE

17. That Kerry Easterfield is, and at all times material herein was, the wife of the Defendant.

18. That any statements alleged by Plaintiff in her first claim for relief to have been made by Defendant concerning Plaintiff were made with the intent and in such a manner that only Plaintiff and Mrs. Easterfield should hear, or could reasonably have been expected to hear, said statements. That Defendant's statements were privileged husband-wife and employer-employee communications.

19. That Defendant's statements were made in good faith, without any malice or intent to injure the Plaintiff.

FOURTH DEFENSE-PRIVILEGE

20. That any statements alleged by Plaintiff in her second claim for relief to have been made by Defendant concerning Plaintiff were made in response to an inquiry from the ABC Employment Agency.

21. That any such statements were made solely in response to questions from the ABC Employment Agency and were not initiated or volunteered by Defendant in any way.

22. That Defendant, as Plaintiff's former employer, had the duty and responsibility to inform the ABC Employment Agency of the honesty and fitness of Plaintiff for employment.

23. That Defendant's statements ware privileged business and community of interests communications.

24. That Defendant's statements were made in good faith, without any malice or intent to injure the Plaintiff.

FIFTH DEFENSE-TRUTH

25. That Defendant had been informed by Reverend MacKenzie Taylor of St. James Episcopal Church that Plaintiff had been convicted of a felony and had been incarcerated in the Women's House of Correction.

26. That pursuant to the statements, representations and urging of Reverend MacKenzie Taylor, and in the interest of Plaintiff and society, Defendant hired Plaintiff as a housekeeper in his home in August, 2001.

27. That on or about July 17, 2002, Plaintiff committed the crime of theft in that she feloniously exerted unauthorized control over a diamond brooch owned by Defendant's wife and valued at $25,000.

28. That any statements alleged by Plaintiff in her Complaint to have been made by Defendant concerning Plaintiff are true.

WHEREFORE, Defendant demands that the Complaint be dismissed and judgment entered in favor of Defendant, that costs of this action be assessed against Plaintiff, and for such other relief as the Court deems proper and just.

MITIGATION OF DAMAGES

29. That any statements made by Defendant concerning Plaintiff were made by him in good faith, believing them to be true, and without any malice or intent to injure Plaintiff.

30. That Defendant acted reasonably under the facts and circumstances known to him.

31. That immediately upon finding his wife's diamond brooch, Defendant informed Lee Marlow that it had been found.

32. That because of Plaintiff's previously existing character and reputation, any and all statements made by Defendant concerning Plaintiff did not materially injure her character and reputation.

WHEREFORE, Defendant prays that, if Plaintiff is entitled to damages, such damages be nominal.

BERRY, MOEHN, FOLEY & MADDEN, P.C.
by

Brian Moehn

Brian Moehn
Suite 1120, First National Bank Bldg.
Nita City, Nita
Attorneys for Defendant

CERTIFICATE OF SERVICE

I hereby certify that a copy of the above Answer was placed in the United States Mail, postage prepaid, addressed to Ms. Marianne Demetral, Armstrong & Demetral, Suite 720, Nita Bank Plaza, Nita City, Nita 99996.

Nora Ella Madden

_____

Nora Ella Madden
1120 First National Bank Building
Nita City, Nita

Deposition of Jesse MacIntyre

Jesse MacIntyre, called to testify on Deposition by Defendant, and having been duly sworn, testified as follows:

My name is Jesse S. MacIntyre. I am twenty-five years old and single. Since August 7, 2002, I have been working as a housekeeper at the Rectory of St. James Episcopal Church, Nita City. Before that I worked as a housekeeper in the home of Ross J. Easterfield, 221 Rolling Hills Lane, Nita City, Nita. It's near 9th Street.

I worked for the Easterfields for about two years. They had a large house, ten rooms, three floors, seven bedrooms, and a swimming pool. Mr. Easterfield is supposed to be one of the wealthiest men in the city. The Easterfields had no children, but they did a lot of entertaining and guests were always visiting them. There were always lots of things to do. I did general housework and cleaning, helped with cooking and serving meals, and generally assisted Mrs. Easterfield.

I was paid $100 a week, plus room and board, when I started working for the Easterfields, and then about a year later it was raised to $120/week. I had my own room on the third floor, and I had Sunday off after breakfast and also three nights off a week. The other housekeeper, Kelly Emerson, also had three nights off, and she and I arranged this between us. The Easterfields treated me fairly well and I was paid $120 a week plus room and board, although the average rate in the area is around $90-$100 a week plus room and board.

Mr. Easterfield owns the Easterfield Realty Co., a large real estate firm in Nita City. I had heard of him before Reverend Taylor introduced us. He is a member of the Board of Directors of the Nita City Athletic Club and formerly president. The club is a nice place and quite large. It has a gymnasium, swimming pool, and other athletic facilities. It also has a nice restaurant and dining room, and rooms for resident members and guests—kind of like a hotel. It is a very exclusive place, only for the rich. Mr. Easterfield told me once that they don't admit Jews or Catholics there. They have a large auditorium where they hold concerts and plays. During the time I worked for the Easterfields, it seems they were always going out with friends to the club.

On Sunday, July 17, 2002, just after I had served breakfast to Mrs. Easterfield in the dining room, she asked me to go up to her bedroom on the second floor to see if she had left her diamond brooch on the dresser there. I said to her, "All right, but I'd rather not. I have to go to church." The church is all the way over on 18th street. She said, "Please, Miss MacIntyre, I'm concerned about it." Kelly Emerson was just leaving the dining room when Mrs. Easterfield said that, and Kelly just rolled her eyes, as if to say, "Here we go again!"

I had seen Mrs. Easterfield wearing it the night before at around 8 p.m. when they left for the concert at the club. It was beautiful and I had always admired it. I heard from the other housekeeper that it was worth $25,000 to $35,000. But Mrs. Easterfield was terribly careless about her jewelry and she was constantly misplacing it and then forgetting where she had put it. She was careless about money too. I was always picking it up and hiding it for her so that some delivery man would not walk off with it. I told her that if she couldn't find some money she should look for it in the video cassette case for "Jesse James Rides Again." That's where I always put it.

I went upstairs and looked for the brooch, but I did not see it anywhere on her dresser. It was about 9:30 A.M. when I went upstairs, and I had planned to go to St. James Church for services at 10:30 A.M., so I only looked for the brooch for about four or five minutes. I came back downstairs and told Mrs. Easterfield that I couldn't find her brooch on the dresser, and that I had to get ready for church. I said to her, "You know it will turn up. It always does." Mrs. Easterfield didn't say anything, and so I left and went upstairs.

I went to my room to get ready for church. I was in my room for about twenty to twenty-five minutes. I came downstairs around 10:15 A.M. to go to church. I was going to the front door to leave when I heard Mr. Easterfield call me from the library. I went into the library and both Mr. and Mrs. Easterfield were there. He was standing next to his desk and he told me to sit down. I told him that it was my Sunday off and I was in a hurry to get to church. I wasn't angry, I was just in a hurry so I wouldn't be late for church.

I told him that I had to catch a bus or I would miss church. He said he knew that, but this wouldn't take long if I told the truth. His emphasis on the word "truth" and angry tone of voice concerned me and made me feel uncomfortable. Also he called me "Miss," which was unusual, as he always called me "Jesse" or "Miss MacIntyre." I became nervous and felt uncomfortable. I didn't have any idea what he was talking about—what he wanted to know the "truth" about. I said to Mr. Easterfield something like, "What's going on here? You're making me feel very uncomfortable."

Mr. Easterfield then asked me if I had seen his wife's diamond brooch at any time that morning. I told him that I had looked for it, but I couldn't find it on Mrs. Easterfield's dresser, where she had asked me to look for it. Then he said in a still angrier tone of voice: "What took you so long, why were you gone so long just to look on my wife's dresser?"

I started to tell him that I was gone for only a few minutes before I came back downstairs to tell Mrs. Easterfield that the brooch wasn't on her dresser, but before I could say anything he said: "Now Miss, tell us the truth, what did you do with the brooch—where did you hide it?" When he said that, he was walking toward me, and he came to within two or three feet of me, for a split second I thought he was going to hit me. I had seen him jump up and shake a temporary housekeeper who had spilled coffee on him at breakfast. He's a big man and he really shook her hard. I was afraid.

From his words and appearance, I felt that he was accusing me of stealing the brooch. I couldn't believe what was happening and I was terribly hurt. During the time in the library Mrs. Easterfield continually pursed her lips and turned her head away "in disgust" whenever I tried to say anything. I told him that he had no right to accuse me of stealing the brooch, that it was probably just misplaced like her jewelry usually is, and he knew better than to accuse me of being a thief. His accusations hurt me deeply. I burst into tears and ran out of the room. I went to my room and packed my bags. I just couldn't stay there under those circumstances.

[At this point in her deposition, the following questions were asked and answers given:

Q. Why do you claim that he was accusing you of theft?

A. Well, it was clear to me that he was.

Q. Why?

A. Well, his threatening actions mainly. And the expression on his face when he talked. What he said, too.

Q. But your conclusion, let us call it, that he was accusing you came mainly from his actions and his facial expressions, right?

A. Mainly.

Q. I'm showing you now what we'll mark as Deposition Exhibit Number 7 and ask you if you recognize this as the Complaint that you filed in this case?

A. Yes, that's the complaint.

Q. Did you read the complaint before it was filed?

A. Yes.

Q. And were the statements in it true to fact and accurate when you read it?

A. Yes.

Q. You didn't tell your lawyer to change it, did you?

A. No.

Q. And it said that "On Sunday, July 17, Mr. Easterfield said within the hearing of Kelly Emerson, `Miss MacIntyre has stolen a diamond brooch.'"

A. Yes, that's right.

Q. Now, did you ever hear Mr. Easterfield say, "Miss MacIntyre had stolen a diamond brooch"?

A. Well, no I didn't.

Q. But you didn't tell your lawyers that did you?

A. What do you mean?

Q. You did not say to them: "Don't put that in there because it isn't true," did you?

A. Well, no. I thought they knew what they needed to put in there.

Q. In order to win this case.

A. I suppose.

Q. And you just said, "Whether it's true or not, just put it in if it will help me get some money from Ross Easterfield."

MR. JANUS.   Objection. I think we're getting a little argumentative now.

Q. You also say in the complaint that Mr. Easterfield did various things "with malice."

A. Yes.

Q. Now, in the two years you worked at the Easterfields', did Ross Easterfield once act maliciously towards you?

MR. JANUS. Objection, calls for a legal conclusion.

Q. I'm not asking it in the legal sense. You may answer the question.

A. No. Not maliciously.]

I finished packing, and when I came downstairs to leave, Mr. and Mrs. Easterfield were in the hall near the front door. I told them that if they thought I was a thief, I just couldn't stay there any longer. I said, "After all this time, now you're calling me a thief." They said nothing. I was walking toward the front door as I said that.

I picked up my bag and went to the front door to leave. When I tried to open the door with my heavy bag, Mr. Easterfield didn't even offer to open the door for me. I had to put my bag down and open the door myself. When I got the door open, Mr. Easterfield reached for the bag, but I picked it up and walked out.

Mr. Easterfield was shaking his head violently back and forth during this time. He stood in the doorway and said in a loud and angry voice: "Miss, you're going to be the sorriest person in the world about what you've done here. You'll regret this the rest of your life." I started to cry again and I sort of ran and stumbled to the street. His words were so cutting and made me feel like I was the scum of the earth. I'll never forget what he said—he hurt me terribly then, and he's continuing to do it by making sure that I can't get a good job. He took away my self-respect and then he wouldn't even let me make a living. His words made me feel lower than I ever have since I left prison. It made me feel like when I was paraded in front of ordinary people in handcuffs or when I had to submit to strip searches when returning from court to the prison.

I walked for quite a ways, I don't remember how far, as I was crying most of the time. I finally got a cab and went to St. James to see Reverend Taylor. The cab driver, a fellow in his sixties with a thick Irish accent took one look at me and said, "Now, now, miss, you've got to stop sobbing and crying. I've been driving this cab for thirty-three years and I've never seen anyone so brokenhearted." When I arrived at St. James, Reverend Taylor calmed me down and I told what had happened at the Easterfields'. Reverend Taylor got me a room in the St. James Home for Women, which the parish runs.

Reverend Taylor made sure that I took it easy for a few days and tried to make me relax and forget what happened at the Easterfields'. Reverend Taylor encouraged me to try and get a job, so that I could go forward and put what happened at the Easterfields' behind me.

The next Friday, July 22, 2002, I saw an ad in the *Nita City Tribune* for a hatcheck or cloakroom attendant at the Nita City Athletic Club, 500 Main St. I went right over and spoke to Lee Marlow, the Manager. The job paid $125 a week, plus tips, which averaged around $50–$75. Marlow said the average daily attendance of guests at the club was about 150, and that almost every night there was a concert, play, or some activity in the club auditorium. If I got the job, I would work from 4 P.M. to 1 A.M., with Thursday and Sunday off. Also I would get my meals free at the club.

Marlow stated that there were other applicants, but that I was exceptionally well qualified for the job. Marlow was in charge of hiring and a lot would depend on my character references. Marlow said they would not employ anybody they could not trust absolutely, because it often happened that guests would leave valuable articles in the items they checked at the cloakroom. Marlow told me that they didn't have a labor union there. This was okay with me, because I never had any use for labor unions anyway, as they've never helped people like me.

Marlow didn't ask me whether I was then employed or anything about past employment. I suppose it was because I said that I was a member of St. James Church and I was presently living at St. James Home. I said I knew Reverend Taylor who had gotten me a room there. Marlow also belonged to St. James and knew Reverend Taylor. Marlow said that if Reverend Taylor would vouch for me, I wouldn't have anything to worry about. Marlow knew of Taylor's fine work and had the highest regard for it. Marlow told me that I would be notified about my application after talking to Taylor and after considering the other applicants. I gave the address and phone number of St. James Home. When I got back, I told Reverend Taylor about my application at the club. Taylor said the job would be good for me and that Taylor knew Marlow and would recommend me. Later in the afternoon I got a call from Marlow's secretary asking me what my social security number was and saying that she had already prepared my W-4 forms. She said the W-4s were on her desk. She described the employee's lounge at the club in detail and told me how lavish it was.

I didn't tell Marlow about my unpleasant experience at the Easterfields' on Sunday, July 17. I didn't say I had worked there because I wasn't asked about my previous employment. Marlow didn't ask for any other character references when I said I knew Reverend Taylor and was living at the St. James Home.

When I talked to Marlow that day in the club, it looked like I would get the job for sure. Marlow would talk to Reverend Taylor and she would get back to me right away, as someone was needed to help out as soon as possible. On the next Tuesday, July 26, 2002, I still hadn't heard from Marlow, and so I called. Marlow said that the job had been filled by another girl. I was shocked and disappointed. I went over to the club that afternoon to ask why I didn't get the job. I needed it so much, as my small savings were running out. I asked if Marlow had spoken to Reverend Taylor. Before getting a chance to talk to Reverend Taylor, Marlow had talked with Mr. Ross Easterfield, my former employer, who was a member of the club. After talking with Mr. Easterfield, Marlow had hired somebody else and the job was now filled.

I asked Marlow about contacting Mr. Easterfield instead of Reverend Taylor, especially since I had given only Reverend Taylor's name as a reference. I also reminded Marlow about not asking me anything about my former employment when I applied. Marlow said that the day after I applied, Saturday, July 23, Mr. Easterfield had come into the club for lunch. Marlow had lunch with Mr. Easterfield, and during lunch happened to remark that I was applying for the job. Mr. Easterfield then stated some things which cast doubt on my honesty. Marlow said that, of course, it was necessary to abide by Mr. Easterfield's remarks, since Mr. Easterfield was a member of the Board of Directors.

Marlow then asked me if it was true that I had a previous conviction for a crime. I asked Marlow how she found out about it, but she refused to say. Mr. Easterfield must have told her. I then told Marlow that, if she had called Reverend Taylor, she could have found out about all of the circumstance connected with it. That was a long time ago and Reverend Taylor would have told her I have had a good record since then, and that I was trying to live, and was living a good, decent, honest life. I had paid my "debt to society," if that's what they call it, and it was terrible for her or Mr. Easterfield to try to destroy somebody who was trying to make good.

Marlow said she was sorry, but that the job had been filled. She told me that she had to abide by what a member of the Board of Directors like Mr. Easterfield says. I told Marlow then that if Mr. Easterfield had accused me of theft while I was employed by him, this was a lie. I told her that I had never stolen anything from the Easterfields. When I said this Marlow looked down at the floor and was just silent. I then told her about the incident that Sunday with the diamond brooch. I told her Mrs. Easterfield had probably mislaid the brooch and that Mr. Easterfield had made a terrible mistake in accusing me. I said to her, "I'm just sure that Mr. Easterfield thought I stole the brooch." I never stole the brooch and it hurts me so that they say I did. I started to cry. Then I said, "You have a good job. You probably have never really been down on your luck. It can happen to you like it happened to me: first you're falsely accused and they never give you another chance. Never. You can't understand how much this hurts me. I didn't commit the original crime. I told my lawyer that and he just said, 'Tough luck little lady. Yeah, you're innocent, but you're poor and you were at the wrong place at the wrong time. Plead guilty and get it over with or you'll face heavy time.' Three years later he was disbarred. Now you're saying the same thing to me, 'Tough luck little lady, you were at the wrong place at the wrong time.' My life is over. There's nothing for me." I started crying and ran out of the club.

I went back to St. James and told Reverend Taylor. He called the Easterfields. He could not reach them. They were out of town, in Paris, the housekeeper told him. Reverend Taylor became very angry. He's such a mild fellow. I've never seen him that angry before. He said, "I've always thought that Easterfield was a self-centered bas—, person. We'd have been better off if he hadn't gotten involved in this program at all. It's pure, thoughtless cruelty. A child pulling the wings off a butterfly. I'm just so sorry, Jesse."

I've tried to get other jobs, at least ten or twenty, and nobody will hire me with Mr. Easterfield's bad character reference. In fact, I even applied at the ABC Employment Agency, despite the fact that they charge a large fee for their services. The Wednesday after I left the Easterfields, July 20, I went to the ABC Employment Agency and filled out an application form. The form asked about my prior employment, so I had to put down Mr. Easterfield, but I was never asked if I had a prior criminal record.

After Marlow told me about Mr. Easterfield's "bad character report" on me, I called the ABC Employment Agency back because I had not heard from them. This was on Wednesday, July 27, the day after I went to see Marlow, when she told me the job had been filled. The employment agency told me they had no jobs available. I asked them if it looked like something might come up soon, as I really needed to get another job and I was getting worried about it. The agency was very curt to me over the phone and said something like, "I don't think we'll have a job for you coming up soon. It looks very doubtful." Actually, they acted as if they didn't want anything to do with me.

In early August, 2002, Kelly Emerson called me and told me that the missing brooch had turned up in the library of the Easterfield home. She called me 15 minutes after she found it, she said. I think that Kelly told me that Mrs. Easterfield admitted leaving the brooch in the library. It was just as I thought—the missing brooch was found where Mrs. Easterfield had mislaid it and then forgotten about it. Just as she had mislaid other articles while I was working for her.

So, because of Mr. Easterfield, I lost out on the job at the club. This job is a small thing for Mr. Easterfield to be bothering about, but it meant bread and butter to me. Why should I be the victim of the carelessness of Mrs. Easterfield and Mr. Easterfield's petty, busybody activity and interference in the club with Marlow? Mr. Easterfield's mistake won't get me the job at the Nita City Athletic Club now.

Yes, I do have a prior conviction and was arrested once before that. The arrest was when I was thirteen for shoplifting. I picked up a blouse and walked past the check-out counters and I was arrested. I didn't intend to steal it. There was a station adjustment and no charges were brought. The conviction was something else. I still can't believe it happened to me; it seems like a terrible nightmare, and it looks like it will haunt me the rest of my life. I was born and raised in Nita City, but I never knew my father and mother, as they died in an automobile accident when I was very young. I had no relatives and so I was brought up in an orphanage in Nita City. They were kind to me there and I went to school through high school. When I was eighteen, I left the orphanage and got a job at Bowles Restaurant in Nita City as a waitress.

While I was working at Bowles Restaurant, I met another girl who worked there, Alice Adams. We roomed together. Alice lives in California now. One day at the restaurant, she introduced me to a man named Frank Holman. He came into the restaurant regularly and we'd usually talk for a few minutes or so. We became friends and occasionally we'd see each other socially. We would go to a movie or a party at a friend's house. It was never anything serious, and I went out with him only a few times, oh, something between 5 and 10 times, I guess. I found out later that Frank Holman had two previous felony convictions, both for robbery, but I didn't know it when I was dating him or I wouldn't have seen him.

One night in May, 1999, I went out with him and we were going to a movie, or so he told me before we went out together. Well, that night Frank Holman tried to hold up a gas station. On the way to the movie, Frank Holman stopped at a gas station. He said that he needed to get some cigarettes. He went into the station and I stayed outside in the car. I swear that I didn't know he was armed or that he intended to hold up the station.

After he was inside the gas station for a few minutes I heard some shooting. I got frightened and I didn't know what to do. I waited in the car for a few minutes and then the police came. When the police came, I was sitting on the passenger's side, as I had been ever since I got into the car that night. A policeman came over to the car and asked what I was doing there. I told him that I was waiting for Frank Holman and that he had gone inside the station to get some cigarettes, but he hadn't come out yet. The policeman told me to turn off the car engine and to wait in the car until he returned. Holman had left the car engine running when he went inside and I hadn't even thought about it until the policeman mentioned it, as Holman had said he'd just be a minute to get some cigarettes. I found out that Holman had tried to hold up the station and that he and the gas station manager had been shot. The station manager was shot in the leg and Holman in the shoulder. I was arrested along with Holman and charged with attempted armed robbery. They charged me with being an accomplice and said that I was the driver of the getaway car. I told them that I had no idea that he was going to rob that place, but they wouldn't believe me. Even after the lab report showed only Holman's fingerprints on the gun, still they wouldn't believe me.

Holman was convicted of armed robbery. It was his third conviction and he was sentenced to fifteen years. I didn't know about his previous record until the police told me about it. I pleaded guilty to a lesser charge of theft, on the advice of my attorney. He said that, from all the circumstances other than my word, it looked bad and that, if I was convicted, I could get ten to fifteen years. So I took his advice and pleaded guilty to the lesser charge that he and the prosecutor had been talking about. Although I denied I knew about Holman's scheme, I was given two years in the Women's House of Correction.

While I was in the House of Correction, I met Reverend MacKenzie Taylor, who took an interest in me. He had started up the St. James Home, which is an institution where they try to give you a chance to readjust to society and get a job. After about thirteen months, in August 2000, I was paroled to Reverend Taylor at the St. James Home. It was Reverend Taylor who then got me the job at Easterfield's. When I took the job, Mr. Easterfield told me he was interested in Reverend Taylor's project. He said he was in favor of the St. James Home and he wanted to help me. During the time I worked at the Easterfields', Reverend Taylor often visited there to see how I was doing, and he talked to Mr. Easterfield. As far as I know, there was never any complaint about me.

I stayed at the St. James Home for about two months before I got the job at the Easterfields'. During that time I had only one problem. I was at the local T-Mart shopping. I picked up a blouse that I liked and noticed that it did not have a price on it. I stuck it in my shopping bag and walked past the check-out counters to the man who was wearing a T-Mart badge standing near the front door to ask him how I could find out the price. Before I could say anything to him, this man said something like, "Where do you think you're going? Come with me." This man and the manager of the store kept me in a room off the store for about an hour and a half while they decided whether or not to call the police. I was really frightened—afraid of a parole violation. Finally they decided to let me go, but were real mean and told me that they didn't want me in the store again. They gave me a copy of some law and told me that they could have prosecuted me if they wanted to. It's below at page 87.

Mr. Easterfield had no reason to believe I stole the diamond brooch. He just jumped to conclusion—thinking about the fact that, after all, I did have a criminal record.

At least six times while I worked at the Easterfields', maybe more that I didn't hear about, Mrs. Easterfield misplaced her jewelry and told Mr. Easterfield that some of the help had stolen it. Each time, it turned up just where she had mislaid it. She would demand that Mr. Easterfield call the police and swear out an arrest warrant, but he never did it, as he knew of her careless habits and, also, he was too smart to get himself involved in any false arrests. He never seemed to take her ravings seriously. Mr. Easterfield certainly knew of his wife's carelessness with her jewelry and her habit of making reckless accusations. He was totally unreasonable in accusing me of theft that Sunday morning, and then he talked to Marlow and made sure I didn't get another job.

I think that Mrs. Easterfield can be just an incredible hypocrite. I couldn't believe that "God just didn't bless us" stuff in her deposition. In the fall of 2001 she became pregnant. I heard her discussing it with her husband one afternoon in the living room. They were speaking in hushed tones but weren't behind closed doors or anything. Mrs. Easterfield was saying that she was not cut out to be a mother and that her "commitments" would not allow her to have the child. By commitments I guess she means her time at the club. Mr. Easterfield seemed a little reluctant but went along.

Although Mr. Easterfield accused me of theft, he never called the police or swore out any warrant for my arrest. He was too smart, and knew his wife too well, to get into any problems like that; he just busied himself with informing Marlow.

Yes, early in July, 2002, I did try to borrow $500 from Mr. Easterfield, but he refused to even talk to me about it—he just flatly said "no." I also tried to borrow the money from the other housekeeper, Kelly Emerson. I wasn't surprised when she said that she didn't have that kind of money. I didn't tell either of them about my troubles with the Fidelity Loan Company and why I needed the money.

About a month or so after I began working at the Easterfields', I borrowed some money from the Fidelity Loan Company. I needed clothes and some personal things, and I just couldn't ask Reverend Taylor for anything more, as he had done so much for me, so I borrowed $300 from the loan company. I had no difficulty making the payments and everything was going fine.

About seven or eight months later, I think it was in June, 2001, I got a call at the Easterfields' from the lawyer who had represented me in my criminal case. At the time he represented me, I could only pay him around $200, and he wanted the rest of his money. He said that his total bill was $1,000, and he wanted to collect the $800 that was still due. He said that he had waited a long time to be paid and he wanted it as soon as possible. I told him that I didn't have that kind of money, but he didn't even listen. I offered to pay him so much each month, but he refused—said that he had waited long enough and he wanted it all in one lump sum. He said that he wanted it within one week or he would go to the Easterfields and take my wages, and then he hung up.

I didn't know what to do—I didn't want him to go to Mr. Easterfield, as I might lose my job, and also I couldn't ask Reverend Taylor, as I knew he didn't have that kind of money. So, finally, I decided to try and borrow some more money from the Fidelity Loan Company. I was only making $120 a week at the time so they wouldn't give me more than $800. They gave me some new papers and a new payment book. I was doing okay for a few months, but the payments were so high that I started to get behind. No matter how hard I tried I couldn't catch up, and then finally, in June and July of 2002 they really started to pressure me. They would call me all the time at the Easterfields', and even though I told them I was doing my best and asked them to please stop calling me at the Easterfields', they kept on hounding me. Then, around the middle of July, 2002, they called me a couple of times at the Easterfields' and threatened me—said that they'd take me to court, take away my wages, and I might lose my job. They had really upset me and I tried everything I could to get the money to pay them. I even asked Mr. Easterfield if he would loan me the money, but he didn't even listen. Finally, a week or so before I left the Easterfields' house, I went to Reverend Taylor. He was very reassuring and said that they maintained a fund to help people in my sort of situation. He loaned me $400 and said I could repay when I could. I was very, very relieved.

The loan application to Fidelity is below at page 85. I signed it. The loan officer typed the information on the form, except for the signature. Yes, when she asked me about my indebtedness, I answered "None." I became confused and said that because I had told them about the debt to the lawyer. I answered "none" because after I got the money from the loan company, I would have no indebtedness, because I would use the loan to pay off my debt.

That's what I meant. No, my salary then was $120 per week, not $150. I wouldn't have said $150. It must have been her mistake.

After I lost my job with the Easterfields, Reverend Taylor talked to the loan company and I got an extension on the loan. I had to sign a new set of papers, and I think Reverend Taylor signed them also.

On August 7, 2002, Reverend Taylor got me my present job at the St. James Rectory. They pay me $70 a week plus room and board at the St. James Home for Women. I've never had lunch in a fancy restaurant with Reverend Taylor. I've never had lunch in any fancy restaurant since I got out of prison.

Mr. Easterfield did me a terrible wrong. He wrongly accused me of stealing, ruined my reputation, and knocked me out of any chance to get a job at the club or anywhere else. What I don't understand is why such a "big man" like Easterfield even bothered with a little person like me or with such a minor thing as the hatcheck and coatroom job at the club. I guess he wanted to get me, and he sure managed to do that. He was wrong and he should have to pay for what he has done. But, even if I do win this case and he has to pay some money, he is so high and mighty that he won't even notice it and will brush it aside like an old suit. He is one of the wealthiest men in the city and what is a few dollars to him—nothing, he won't even notice it. He can forget about his mistake right away, but I can't, as I won't be able to get a job or forget what happened for a long time because of what he did.

Yes, I know about the letter Reverend Taylor received after I was let go by the Easterfields. I swear that I've never seen it. If you ask me it was Mrs. Easterfield's work or maybe Mr. Easterfield's. It bears the mark of her meanness. He may have just wanted to improve his case against me a little.

The Deposition was concluded and Ms. MacIntyre was excused.

This Deposition was transcribed, and then it was signed by the Deponent, Jesse MacIntyre.

Certified by

A. Marie Lane

Certified Shorthand Reporter (CSR)
Nita City, Nita

Deposition of Ross Easterfield

ROSS EASTERFIELD, called to testify on Deposition by Plaintiff, and having been duly sworn, testified as follows:

My name is Ross J. Easterfield, and I live at 221 Rolling Hills Lane, Nita City, Nita. I am married and we have no children. I was decorated for heroism while serving with the Marines. I own and operate a real estate firm, Easterfield Realty Co., the largest in Nita City and one of the largest in the state. I have an annual income of approximately $820,000 from my business and investments.

Jesse MacIntyre was a housekeeper in our home. She worked for us for about two years until she quit on Sunday, July 17, 2002. She claims I falsely accused her of stealing a $25,000 brooch belonging to my wife. This is a ridiculous claim, an attempted holdup, and I won't pay a cent. I have made no offers and I will not make any offers. I would never have hired her but as an act of charity to the church. No good deed goes unpunished.

This girl is an ex-convict who served time for attempted armed robbery. How can a person who has served time as a convict for a serious crime have a character for honesty which can be damaged? You have to have something to lose before you can lose it. She can't get a job because she's an ex-con, not because of anything I've done.

I was willing to give Miss MacIntyre a job when other employers wouldn't because of her record. I tried to help Miss MacIntyre by giving her a job and bringing her into our home—to help her get started again in building a new life and a good reputation after that prison experience. Even during that incident with the brooch when things looked so bad for her, I didn't fire her—she quit.

In August, 2000, I gave Miss MacIntyre a job as a housekeeper in our home even though we already had a housekeeper and really didn't need another one. I gave her the job at the urging of Reverend MacKenzie Taylor of St. James Episcopal Church, which I attend. I knew Reverend Taylor and had heard about some of his projects. Reverend Taylor had a project at St. James, where the parish had set up a home and he takes in paroled convicts to help them find jobs and readjust to society. He has some kind of working arrangement with the state prison authorities. I thought this a humane project. His work is partly paid by the parish and partly by outside funds. I have contributed to it.

I felt sorry for Miss MacIntyre and I gave her a job in our home as part of Reverend Taylor's plan for her rehabilitation and re-entry into society.

We have a large home with ten rooms, seven bedrooms, and three floors on about an acre lot, with swimming pool and a tennis court. We had, at the time, a cook, gardener, chauffeur, and then with Miss MacIntyre, two housekeepers. Miss MacIntyre did general housework and cleaning, and generally helped my wife. I paid her

$100 a week plus room and board and had raised her wages to $120 a week plus room and board about a year after she started. This is above the average for housekeepers in Nita. I know because I ask around at the club every so often. Also, she had Sunday and three nights a week off. She had her own private room on the third floor of my house. We treated her well and her wages were above the average for housekeepers in Nita City.

Due to my active work in community affairs, I have had many meetings and guests in our home. I have been active in United Fund drives, Police Foundation drives, Good Government League, Muscular Dystrophy Fund, and other community groups. As a result, our house was often like a hotel with all those meetings and guests. I don't make any money out of these activities. I do my duty as a citizen, contributing my time and efforts. I have always taken an active interest in politics and contribute to conservative causes. I currently contribute to the Republican and Libertarian parties. There was a time fifteen or so years ago when I thought the country was in really deep trouble and I was more radical in my politics. At that time I made some contributions to Lyndon LaRouche's party. I think that was really foolish of me.

When I took in Miss MacIntyre, I knew from Reverend Taylor about her criminal record. Reverend Taylor told me that Miss MacIntyre had served about thirteen or fourteen months of a two-year sentence at the Women's House of Corrections for her part in an armed robbery of a gas station. She had pleaded guilty to a lesser charge, while her companion, a guy named Holman, was convicted and got fifteen to twenty years as a second offender.

Reverend Taylor said that she was a victim of circumstances—that she was, in fact, innocent. He said that Miss MacIntyre's friend, Holman, had taken her out on a date and they were in his car when he stopped at a gas station and tried to rob it. She claimed that she didn't know that Holman had a gun or that he intended to rob the station. Apparently she just sat out in the car during the robbery. There was some shooting and both Holman and the gas station attendant were hurt. The police arrested both Holman and her. She pleaded guilty to some lesser charge on the advice of her attorney. This was her story, according to Reverend Taylor. The police claimed she was the getaway driver. I thought perhaps that Reverend Taylor was a bit naive. I didn't have to believe that she was completely innocent before I offered to help. I was not so sure as was Reverend Taylor that she didn't know what Holman planned to do, but felt it was still my obligation as a Christian to do what I could.

Miss MacIntyre's work for us was generally satisfactory. Reverend Taylor often came to see us and check up on her. I recall telling him that I had no reason to complain about her work. And, oh yes, Reverend Taylor did tell me that she had been brought up in an orphanage. Her parents had died when she was very young and she had no relatives to care for her.

On Sunday, July 17, 2002, I slept in a little late and around 9:45 A.M. I came downstairs. My wife was in the dining room, and when I greeted her it was obvious that she was upset and distraught about something. She told me that her diamond brooch was missing and that she was concerned about Miss MacIntyre's conduct earlier that morning.

My wife said that she had left the brooch on her dresser the night before when we returned from the concert at the club, and that when Miss MacIntyre had finished serving breakfast, she had asked her to go to my wife's bedroom and bring the brooch to her. It would normally take about five minutes or less for Miss MacIntyre to go to Mrs. Easterfield's bedroom and return to the dining room. My wife said that Jesse was gone fifteen minutes or so, and when she came back she said the brooch was not there, that it was missing. My wife said she asked Jesse what took her so long, and Miss MacIntyre replied rudely and angrily that she had been busy and walked out. I confess to having mixed feelings when my wife explained what happened that morning. On the one hand I felt that my wife may have exaggerated a problem with lost jewelry once more. Still, I thought it wrong to discount her suspicions without a hearing.

My wife and I went to the library and we talked about the brooch and what had happened that morning. I had given the diamond brooch to my wife as a wedding present. It is insured for $25,000. My wife had worn it the night before when we went to a concert at the Nita City Athletic Club. After the concert we had some drinks with friends and we got home around 1 A.M. I remember my wife wearing the brooch that night, but I don't remember anything special about what she did with it when we got home.

We were married on June 7, 1980. In response to discovery I produced a bill of sale for the brooch. I know the bill of sale is dated May 15, 1975. The bill of sale is just wrong: that's all I can say. The company is out of business. We recently had the brooch appraised and it appraised at $25,000. [The bill of sale is below as at page 109.]

At around 10:15 A.M., I heard Miss MacIntyre in the front hall. I called out for her to come to the library and she did so. Yes, it did appear that she was dressed to go out—she had her good clothes on, and yes, I did know that she always went to church about that time on Sunday.

When Miss MacIntyre came into the library, I told her that I just wanted to ask her a few questions and it would only take a minute or so. She was obviously annoyed and acted rude to us. She snapped that she was in a hurry and that this was her day off. She turned her back and was about to leave the room. She actually turned her back on us. I called to her to sit down, but she refused. When she turned toward us again, her face was flushed and she avoided looking at us. She was nervous and was fidgeting with a small handbag. She was trying to keep the handbag out of view.

I asked Miss MacIntyre if she had seen Mrs. Easterfield's diamond brooch that day. Her face flushed red and she said: "You mean the one she wore last night?" I said: "Yes, the one you were sent to look for this morning." She looked down at the floor and didn't respond. So I asked her again to tell me if she had seen it or knew anything about what had happened to it. She flared up in anger and said that I had no right to call her a thief and accuse her of stealing the brooch. She ran out of the room and I heard her run up the stairs. I never accused her of stealing the brooch and I most certainly didn't call her a thief. She said it; I didn't. My wife then flared up and said, "That vulgar little tramp!"

The diamond brooch was missing and all I did was ask Miss MacIntyre if she had seen it. I didn't accuse her of stealing it. Whenever anything of value is missing, I ask the employees if they have seen it and to help look for it. That was all I expected of Miss MacIntyre when I asked her about the missing brooch.

I may have spoken sharply to her, but I didn't lose my temper. I tried to be calm. At first I didn't suspect her of having anything to do with the missing brooch, but after she acted so strangely then, yes, I did begin to suspect her. When she didn't respond at all to my simple question of whether she had seen the brooch that morning, and then suddenly rushed out of the room, it did appear quite suspicious.

Also, about a year before Miss MacIntyre came to work for us, our cook disappeared with some of my wife's jewelry. I reported it to the police and swore out a warrant for her arrest. The police caught her and the jewelry was recovered and returned to us. That incident was probably in the back of my mind also.

After Miss MacIntyre ran out of the room, my wife and I stayed in the library. We talked about Miss MacIntyre's strange and suspicious behavior and how it was similar to the trouble we had with our cook, Miss Alice Brown, a few years ago. I then told my wife about Miss MacIntyre's past and her prior conviction and serving time in prison. Up to that point, I had not told my wife about her criminal past. I hadn't thought that she would handle the thought of an ex-convict living in the house very well. So the combination of her strange behavior that entire morning coupled with the fact that she was an ex-convict and the Alice Brown incident a few years ago made us both a little suspicious.

A little while later, Miss MacIntyre came down the stairs. We went out into the hall. She had a suitcase and she rushed past us to the front door. As she did so, she shouted at both of us: "If you think I'm a thief, I am quitting right now—you can have your job," or something like that. I shook my head "no" to her statement that we were calling her a thief. Then she put the bag down on the floor to open the door. I reached down to help her with the bag, to lift it up and help her carry it out. She hurriedly snatched it from me and went out the door. As she was walking down the steps, I told her that she could stay and she said, "No." I then told her that she was walking out on a good job—that she would regret it, as we've been good to her and helped her when others wouldn't. I most certainly did not threaten her with any reprisals. I was just telling her how good she had it here and how tough life can be for a person with a criminal record.

I had not fired her. She herself quit. I had not accused her of theft; that was her inference. I suspected her, from her behavior and actions, but I didn't accuse her of stealing the brooch. I asked Ms. Emerson about the brooch that morning and she didn't take offense. In fact, after this madness with Ms. MacIntyre, I approached Ms. Emerson a few days later in the dining room and said something like, "Kelly, I hope you know that I did not mean to imply anything by asking you if you had seen the brooch on the morning Jesse left." She said, "No, of course not, Mr. Easterfield. I didn't feel that you were accusing me at all."

I don't think I was unreasonable in thinking that she had acted suspiciously. I thought that she was trying to hide something, and this something had to do with the missing brooch. What else could I think from her unusual conduct?

Also, earlier in July she had asked me to loan her $500. I refused. I thought it inappropriate for a person's employer also to be her creditor. There's just too much confusion of roles in this situation. She did not tell me what this was for. All she said was that she needed it desperately. A few days later my wife told me that she happened to pick up the phone on the upstairs extension in our bedroom and had heard Miss MacIntyre on the line in the kitchen. According to my wife somebody on the other end of the line was threatening Miss MacIntyre if she did not pay them some money. Miss MacIntyre, according to my wife, replied something about getting the money "even if she had to steal it"—or words to that effect. My wife had told me about this before the episode with Miss MacIntyre that Sunday.

No, I did not report the loss of the brooch to the police. I had my suspicions about Miss MacIntyre, but I wanted more facts and I didn't want to risk a false arrest suit.

Yes, I did report the loss to the insurance company, first by phone and then by letter. In the report to the company, I said the brooch had probably been lost. My copy of the letter is below at page 113. I didn't say anything about Miss MacIntyre. Later when the investigator called, it was after the brooch had been found, and so the claim was withdrawn. When I called them to withdraw the claim, they mentioned that they hadn't received my claim letter.

It is true that my wife has on a number of occasions mislaid or misplaced articles of jewelry and forgotten where she put them. Yes, she did suspect that somebody in the house had stole them, and the jewelry later turned up in the house. But in the case of Miss Brown, my wife's suspicions turned out to be true and well-founded. I remember that, when Miss Brown disappeared with the jewelry, I asked the other housekeeper, Kelly Emerson, if she had seen the jewelry. She cooperated with me calmly in helping me search for it.

That was all I expected of Miss MacIntyre when I asked her about the missing brooch that Sunday morning.

Late in the afternoon on the seventeenth I had a conversation with the handyman/ gardener whom we had working for us last summer, Peter Zanoni. He asked me what all the shouting had been about. I told him. This is what he told me then. He told me that he was doing some electrical work on the second floor when he saw Jesse go into our bedroom about 9:35 A.M. He said Jesse didn't see him. Before she left the bedroom she poked her head out of the door "to see if anyone was watching." Zanoni said it looked like she had some small object in one hand. "She kind of ran into me and seemed surprised—gave a little jump. I said, 'Why so secretive? What have you got there?' She said, "Nothing. Nothing at all." and ran up the stairs." Mr. Zanoni died last fall.

On the Friday after Miss MacIntyre quit her job with us, July 22, I received a call from the ABC Employment Agency concerning Miss MacIntyre. Yes, I've seen the ABC Application Form and the supervisor Winsor's notes on it. I didn't make those statements to her.

When the agency called, Ms. Winsor introduced herself and told me that they were inquiring about Miss MacIntyre, as she had applied for job placement with their agency. She explained that it was standard business practice and absolutely essential that the agency get as much information as possible from an applicant's prior employers. Ms. Winsor then asked about her employment with us. Such as the position she held, for how long, whether her work was satisfactory, and questions like that. I answered those questions, and then they asked why the employment was terminated. I explained what happened that Sunday morning and that Miss MacIntyre quit her job with us and walked out. I specifically said that I had not fired her. They asked if I would recommend her and I told them quite honestly, no, I could not. They also asked if I would have her back in our home and I told them, no, I would not. They called me and asked the questions; I had to tell the truth.

On Saturday, July 23, 2002, I stopped in for lunch at the Nita City Athletic Club. I was formerly president of the club and am now a member of the Board of Directors. By chance, I met Lee Marlow, the manager of the club, and we lunched together. Naturally, as a member of the Board of Directors, I'm vitally interested in the club's welfare. During lunch, Marlow happened to mention that she was hiring a new hatcheck or cloakroom girl, and that a woman from the St. James Home named Jesse MacIntyre had applied along with some others. As I recall, Marlow described her appearance, I recognized her, and I said that she had worked for us as a housekeeper and that she had quit last Sunday.

Marlow told me she had not asked Jesse about her previous employment because she had mentioned Reverend Taylor of St. James, whom Marlow knew, and that was enough. Marlow said she had not asked for any other references. She said he had tried to reach Reverend Taylor, but had not yet succeeded.

About two years ago, a cashier at the club had walked off with about $1,000 of the club funds. We never got it back. I remember this and I told Marlow then, during our lunch, that she ought to be careful about the person she hired.

I told Marlow that Miss MacIntyre had worked for us as a housekeeper for two years on the recommendation of Reverend Taylor because we wanted to give her a chance and help her get started again. I told Marlow that, as reported by Reverend Taylor, Jesse MacIntyre had served time in the Women's House of Corrections for having taken part in an armed robbery attempt of a gas station, and that she had pleaded guilty to a lesser charge and got two years and her boyfriend had gotten fifteen years. I told Marlow how Reverend Taylor got her out on parole and took her to the St. James Home. Marlow said that Jesse had not said anything about her prior criminal record. I then told Marlow about what had happened that past Sunday.

As a member of the club's Board of Directors, I had the right, and even the duty, to make known to the club Manager what I knew of the applicant for the job. It certainly is a fact that Miss MacIntyre had a criminal record. That can't be denied or disputed. Also, she acted very strangely that Sunday morning when I asked her about the brooch.

On August 3, 2002, our other housekeeper, Kelly Emerson, found the diamond brooch while she was cleaning in the library. I was in the living room and she immediately brought it to me. She told me that she had found it behind a book on the library shelves. I asked her to show me where she found it and she showed me the book *Modern Physics* by Henry P. MacIntyre. That book is larger than the other books around it, and it isn't used very much. I called to my wife, who was in another room, and showed her the missing brooch and told her where it was found. She said that she had stepped into the library for a few moments that Saturday night after the concert, but that she didn't remember putting it behind a book on a shelf in the library. She said she remembered taking it off and putting it on the dresser in her room.

A day or so after the brooch was found, I called Marlow at the club and explained that the missing diamond brooch had been found. I said that our other housekeeper, Ms. Kelly Emerson, had found it in the library while she was cleaning. Yes, I'm almost positive that I mentioned where the brooch was found—after all, it was quite remarkable and unusual that it was behind a book authored by MacIntyre, especially when there are over a thousand books in the library. I am aware of the average levels of tips earned by coatcheck girls at the club: about $75 per week.

I recall either wanting to call the ABC Agency or actually calling them: I really can't remember which. You see my own mother suffered a stroke a few days after the brooch was found. I flew to Cleveland and stayed with her until her death ten days later. When I got back I was personally disoriented and way behind in my work. I found a note on my desk calendar that suggests that I did call ABC about Jesse. It's below at page 111.

I did discover Miss Emerson eavesdropping once before. My wife and I were having a conversation about some of our personal financial matters in our bedroom and I heard a soft sound outside. I walked outside and found Miss Emerson standing there in the hall pretending to dust. I confronted her directly: "Miss Emerson, were you listening to our conversation?" I guess I sort of shocked her with my directness, and she said a meek, "Yes." I lectured her for a good ten minutes about that. I was sure that she would never do that again after that lecture. That's why I was surprised to hear that she did.

Miss Kelly Emerson left our employ in October, 2002. She said that she had been happy and well treated, but she wanted a change and to live alone.

The Nita City Athletic Club is incorporated. The duties of the Directors of the club are general supervision, determination of the policies of the club, approving budgets, and matters like that.

Yes, I am aware of the letter Reverend Taylor received. It looks like a bit of remorse that Miss MacIntyre didn't have the courage to go through with. Of course I had nothing to do with its creation and I resent even that suggestion. I did not receive the "note" that Reverend Taylor says he sent to me about being nice to Jesse. My wife told me that she never got such a note either.

I have read over Winsor's description of my problems with the law and they are true as far as they go. That is what the indictment said and I did plead guilty. I deny doing what it alleges, but how could I turn down the kind of offer they made when facing twenty years in jail. I was tempted to go to trial, but the risk was just too great. The fact that the State agreed to probation shows that the prosecutor knew how weak her case was. She was up for re-election when she brought the case and after she was re-elected he just wanted to get out of it. It's true that two civil suits have been successful in rescinding real estate contracts based on alleged misrepresentation, but that's two out of thousands of transactions. I have spoken at scores of real estate brokers' seminars but I have no specific recollection of the talk that Winsor describes. It's possible I gave it. As to the remark she quotes from me, I don't remember saying it, though there's some truth to the sentiment.

Yes, when discovery turned up Miss MacIntyre's fraudulent loan application, I did call up the Loan Company and demand that they do their duty and file a criminal complaint against her. I had gotten my Notice for Deposition that day and I was angry. Yes, I did tell them that if they did not take such action, I would take it as a sign of fiscal irresponsibility and make sure the clients of my real estate company did not do business with them again. My action might seem petty to you, but Ms. MacIntyre's exploitation of decent people has to end somewhere.

The deposition was concluded and Mr. Easterfield was excused.

This Deposition was transcribed, and then it was signed by the Deponent, Ross Easterfield.

Certified by

A. Marie Lane

_____

Certified Shorthand Reporter (CSR)
Nita City, Nita

SUMMARY OF KERRY EASTERFIELD'S DEPOSITION

KERRY EASTERFIELD, called to testify on Deposition by Plaintiff and having been duly sworn, testified as follows:

My name is Kerry Easterfield. I live at 221 Rolling Hills Lane, Nita City, Nita, with my husband Ross J. Easterfield. God has not blessed us with children. It's a source of some sorrow.

I understand that Jesse MacIntyre is suing my husband for damages, claiming that he made certain accusations or charges that injured her reputation, particularly that he made statements to Lee Marlow, the Manager of the Nita City Athletic Club, and the ABC Employment Agency, and that these statements resulted in her not obtaining employment.

Yes, my fur coat is young seal fur. Why do you ask?

I was astonished at these outrageous claims. There is no basis for them whatsoever. This girl was a former employee of ours—worked for two years as a housekeeper in our home before she quit on July 17, 2002. I think she is just trying to "take" my husband for a pile of money. I agree with him that he should not offer to pay one cent by way of settlement of any claim this young woman may make. We have not made any offer and will not.

Jesse MacIntyre, unmarried, worked for us as a housekeeper for about two years prior to July 17, 2002. She then quit. She was not fired by us. Neither my husband nor I had any intention of firing her.

My husband had given me a wedding present—a diamond brooch—it was valued at from $25,000 to $30,000. I understand he had it insured with the Providential Insurance Co. for $25,000. The night before she quit, Saturday, July 16, my husband and I went to a concert at the Nita City Athletic Club (my husband was a former President of the club and is now a member of the club Board of Directors). I wore the brooch that evening. After the concert, we had cocktails with some friends and we got home around 1 A.M.

The next morning, Miss MacIntyre served breakfast in the dining room at about 8:30 A.M. or so. I had eggs Benedict, a croissant, a cup of espresso, and a Bloody Mary. My husband was not up yet. I think it was around 9 A.M., when I was still at the table, that I suddenly thought of my diamond brooch. I remembered that I had left it on the dresser in my bedroom on the second floor. I asked Miss MacIntyre to go up to my bedroom and bring the brooch to me. She left the dining room and did not come back for about fifteen or twenty minutes. When she returned, I asked her if she had the brooch. She was extremely rude to me and snapped out that the brooch was missing. I asked what had kept her so long and she snapped at me that she was in her own room. She left the dining room without saying another word. Yes, I knew she had Sunday off and that she was probably going to church.

[At this point in her deposition, Mrs. Easterfield was asked about a conversation with her husband which took place just after Jesse left the dining room. The following questions were asked and answers given. After these questions and answers, attorneys for Mr. Easterfield interposed objections to all questions concerning conversations between the Easterfields out of others' hearing, but allowed Mrs. Easterfield to "answer over" the objections.]

Q. What happened then?

A. Mr. Easterfield came downstairs and walked into the dining room.

Q. What, if anything, did he say to you or you to him?

A. Well, I was very upset at the uppity way in which Jesse had acted and as soon as Ross came into the room, I blurted out, "Jesse took my wedding brooch."

Q. And what did Ross then say?

A. Well he looked sort of angry and he said, "Why do you say that?"

Q. Who was he angry at?

A. Jesse, of course.

Q. Then what did you say?

MR. JANUS. At this point I am going to interpose an objection of privilege . . . the husband-wife privilege. And I'm instructing my witness not to answer that question or any other question concerning the contents of this conversation.

Q. Okay. Who else was in the dining room with you when you had your conversation?

MR. JANUS. OBJECTION . . . uh, assumes facts not in evidence. There's been no testimony that anyone else was there.

Q. You can answer the question now.

A. No one else was there, I don't think.

Q. Where was Kelly Emerson?

MR. JANUS. If you know.

A.   Well, she was in and out of the dining room serving breakfast. By the time Ross came down, she had served breakfast, pretty much, and had gone back to the kitchen. She was clanging around out there. About that time she was coming into the dining room occasionally to pick up dishes.

Q.   How loudly did you say the words, "Jesse took my wedding brooch!"?

A.   Well, I was angry, but I don't scream.

My husband came downstairs a little while later and I told him what had happened with Miss MacIntyre. Then I went up to my bedroom myself, and the brooch was not there. I came back to the dining room and I told my husband that the brooch was missing. We went to the library and discussed what had happened that morning.

A little later, we heard Miss MacIntyre in the front hall. My husband called to her and she came into the library. She had her coat and hat on and was dressed to go to church. My husband asked her to sit down. She replied in a rude and angry tone: "I'm in a hurry. You ought to know I'm going to church and I don't want to be late. This is my day off, isn't it?" She refused to sit down when my husband asked her to do so. She started to walk out of the room—turned her back on us. She would not look at us and seemed to be avoiding us. She had a small handbag with her. It seemed to me that she was trying to keep it out of sight. Her face was flushed red. She was in an angry mood.

My husband asked Miss MacIntyre if she had seen my diamond brooch that morning and she replied, "You mean the brooch she wore last night?" He said, "Yes, that's the one, I see you know it." It was obvious that she knew what we were talking about, and she was being evasive. My husband asked her what took her so long when she was asked to look for it that morning, and she simply said that she was "busy." That curt and smart-alecky remark exasperated my husband and he said something like, "Just tell us the truth. Have you seen the brooch this morning?" She flared up in anger, snapped at us that we had no right to call her a thief, and ran out of the room. Of course, my husband was a bit upset by her conduct. He did speak in a louder than normal tone of voice, but I wouldn't say that he lost his temper. My husband did not accuse her of stealing the brooch. She put those words in his mouth.

We stayed in the library and talked about what had happened, both with the brooch and Miss MacIntyre's unusual conduct. I told my husband that I remembered thinking about the brooch when I was in the library for a few moments the night before, and how he had given it to me for our wedding, and that I was almost positive I went upstairs to our bedroom, took it off and put it on my dresser. I also told him that, in my opinion, Miss MacIntyre's conduct was very suspicious—both her conduct in the library and the fact that, when I asked her to look for the brooch earlier, she was gone for about twenty minutes.

I also reminded him of the trouble that we had with Miss Brown a few years ago. (Miss Brown had worked for us as a cook and one night she disappeared with my jewelry. Thank God, they caught her and we did get the jewelry back.) I told him that maybe we had another Miss Brown case here. My husband then told me that Miss MacIntyre was an ex-convict and had served time in the state penitentiary for armed robbery. He said that he hired her on the recommendation of Reverend Taylor as part of her rehabilitation program. My husband hadn't mentioned a thing to me about her past criminal record before that time, but it certainly explains why Reverend Taylor was here so much checking up on her. I was angry that my husband had brought this woman into my home without telling me about her background. I told him that I was angry at him. He then got angrier for being accused of making unilateral decisions. I saw right away that it was his childlike good heart that had led him to do this. I told him this and that I couldn't stay mad at him for being such a good man.

And then we heard Miss MacIntyre out in the hall. We went out and there she was—with her suitcase or traveling bag. She was on her way to the front door. She just rushed past us both and, as she did so, she said something like "If you think I stole the brooch, I'm quitting right now. You can have your job." Her face was flushed red with anger. Ross shook his head "no" to her statement. She put her suitcase down on the floor to open the front door. When my husband reached for it to help her with the suitcase she suddenly grabbed it from him and went out the door. As she was leaving, my husband said, "You're leaving a good job— we've been good to you." She just kept on and she hasn't been back since then.

We paid her $120 a week plus room and board, and she had Sundays and four nights a week off. During her time with us, she had been generally satisfactory in her work, but, during the last month she had become very rude and was slackening off in her work.

I was convinced that she had stolen the brooch. I told my husband that when we were talking in the library.

I never saw her after this. I understand she went to Reverend Taylor's place at St. James Church. We belong to that church also. I understand that Reverend Taylor gave her a room there. Reverend Taylor has an establishment—a home there—that he operates and has rooms for single women working in Nita City. He also takes women who are "paroled" from prisons and gives them a place there and tries to get work for them as part of their "rehabilitation."

As I told you, this girl Alice Brown had stolen some of my jewelry two years ago. On that occasion, my husband swore out a warrant for her arrest. She was caught by the police. She pleaded guilty and was put on probation. The jewelry she admitted taking was recovered by the police and returned by them to us.

About a week or so before this episode, at about 10 p.m. one night, I happened to pick up the phone on an extension in my bedroom to call out. I recognized Miss MacIntyre's voice on the kitchen extension, talking to a man whose voice I did not recognize. He sounded like a real thug. I did hear this person say: "If you don't get the $500 by next week, you'll be sorry," and, before I could hang up, I heard her say, "I'll get it for you even if I have to steal it." Again, I can only give you the substance of what I heard. I am not an eavesdropper—I hung up immediately when I realized she was on the phone. I mentioned this conversation to my husband prior to the episode with Miss MacIntyre that Sunday. I did not mention it to Miss MacIntyre.

After she quit, my husband and I discussed the matter between the two of us. We agreed he did not have enough to swear out an arrest warrant, or even to report the incident to the police, as we had done in Alice Brown's case, so he did not. I did not want him to do so, anyway. I felt sorry for Jesse. My husband told me, "I was willing to forgive her if only she would have been honest."

Yes, I remember a conversation with Marlow in which we discussed the Alice Brown matter. She said some things about what they do at the club to try to avoid such problems, but I just don't remember what she said. I don't remember whether she mentioned their policies on hiring ex-convicts.

On August 3, 2002, our other housekeeper, Kelly Emerson, was cleaning the library—dusting the books in the study—and she found that brooch. She brought it to my husband in the living room and then he called me to come into the living room. She explained that she had found it hidden behind a book in the study—on the shelves there—and the title of the book was *Modern Physics* by Henry MacIntyre. We have over a thousand books in the study there.

I most certainly didn't put the brooch behind that MacIntyre book in the library. I do recall that I went into the library for a few moments when we got back from the concert at around 1 a.m. I don't recall taking the brooch off and leaving it in the library that night. I admit that it is possible that I took it off and left it in the library, but my recollection is that I had left the brooch on the dresser in my room.

No, I did not tell Miss Emerson when she found the brooch that I remembered putting it there in the library. If that is what she says, then she misunderstood me. When she brought me the brooch and told me that it was found in the library, I said something like, "Oh, I may have left it in the library that night." Leaving it in the library and hiding it behind a book are quite different things. I think Miss Emerson is "remembering" things in a way that will help her friend.

It is perfectly possible that Miss MacIntyre took the brooch from the dresser when I sent her up to my room that morning to look for it, and on her way back to the dining room, she put it behind the book where Miss Emerson found it—putting it behind a book written by a person named MacIntyre would, of course, make it easier for her to find it later among the some thousand books we had there. Maybe she planned to take it from the house later on, but never got the chance. Even if I had left it in the library, she might still have hidden it behind that book.

Yes, Miss MacIntyre had embarrassed me terribly at a cocktail party I had given toward the end of June last year. I had invited the Executive Wives Club over one hot Saturday afternoon. Miss MacIntyre put the crab meat canapés out on the kitchen counter too early and they just sat in the heat. Everyone at the party had stomach cramps by 7:30. The president of the club had to go to the hospital emergency room and they had to pump her stomach. What an embarrassment. Anyway, I said to my husband, "I want that woman fired!" He told me that she needed the work and that we should keep her on. He also said that we didn't know for sure that the crab meat wasn't bad already. I shouted at him, "I'm getting rid of her if it's the last thing I do!" We were alone in our bedroom when I said that.

I admit that, in the past on a number of occasions, I mislaid or misplaced articles of my jewelry. On those occasions I did suspect thievery by one of the housekeepers and I did state my suspicions to my husband. On most of those occasions (except in the case of Miss Brown), the missing or misplaced jewelry did turn up later in the house where I had left it and forgotten about it. I guess I have been a bit careless on some occasions. Yes, Miss MacIntyre did occasionally give me amounts of cash that I'd left here or there around the house.

It was after the brooch was found, as I told you, that my husband told me for the first time about meeting Marlow and talking about Miss MacIntyre and the episode in the house that Sunday. My husband was doing his duty to the club. We had no intent to injure Miss MacIntyre, no malice or bad feelings toward her at all.

Her services as a housekeeper in our home were generally quite satisfactory, except, as I told you earlier, for the last month before she quit, when she became quite rude and impertinent in speaking to my husband and myself. I also noticed that she was depressed or melancholy at times and did not seem to be working efficiently. The incident with the crab meat happened during this time. She seemed to be worrying about something. I never found out what the nature of the transaction was between her and the unknown person who was talking to her on the phone that night when I overheard them. I mean the time that person was threatening her and demanding $500.

I was friendly with George Williams, my tennis coach. We had lunch occasionally. Yes, he was young and handsome but I was interested in tennis not in him. There is absolutely no evidence that we were having an affair. It was a shock when he died suddenly, but I can't say I mourned his passing. I guess that shows we weren't close.

Yes, it is my responsibility to insure my jewelry since the general homeowner's insurance doesn't cover pieces of a value of more than $1,000 and I have quite a few of those. My understanding with Ross is that if I lose a piece of jewelry, the insurance proceeds are mine to do with as I please. I did lose a ring once and the insurance company paid off $3,500. I bought another ring with the proceeds.

Yes, that's right. Miss Kelly Emerson is no longer working for us. She resigned in October, 2002. She said that she had been happy working for us, but that she wanted a change and to live alone.

It's true that Miss MacIntyre told me to check the video box of "Jesse James Rides Again" if I misplaced cash.

I belong to Citizens for Effective Law Enforcement and to Citizens for the Punishment of Criminals, a group that opposes the "rehabilitative ideal." I think that our courts are altogether too lenient in the sentencing of criminals and I am completely against parole. Doesn't all this prove me right? If there hadn't been parole all this wouldn't have happened. I am a bit of a single issue voter on this. I contributed heavily to the campaign of a local judge who promised as part of his campaign to impose the maximum sentence on every criminal before him. Some judges' disciplinary group screamed and he lost the election.

I saw the letter Reverend Taylor received. If she was so sorry why is she putting us through this hell? Pure greed and ingratitude. Of course I had nothing to do with its being sent.

Contributions to organizations? Well, I supposed I must answer honestly. For the past six years I have contributed anonymously to the local food pantry.

The Deposition was concluded and Mrs. Easterfield was excused.

This Deposition was transcribed, and then it was signed by the Deponent, Kerry Easterfield.

Certified by

a. Marie Lane

_____
Certified Shorthand Reporter (CSR)
Nita City, Nita

SUMMARY OF REVEREND MACKENZIE TAYLOR'S DEPOSITION

REVEREND MACKENZIE J. TAYLOR, called to testify on Deposition by Defendant, and having been sworn, testified as follows:

My name is Reverend MacKenzie J. Taylor. I am an ordained priest of the Episcopal Church. I am a graduate of the Yale Divinity School, and I was ordained to the priesthood in 1997. At Yale, I took graduate courses in sociology and served as an assistant to the chaplain at the Connecticut State Prison.

After I was ordained, I became an assistant pastor at St. James Church, Nita City, Nita. I did graduate work at Nita University and received an M.A. in criminology. My master's thesis was a study of the relationship between pastoral care in a parish and the rehabilitation of former convicts. Since 1998, I have been an assistant chaplain at the Nita Women's House of Corrections, which is a penal institution operated by the State of Nita.

In 1999, I established the St. James Home for Women. The parish owns the building and maintains the Home with some help from the United Fund and private donations. The Home was organized and set up to provide a place where young women who need assistance can turn for help. We provided rooms, meals, a family community-type atmosphere, and, if necessary, guidance and counseling. We assist the women in obtaining employment or furthering their education or job skills, so they can eventually make it on their own. The Home is meant to be a short term, halfway-house type of facility to assist young women, in whatever way we can, in achieving a normal and productive life for themselves. Some simply need temporary shelter and assistance between jobs or during a family crisis, while others need the suppor t and encouragement of the community atmosphere, guidance and assistance in obtaining employment, or counseling in helping them put their lives back together again.

In conjunction with the St. James Home, I also established a program under which we accept young women on parole from the House of Corrections by arrangement with the state authorities. St. James accepts them only after careful sociological screening. Upon their release to us on parole, our role is to find jobs for them and help them readjust to society. Under our arrangement with the State, they will be paroled to us if we will provide general supervision and assist them in obtaining employment. I am primarily responsible for this program.

Over the past four years, we have accepted about fifteen or twenty young women in the program. Pending our placing them in jobs, we counsel them and provide work and some income for them in the Home preparing meals and general upkeep duties. All of the women have been remarkably successful in readjusting to society, and we have yet to lose a single woman who's been in the program. We've trusted them and they have returned that trust. After our screening and their acceptance in the program, we've attempted to build up their confidence and demonstrate our trust in them, and every single one of them has certainly more than returned that trust and confidence. This "zero recidivism" rate has been what has most impressed our private funding sources. Of course, I'm very happy about that as well. I think that we've developed a program of spiritual counseling, group reinforcement, and community involvement that makes falling back into criminal patterns very, very unlikely. I've recently published a short book outlining our methods.

No, the St. James Home is not exclusively for parolees from the Women's House of Corrections. The Home serves women from all parts of society and the parole program is only a small portion of the Home's service to young women. Of all the women that have utilized the Home over the past four years, I would estimate that less than ten percent were in the parole program.

In May 2000, I met Jesse MacIntyre in connection with my work at the Women's House of Corrections. She was serving time for complicity in an attempted robbery of a gas station. From the prison officials and the court records, I determined that a man named Holman attempted to rob a gas station, and both he and the gas station attendant were shot. When the police arrived, they arrested Holman inside the gas station and Miss MacIntyre outside in Holman's car. Holman was charged with attempted armed robbery and assault, and Miss MacIntyre was charged as an accessory—apparently on the theory that she had helped plan it and was the getaway driver. Holman was convicted and received a sentence of fifteen years. Miss MacIntyre's attorney worked out a plea bargain and she pleaded guilty to a lesser charge and was sentenced to two years in the House of Corrections. The lesser charge was simple theft, which is a class 5 felony, the lowest in Nita.

I talked to Miss MacIntyre and counseled her. I learned that she was an orphan from early childhood—both parents killed in an automobile accident—and that she had been brought up in a Nita City orphanage. She left the orphanage at age seventeen and began working as a waitress in a Nita City restaurant. Through a friend, she became acquainted with Holman and dated him a few times. Miss MacIntyre told me that she had no idea whatsoever of Holman's plan to rob the gas station, and that she was with him that night because he had asked her out on a date to go to a movie. That when he stopped at the gas station, he had said that he needed cigarettes and he would be right back. The next thing she knew, she heard shots, she waited and became more and more frightened, and then the police came and arrested her while she was still sitting in the car. She said that she pleaded guilty because her attorney told her that if she didn't, she would be found guilty anyway and would be sentenced to fifteen years.

I learned that Miss MacIntyre's lawyer was a local courthouse "hustler." This means that he took a large volume of cases, many from first time criminal defendants who didn't know better. Jesse's parole officer told me that he had managed not to try a case from 1992 through 1999. He just pled them all out. I learned this from reading the Memorandum Opinion of the Attorney Registration and Discipline Commission disbarring him. Jesse came to realize only later how she had been taken advantage of by this guy.

Miss MacIntyre maintained her innocence with such firmness and conviction that I decided to do some checking on her background and the circumstance surrounding the incident. I determined that everything she had told me was true. The more I learned about Miss MacIntyre and the incident that sent her to prison, the more I become convinced that she had told me the truth and she was in fact innocent. I evaluated Miss MacIntyre as a good, decent, hardworking person who became a victim of circumstances and a bad lawyer. I did that evaluation as part of my professional work as a criminologist to determine the appropriate rehabilitative environment for Jesse. In making this decision, I reviewed quite a bit of material: the sorts of things that are generally, and in my opinion, appropriately relied upon by criminologists designing rehabilitative programs. One of the documents I reviewed was a sworn statement by a friend of Holman's who had died before Holman's case went to trial. For some reason they wouldn't have allowed it into evidence at Jesse's trial, if she had had a trial, but it was important to me, as it would have been to any criminologist. Anyway, this friend of Holman had sworn that he had spoken to Holman before the robbery and, in effect, that Holman intended to do the robbery with Jesse as an innocent dupe. I made a photocopy of the statement. It's below at page 95. It was consistent with my own impressions of Jesse.

In July 2004, Miss MacIntyre was paroled to me at the St. James Home. Her parole was granted unanimously the first time her case was considered by the parole board. This is a group not noted for its leniency, believe me. Its order is below at page 97. At the time of her release, she had served thirteen months. Upon her release, Miss MacIntyre lived at the St. James Home, and she was immediately accepted and became part of the group that was living there at the time. She was well liked by everyone and her transition was progressing even faster than I had expected.

About a month after she was released, I succeeded in getting her a job as a housekeeper in the home of Ross J. Easterfield, 221 Rolling Hills Lane, Nita City. Mr. Easterfield is a member of St. James Parish and had expressed interest in my work and the St. James Home. I told Mr. Easterfield about Miss MacIntyre and made a full disclosure of her past record—the conviction, the time she had served in prison, and that she was on parole. I also told Miss MacIntyre that I was making a full disclosure of her past to Mr. Easterfield, so that both parties would have a clear understanding. Mr. Easterfield agreed to hire Miss MacIntyre by employing her. Thereafter, I frequently visited the Easterfield home, and Mr. Easterfield assured me that he was well satisfied with Miss MacIntyre.

I am very reluctant to pass judgment on someone's motivations, but I have come to have a very firm notion of Mr. Easterfield's motives in the matter of Miss MacIntyre's employment. This judgment is based on years as a spiritual director and pastor. I now believe that Mr. Easterfield was not motivated by a sincere desire to help Ms. MacIntyre but by a "Pharisaical" desire to appear virtuous and generous in the eyes of the community and ultimately in his own eyes. This is a common pitfall that all the moral and spiritual writers comment on. Writers in the Lutheran tradition, recently Bonhoefer and Paul Ramsey, are particularly eloquent on this. Classically, it is intertwined with a desperate need for self-justification that cares just nothing for the truth. Such people can be terrible liars. Worse, perhaps, they are so self-absorbed that even their perceptions of events are really badly skewed. My own pastoral experience confirms this. I know that this is harsh, but I'm driven to that conclusion. I recall a conversation I had with Mr. Easterfield in April of 2002. It took place at the church after Mass one Sunday. Mr. Easterfield was asking my advice on a number of matters. We were alone. At the end of the conversation, I asked him if he might be able to employ another young woman from the St. James Home. Easterfield said something like, "Well, Reverend, to tell the truth I don't think I'm really getting enough credit for this sort of thing and I think I'll direct my charity to places where it might be more publicly appreciated. You know, Reverend, what the Good Book says: `Don't put your light under a bushel basket!'" I think this fellow has been getting his name on plaques at public buildings for so long that he had come to expect it.

Based on my observations, I can say that I was well acquainted with Miss MacIntyre's reputation while she was at St. James and while she was working at Easterfield's. Her general reputation for honesty and integrity—for truth and veracity—was good. It seems to me that she had been completely rehabilitated after her parole to us. Her character and reputation had been completely restored. It seems perfectly plausible to me that a person who has once been convicted of a serious crime can still regain his character and reputation by a blameless life thereafter. It would be atrocious to say that, because a man or a woman had been convicted of a serious crime, he or she could never again have or acquire a reputation for honesty and integrity, for truth and veracity which could be destroyed by slander or libel. So, in my opinion, in July, 2002, and long before that, Miss MacIntyre had reacquired her reputation for honesty, integrity, for truth and veracity.

Around the 7th of July of 2002, Jesse came to the rectory and told me that she had fallen behind in the payments to the Fidelity Loan Company. She said that about $300 was due and that another payment of $100 was coming due in July. The Home maintains an emergency fund for exactly this sort of thing and I told Jesse not to worry, loaned her the money, and she seemed much relieved. We haven't discussed repayment. We'll leave that to her conscience.

On Sunday July 17, 2002, Miss MacIntyre came to the rectory at St. James and she was quite upset, almost hysterical. She kept calling Kerry Easterfield "Isadore Easterfield." I managed to calm her down and discovered that she had left her job at the Easterfields'. When I asked where she had last seen the brooch she shouted, "Do you think I took it?" and then started crying and said, "Oh, I'm sorry." I really don't know if she quit or was fired by Mr. Easterfield. She told me that she had left the Easterfields' because Mr. Easterfield had accused her of stealing some of his wife's jewelry and that she just couldn't stay there any longer under those conditions. I arranged for a room for her at the Home, and tried to help her get her life back together again as best I could. She was quite shaken by the incident at the Easterfields', and I was quite concerned about her.

I did receive this strange letter during the week after this lawsuit was filed. I didn't quite know what to make of it. Did Jesse send it? Did the Easterfields? Did someone else? I just don't know. It's below at page 91. I produced it in response to a question at this deposition. No privilege objection was made. That was something I wondered about. Since Jesse denied sending it, I didn't think there was any confidentiality problem from my point of view. Mr. Easterfield told me that his private detectives had determined that it had been typed on the typewriter at the Nita Public Library, a machine to which everyone has access. No one down there saw any of the parties type it.

I recall that several times when I visited the Easterfields, Miss MacIntyre mentioned that Mrs. Easterfield had raised a storm about someone stealing her jewelry, only to have the missing jewelry turn up in the house where she had mislaid it. Also, on one or two occasions while visiting the Easterfields, I talked to Mr. and Mrs. Easterfield about this. Both of them confirmed that several times Mrs. Easterfield thought the employees were stealing her jewelry and it was later found where Mrs. Easterfield had misplaced it. Mr. Easterfield indicated to me that he never took his wife's complaints very seriously. I don't remember his exact words. From what Miss MacIntyre told me, it appeared that this is what happened again that Sunday, July 17. Also, not once in all the times I visited the Easterfields while Miss MacIntyre was working there did either Mr. or Mrs. Easterfield mention or even allude to any theft, dishonesty, or any problems at all with respect to Miss MacIntyre. In fact, they had very positive things to say about Miss MacIntyre and were quite satisfied with her. After visiting with the Easterfields one time it occurred to me that Jesse had told me that the Easterfields rarely told her anything positive about her work while they were very positive about her to me. I sat down and wrote them a little note about it. In response to your subpoena I printed it out of my word processor where I had saved it and it is marked below at page 95. I put the original letter into a St. James parish envelope, which has the rectory's return address on it, and put it in the out mail box in the rectory's reception area. The secretary who also acts as the receptionist should know the procedure about what happens from there to get the letter mailed. I've never had any problem with getting mail sent out. The next time I saw Mr. Easterfield after I mailed the letter was a couple months later, after church. People were streaming out of the church and he stepped over to talk to me. I don't expect that anyone could hear the conversation. He asked me how I was doing and then said that Jesse seemed to be doing fine and that they had "discovered" that she really responded well to positive feedback. I took this to be a reference to my note, though I thought the word "discovered" was a little funny.

The Friday after Miss MacIntyre left the Easterfields, Jesse told me that she had applied for a job at the Nita City Athletic Club. She said that the job was as a coatroom attendant and that she had given my name as a character reference to Lee Marlow, the general manager at the club. Jesse told me that Marlow had said that a positive recommendation from me would assure her the job, regardless of anything else in her background. Marlow never contacted me. If she had, I would certainly have recommended Miss MacIntyre to her as a person of honesty and one who could and should be trusted. Most people don't have to go through what that young lady has gone through in her short lifetime, and she has certainly earned an excellent reputation. I would have given her a strong recommendation, with my firm and unqualified conviction in her honesty and integrity.

I have never had any reason to distrust her. Oh, once while she was living at St. James we thought that two twenty dollar bills had disappeared from the collection box into which the baskets had been emptied, but we weren't sure. The initial count had been done by an usher who had been wrong before and was probably wrong this time. Jesse was the only person in the rectory during the time between the two counts. I concluded that we had miscounted and that there had been no theft by anyone.

I received only one direct inquiry about Jesse. I'm not sure how serious they were about hiring her: perhaps the request for a letter was pro forma. She had submitted an application for a job as a bus driver with the Nita Transit Authority. They asked me for my opinion as to her suitability for the job. It's sort of funny that they did since my father drove a bus for a city transit authority and I know a little about the job from him. I knew that for the first few years, until she gained some seniority, she would have the worst routes—very heavy traffic in the downtown areas. I also knew that every other day or so someone would accuse her of shortchanging him and there would either be a heated argument or she would have to make up the change from her own pocket. Anyway, I really didn't think that it was the job for Jesse at this time in her life. This was a hard decision for me since it would have been a relatively well-paying job. Still, I thought it would have been a mistake. I wrote a letter back to them and it is below at page 99. I wrote it, but I never sent it. I decided that just because this job wasn't ideal, I shouldn't interfere with what might be the best opportunity Jesse might have in a very much less than ideal world.

Lee Marlow belongs to St. James Parish and I know her fairly well. On several occasions, she has expressed interest in my work and has also made donations to the Home. I remember talking to Marlow after church one Sunday early in 2002. We were talking specifically about our work with ex-convicts. She told me that the club hires quite a number of people with "limited skills" (I remember the phrase she used) and said that I should feel free to refer some of our people to her. I was somewhat offended when she said, "Of course, they're mainly minorities, I expect," in a way that led me to think that she wasn't enthusiastic about that prospect. I didn't make an issue of it, since I thought to myself that the club might be able to provide the most important thing for ex-convicts, a steady job. I'm sure that she meant that we could refer people with criminal records to her.

The week after Miss MacIntyre applied for the job at the Athletic Club, she told me that she had gone back to see Marlow and Marlow had informed her that the job was filled. Miss MacIntyre said that she couldn't get a job there because Mr. Easterfield had given a bad character report on her to Marlow. She said that Mr. Easterfield had repeated his charge of theft—that she had stolen Mrs. Easterfield's jewelry—and had also told Marlow about her having served time in the Women's House of Corrections. Miss MacIntyre was quite upset about this and began to doubt her ability to ever get a job in Nita City. I tried to reach Mr. Easterfield, but both he and his wife were out of town.

In early August, 2002, Miss MacIntyre told me that the brooch had been found, but since Mr. Easterfield had called her a thief, she couldn't get a job and she couldn't go on being thought of as a thief, especially when she had done nothing wrong. Miss MacIntyre was in despair and she was planning to leave St. James. It was my opinion that the shock she had received would retard her rehabilitation and could possibly cause her to slip into criminal habits and associations. I was afraid that within a few months she might be involved with some of the wrong people. After all, having been in prison, she had met a number of undesirable persons there, and if she left St. James and renewed those acquaintances, we could expect the worst. All the good work we had done would be lost, perhaps irretrievably. It would be another tragic instance of unnecessary recidivism.

In the case of an ex-prisoner, there are always two strong psychological pulls—one toward a decent life and the other toward crime. The pull toward crime unfortunately often becomes a push when an ex-prisoner is trying hard to re-enter society in a fully normal and law-abiding capacity and society turns its back and refuses to give the person a fighting chance. When this occurs, the disappointments and frustrations experienced by the ex-prisoner are overwhelming, particularly when the person had made substantial efforts to go "straight." It is a cruel thing to observe.

I was quite concerned about Miss MacIntyre and her ability to adjust to the incident with Mr. Easterfield and its continuing ramifications, so I got her a job in our Rectory as a housekeeper. We can only afford to pay her $70 a week plus room and board.

Miss MacIntyre has been with us at the Rectory for some time now, and she is managing quite well emotionally, but is concerned about her future. She wants to be more than a housekeeper the rest of her life, both for personal satisfaction and economic reasons.

Among the clergy at the Rectory—there are four of us—she enjoys an excellent reputation for honesty, integrity, diligence and devotion to her humble tasks. There has not been a single instance of dishonesty on her part and she has had numerous opportunities to do so. For example, church collections are frequently brought by the ushers to the rectory right after the service, and frequently Miss MacIntyre is the only one in the rectory when this occurs. She has had access to money and valuables on a daily basis since she has been with us, and nothing has been missing. When the count on our collection was off, I never entertained even a thought that Miss MacIntyre might be at fault. I trust her implicitly.

A short time after Miss MacIntyre came back to the St. James Home, she told me that she had a loan with the Fidelity Loan Company and that they were giving her a hard time about the payments. I helped her renegotiate the loan and, to my knowledge, she has not had any more difficulties with them.

Miss MacIntyre is a very fine person who had a bright and promising future, and I certainly hope and pray that this incident with Mr. Easterfield doesn't scar her for the rest of her life. I've been quite concerned that the incident will follow her and continue to hurt her, both personally and in obtaining employment.

This Deposition was concluded and Reverend Taylor was excused.

This Deposition was transcribed, and then it was signed by the Deponent, Reverend MacKenzie Taylor.

Certified by

A. Marie Lane

Certified Shorthand Reporter (CSR)
Nita City, Nita

SUMMARY OF KELLY EMERSON'S DEPOSITION

KELLY EMERSON, called to testify on Deposition by Defendant, and having been duly sworn, testified as follows:

My name is Kelly F. Emerson. I am now employed as a housekeeper in the Sheraton Hotel, Nita City. I have been working there since January, 2003. Before that I worked as a housekeeper in the home of Mr. and Mrs. Ross J. Easterfield, 221 Rolling Hills Lane, Nita City, Nita.

While I was employed in the Easterfield home, I met Jesse S. MacIntyre, who was also employed as a housekeeper there for about two years up to July 2002. We became close friends. We occupied rooms on the third floor of the Easterfield residence. Each of us had general housework—cleaning, assisting in serving meals, and generally assisting Mrs. Easterfield.

Mr. and Mrs. Easterfield always treated me fairly. When I started there, I was paid $90 a week plus room and board. I had three nights a week off, also Sunday after breakfast. Twice while I worked there, Mr. Easterfield raised my wages from $90; and when I left in October 2002, I was getting $130 a week.

I now understand that Jesse MacIntyre is suing Mr. Easterfield for "defamation of her character." I am very sorry to hear this. I like Mr. Easterfield. Also, I like Jesse MacIntyre. If I have to come to court and testify in this case, I can only try to be fair to all of them and tell all the "facts" I know of as I recall them. I only want to see justice done—whatever that is—according to the law. I don't have any prejudices against anybody. I have no other interest in the way this case turns out, no matter who wins.

I think I understand what this case is all about. As I understand it, Jesse claims that Mr. Easterfield falsely accused her of stealing a diamond brooch belonging to Mrs. Easterfield and that he made this accusation to Lee Marlow, the manager of the Nita City Athletic Club, where Jesse was trying to get a job as a hatcheck or cloakroom girl or attendant, and that, because of what Mr. Easterfield said, Marlow refused to give Jesse the job and hired somebody else. And that Mr. Easterfield also gave a bad reference on Miss MacIntyre to the ABC Employment Agency.

I do remember the diamond brooch involved. I often saw Mrs. Easterfield wearing it. I admired it. It was very expensive. I understand it was worth around $25,000. I recall that a cook who worked at the Easterfields for a few months, Sarah Washington, told me that when Jesse had first seen the brooch, she had exclaimed, "My God, that's beautiful. I wish I had something half that gorgeous." I myself recall that Jesse told me once how "high class" the brooch was. I think she had a bit of a fixation on it.

While I worked in the Easterfield home, I did observe on many occasions (at least ten or twelve times) that Mrs. Easterfield had a careless habit of mislaying or misplacing her jewelry, including this diamond brooch. She was careless about where she left it. As I recall, sometimes she kept the brooch in a box on a dresser in her bedroom on the second floor of the house. On these occasions when she mislaid the brooch or other jewelry, she would lose her temper and make wild and angry accusations that the brooch or the jewelry had been stolen by somebody in the house. She was always losing things—keys, jewelry, rings—and then she'd get frantic about it because she would say somebody had stolen these things. But every time this happened, the missing brooch or jewelry would "turn up" somewhere in the house where she had carelessly mislaid them and forgotten them. I know this because on several of these occasions, I was the one who found the things and returned them to her, and then she would be full of apologies for making the wild accusations about somebody stealing them. Word was among the staff when I got there that Mrs. Easterfield simply couldn't admit that she was wrong. Word was that when she lost her jewelry and it was later found where she left it, half the time she would say, "Well, I'm sure that I didn't leave it there. Who moved it and why?" They said she did this even when someone had seen her put it in the place where it was found. People thought she just lied about it. With me, she always apologized. I found her a truthful person.

I remember one time when I was cooking for a dinner party that Mr. Easterfield was having for some very important business associates whom he was very eager to please. I put the roast beef in the oven at 4 P.M. and went about my other work. The guests arrived at 6:15 P.M. and when I went to check on the roast, I found it was still raw. Somehow the oven had not gone on or had been turned off. Mr. Easterfield was furious. Well, Mrs. Easterfield told us all that it was her fault—that she had turned the wrong dial on the oven and turned it off while trying to do something else with the stove. She didn't have to do that—she could have let me take all the blame. I was very grateful to her for that.

On a number of these occasions—the last time was in spring 2002—Mr. Easterfield was present when his wife claimed that somebody had stolen the brooch, and he was also present then, when the missing brooch turned up where she had misplaced it. So, I must say that Mr. Easterfield knew of his wife's careless habit of misplacing jewelry and then accusing someone of stealing it. Seems to me that Mr. Easterfield should therefore have been more careful himself about accusing Miss MacIntyre of stealing the brooch in this case.

I recall one specific incident during December of 2001. Mrs. Easterfield had put her very large diamond engagement ring on the pinky of her right hand to remind her to get their season tickets to the opera. She was sitting at the dining room table with her husband. This was the month after the cook had disappeared with some of her jewelry. She looked down at her left hand and didn't see the ring on her ring finger. She gave a jump and shouted in a loud voice, "Oh my God, who took my engagement ring?" She was looking at me when she said this and I felt that I was being accused. Her right hand was on her lap and so Mr. Easterfield started asking her, "Where did you see it last?" That sort of thing. After about a minute of this, she lifted her right hand to gesture. Ross Easterfield said, "What's that?" They saw it was the ring. He threw down his Wall Street Journal and walked out. Mr. Easterfield was only harsh with me once. That was a time when I guess I deserved it. The Easterfields were in their bedroom talking about all their money and I became a little too interested in what they were saying. Anyway, Mr. Easterfield came out into the hallway and really let me have it for eavesdropping. I was afraid that he was going to fire me right then and there.

There was one other time when I thought I was in big trouble, though nothing ever came of it. The cook, Maureen Hainer, had taken home a box of a dozen lobsters that Mr. Easterfield had put in the basement freezer about six months before. She told me about "borrowing" them for a family party for which she didn't have money to "do right." She told me that she was sure that Easterfield had forgotten about them. "Nice to be so rich that you forget about a dozen lobsters," she said. Well, Easterfield realized they were gone and asked me if I knew anything about it. I told him that I had "no idea about what happened." Later Easterfield asked Hainer about the lobsters and she admitted "borrowing" them but convinced Easterfield that she always intended to replace them. She told me that she told Easterfield that she had told me about taking them, in order to convince him that she intended to return them. Well, I figured he'd take it out on me that I had not told him what I knew, but he never followed up on it.

Yes, I recall Sunday, July 17, 2002. Mrs. Easterfield had asked me to stay on duty that day because she was expecting guests—so I was not taking that Sunday off. Jesse had the day off after she served breakfast about 9 A.M. to Mrs. Easterfield in the dining room on the first floor. Jesse told me that she intended to go to church (St. James) that Sunday, and then go to see some friends. I remember specifically that Jesse told me that she didn't want to be late that day, since the opening hymn was one of her favorites and always gave her the courage to go on. I came down that morning to the kitchen and was having my own breakfast at about 9:30 A.M. or thereabouts. I did not see Jesse or Mrs. or Mr. Easterfield.

Later, after I had finished breakfast—maybe about 10 A.M. or so—I went to the front door to see if the Sunday paper had come. The library is near the front door and as I passed the door to the library I noticed that it was open. I heard voices in the library—it was the Easterfields and Jesse MacIntyre. Mr. Easterfield was shouting in a loud and angry tone of voice. From what I could make out he was saying something like "Where is the brooch? Have you seen it today? Just tell me the truth and you have nothing to be afraid of." It was quiet for a few seconds, or I was too far away to hear, and then I heard something about being a thief and stealing the brooch. Suddenly Miss MacIntyre ran out of the room and up the stairs. She was crying and was quite upset. She ran right by me, but I don't think she saw me—she was too upset. She had her handbag with her.

Who said the words "thief" and "stealing"? I couldn't tell exactly, as everyone was talking at once; those words weren't spoken as loud as the ones before, and also, I was further away from the door of the library. It could have been Mrs. Easterfield, Jesse, or even Mr. Easterfield.

It was an ugly scene, and I went upstairs to the second floor to do some work. A little later, I was in the hall on the second floor and I heard Mr. Easterfield's voice; he said: "Miss, you are going to be the sorriest person about all this," or something like that. I hurried down the steps and just as I got down into the front hall, I saw Jesse walking down the walk with her suitcase. Mr. Easterfield was standing in the doorway and he said to me: "Jesse quit her job—Mrs. Easterfield's brooch is missing—all I asked Jesse was whether she had seen it this morning."

He then asked me if I had seen the diamond brooch. I said I had not. Then I said to him: "Maybe Mrs. Easterfield has mislaid it again. I will look around for it." I did look around for it in the house, but I did not find it. No, I don't remember how I felt when Mr. Easterfield asked me if I had seen the brooch. I don't remember Mr. Easterfield later asking me how I felt, but I can't deny that he did.

But the brooch finally did turn up. On August 3, 2000, I was dusting in the library—dusting the books. All around the walls of the library they had bookshelves—about a thousand books. I remember there was one large book called *Modern Physics* by Henry P. MacIntyre—I took this book out to dust it and, right next to it, I found Mrs. Easterfield's diamond brooch. The book was just above eye level. I took it to Mr. Easterfield right then—it was around 10 A.M. and he was in the living room. He called Mrs. Easterfield and I heard her say that now she remembered putting the brooch there next to the book when she and Mr. Easterfield had returned home from the concert at the Nita City Athletic Club on Saturday night, the night before the Sunday when Jesse quit her job. I admit that when I first found the brooch behind the book, I recalled a practice that Jesse had. Mrs. Easterfield often left what I considered rather large amounts of money around the house—thirty or forty dollars at times. A couple times I saw Jesse pick up the money and put it inside the plastic jacket for one of the video cassettes in the Easterfields' rather extensive film library in the living room. She would put the money in the cassette entitled "Jesse James Rides Again." She always seemed a little nervous when I walked into the room while she was doing this. She told me once that she didn't want to have the money lying around the house when so many workmen and delivery men were always coming through and she just didn't want to put it into the Easterfields' bedroom without explanation. She said something like, "Well, I guess I could write a note, but it always seems like too much trouble."

I called Jesse and told her that the missing diamond brooch had been found. She was, of course, quite happy that it had been found, but I could tell, even on the phone, that she was still sad and upset about what had happened. She told me that she couldn't get a job and that everywhere she turned Mr. Easterfield had ruined her chances for the job. She said "I just feel so, so bad. There's nothing for me, just nothing."

When I called Jesse, she was staying at the St. James Home. She got a job there being a housekeeper in the Rectory, but it didn't pay very much and there wasn't much of a future for her there. I've talked to her on the phone a few times and also have seen her in person a couple of times since she left the Easterfields'. I thought I saw her once downtown in a fairly ritzy restaurant having lunch one day. I couldn't see who she was with. It might have been Reverend Taylor, but I'm not sure. They were sitting in a darkened booth away from the windows. I didn't approach them. I saw them through the front window of the restaurant from about 100 feet away. I could be mistaken.

At the time when I worked for the Easterfields with Jesse MacIntyre I considered her to be a girl whom anybody could trust and respect. I didn't know of anything in her conduct that would lead me to think otherwise. Several times, she borrowed small sums of money from me and she paid them back promptly. I never even had to ask her or press her for repayment. From all my dealings with her (we were most friendly and got along well together), I would believe her word, not only when she was under some oath to tell the truth, like a witness in court, but any other time, and I would believe her and have confidence in her truthfulness at all times. I thought she was both truthful and honest.

Jesse and I became good friends while we worked together at the Easterfields'. We talked a lot and got to know each other quite well.

After I got to know her, she told me about her background and her early life—that she had never known her parents and had been raised in an orphanage. She also told me about the unfortunate relationship with Mr. Holman and the attempted robbery of the gas station. She said that she didn't know anything about his plans for the robbery or that he threatened her and made her participate—I forget which—and that she was a victim of circumstances. She was terribly frightened of the court and going to trial. So, on the advice of her attorney, she pled guilty to a lesser charge. She was sentenced to two years in prison, but was released on parole to Reverend Taylor after about a year in prison.

As far as her prior conviction is concerned, it won't make any difference in my opinion of her character. I am basing my opinion on her conduct in the Easterfield home while she worked with me there. If she did in fact have anything to do with that crime, she has certainly paid her dues to society, and there is nothing to lead me to believe that she had not begun a new life after her unfortunate earlier experiences.

Yes, it is true (and maybe Jesse has forgotten about this now) that she did ask me for a loan of $500. This was, I think, in June 2002. I told her I certainly did not have that kind of money. She said she needed it desperately—that was her expression. I felt sorry for her. She seemed so distressed and depressed about it. I personally appealed to Mr. Easterfield and Mrs. Easterfield—told them about her request of a loan of $500 from me and asked them if they could help Jesse. I did not tell Jesse I had done this. I don't know if Easterfield loaned her the money or not. Probably not.

Usually the Easterfields got along all right though they were a little aloof perhaps. There was one time during the first year I worked there when they really did have a big fight. Mr. Easterfield moved out for ten days and lived at the club. They were really screaming at each other in the dining room. Mrs. Easterfield had caused $2,500 in damage to the Lincoln in the parking lot of Saks just after letting the collision insurance on the car lapse. The same day she had lost a stock certificate (which later turned up in a waste paper basket) which she was bringing home from the safety deposit box at the bank. There was a whole lot of screaming. She called him, "Philandering trash" and said something like, "Without my pushing you, you would be sweeping floors." He called her a "Pampered brainless bitch." My impression was that she was the one who was the more eager for the reconciliation.

About a year before Jesse came to work at the Easterfield home, there was another girl employed there—a cook—her name was Alice Brown. I do recall that one morning Mr. Easterfield came to me and told me that Alice Brown had left the house the night before and that certain jewelry belonging to Mrs. Easterfield was missing. Mr. Easterfield told me that he strongly suspected that Miss Brown had stolen it. He told me that he had reported the matter to the police. A few weeks later, Mr. Easterfield told me that the police had caught Alice and that she pled guilty to stealing the jewelry and was put on probation. Mr. Easterfield told me the police had returned the jewelry to him.

I left the Easterfields' in October 2002. I had been fairly happy there, but I wanted a change. Also, I was getting tired of the hassle with Mrs. Easterfield always misplacing her things and the resulting accusations and tense atmosphere. I guess I wanted to be more on my own and have more time alone.

The Deposition was concluded and Miss Emerson was excused.

This Deposition was transcribed, and then it was signed by the Deponent, Kelly Emerson. Certified by

A. Marie Lane

_____
Certified Shorthand Reporter (CSR)
Nita City, Nita

SUMMARY OF REEVE WINSOR'S DEPOSITION

REEVE WINSOR, called to testify on Deposition by Defendant, and having been duly sworn, testified as follows:

My name is Reeve Winsor. I am thirty-seven years old—I was born in upstate New York and my family moved to Nita City, Nita, when I was in grade school. I am married and we have four children, ages three, five, eight, and ten. I got a B.A. degree from Nita City Community College in 1988 and I taught in a Nita City high school for three years. I left teaching for financial reasons and have been working in business and administrative jobs since then.

I started working with the ABC Employment Agency about four years ago. I was hired as a supervisor and then, in May, 2002, I was promoted to Assistant Manager. As Assistant Manager, I supervise the employees and am in charge of the day-to-day operations of the office. When we are busy and if I have time, I help out on taking applications and interviewing the applicants. My primary responsibility is overseeing the background checks and placements, and in general making sure that the office runs smoothly.

Yes, I am aware of the office's record keeping process; in fact, that is one of my responsibilities. As Assistant Manager I am responsible for making sure that the records are made accurately and then filed correctly. Also, I am responsible for implementing any changes in the procedures that may be initiated by the Manager or our accountants.

Ms. Jesse MacIntyre applied for placement with our office in July 2002. She was interviewed, and an application was completed and signed by her. I did the background check on her. As I recall, I did that a few days after she applied. I called her former employer, Mr. Ross Easterfield, and he gave a very negative report. I don't recall exactly what he said, but it was about a very expensive item of jewelry that was missing and Ms. MacIntyre leaving his employment under the suspicion of theft. Mr. Easterfield also informed me that she had a prior criminal record and had spent time in prison.

After I had spoken with Mr. Easterfield, I negatively evaluated her file and placed it in our low priority for placement category. We couldn't encourage Ms. MacIntyre, as her chances for placement were quite slim. I believe we informed her of that shortly thereafter.

While I was talking with Mr. Easterfield on the phone, I made some handwritten notes. I don't recall when I typed the information on the application form. I know I typed it, but it could have been that same day or, if I was busy, the next day, and, yes, even possibly the day after that.

No, I don't do all the background checks. I do some of them, but most are done by our supervisors. I oversee them, but I don't actually do each one. When an application is made and the form is completed, the file for that applicant is routed to me. Automatically, all the files come to my desk. I assign them individually to the supervisors for a background check. I usually retain some for myself to do the background check, but the number will depend on how busy I am. After the background check is completed, the supervisor will record his or her notes on the application form and give their recommendation for placement priority and type of employment. The files come back to my desk, and I review them and then assign them back to the supervisors for placement and any future relationships with the applicant.

I have lived in Nita City most of my life and so, yes, I knew who Mr. Ross Easterfield was. You see, before I took my current job I worked in the real estate business for five years here in Nita City. I knew Mr. Easterfield's reputation there quite well. Before Easterfield came to Nita City he had already made himself a fair amount of money in a small city in Ohio. I heard from a broker here that he had been involved in managing slum properties in Ohio and was under continual suspicion of engaging in some arson for profit schemes. His properties seemed to have a higher than average arson rate and toward the end of his time there he was having a hard time getting insurance. That's what I heard.

In Nita he is known as a very aggressive deal maker and a very hard, even slick, bargainer in the real estate world. Many people in the real estate business community refuse to do business with him.

Easterfield's reputation is as someone who goes beyond acceptable "puffing" in real estate sales and is willing to conceal material information and even misrepresent facts. During the past five years I know of two successful civil suits against Easterfield to rescind real estate contracts on the basis of misrepresentation in the course of the transactions. Twelve years ago the State's Attorney's Office of Consumer Fraud brought ten related criminal actions against him for criminal real estate fraud, allegedly committed in the reselling of houses on which an FHA. Mortgage had been foreclosed and which his company had bought in sheriff's sales. Six months after the charges were filed, in 1993, Easterfield pled guilty to one count. My company had the bad fortune to be the buyer's agent in one of these cases so I was sent each court date to monitor what took place. I read one of the indictments, the one to which he eventually pled guilty. It charged that he had told a prospective buyer, a fifty-seven-year-old widow whose only income was social security and whose life savings were going into the house, that the heating system was two years old and had just been inspected and certified in good repair by federal inspectors. In fact, the indictment continued, it was thirteen years old (though it had been cleaned nicely) and there were dangerous cracks in the boiler. Half the radiators on the second floor of the house had cracked in a cold spell the winter before while the house was empty and the thermostat malfunctioned. It had not been inspected by government inspectors. The statute imposed a maximum two-year penalty and a maximum fine of $10,000 for each count. The nine other counts were dismissed, and I was there when he pled guilty to the one count I described. He was given four years probation, which ended in 1997. About six months after his plea there was a real howl because Easterfield had been a contributor to that judge's reelection campaign and hadn't revealed that to the prosecutor.

The prosecutor told the press that his agreement to the mild sentence was the result of the judge's telling him that the state would "get nowhere" in the trial of these cases.

During the last year that I worked in real estate I attended a real estate brokers' seminar at which Easterfield spoke. Easterfield called his short talk, "Greasing the Deal." I can't quite remember the specifics of the methods he advocated. I just recall that they made me very uncomfortable. In response to a question that challenged some of the methods that Easterfield proposed, Easterfield said, "Look, truth is the first casualty of this business. If you want to be a saint, join a monastery." I started looking for a job in another field soon after Easterfield's talk.

I have never met Ms. MacIntyre. When she applied at our office, she was interviewed by Bob Papa and I never saw or talked to her personally. All I know about her is what I read on her application form and what Mr. Easterfield told me. I haven't met or talked to her since then, either. An investigator called me and set up a meeting with him regarding what had happened with Ms. MacIntyre when she applied with our office. I met with him and told him what happened. Yes, the statement I signed when he was here is below at page 107. The handwriting in the paragraph is his and the signature is mine. Frankly, he caught me on a very busy day when the phone was ringing off the hook. I just wanted to get rid of the guy and I read over what he had written very quickly. I figured we had no exposure so I wasn't as careful as I should have been. Then I came here today because I received those papers from you telling me I had to come and testify at this deposition.

The Deposition was concluded and Reeve Winsor was excused.

This Deposition was transcribed, and then it was signed by the Deponent, Reeve Winsor.

Certified by

A. Marie Lane

Certified Shorthand Reporter (CSR)
Nita City, Nita

SUMMARY OF LEE MARLOW'S DEPOSITION

LEE MARLOW, called to testify on Deposition by Plaintiff and having been duly sworn, testified as follows:

My name is Lee Marlow. I am General Manager of the Nita City Athletic Club, 500 Main Street, Nita City, Nita. I was hired by the Board of Directors and have held this position since 1999. The club is a private social club with approximately 600 members. We have a large building with a gymnasium, swimming pool, auditorium, restaurant, and rooms for members and their guests. I am in charge of hiring all employees.

In July, 2002, I placed several advertisements for a hat check/coat room attendant. The ad we placed in the *Nita City Tribune* is below at page 123. I told my secretary to place the ad, but didn't give her the exact words to include. The second-to-last sentence in it is not really accurate and I didn't tell her to include it. The person we had, resigned. The hatcheck/coat room is on the first floor in the lobby, and is used for members and guests to check their coats and other articles. We rent the auditorium, 3,500 seats, for concerts, plays, and other activities.

When Miss MacIntyre applied for the job, we had already received four applications and I was considering them. On Friday, July 22, Miss MacIntyre came to the club and I talked to her. She didn't make a written application and I did not require one. We discussed the job. I told her it would pay $125 a week plus tips averaging around $50-$75 a week, and that it would also include meals at the club. I used the latter figure because I had inquired of the other people employed there in the context of their salary reviews. I wanted to know how much they made from tips in order to determine their base salary. The hours would be from 4 P.M. to 1 A.M., with Thursdays and Sundays off.

Yes, I was impressed with Miss MacIntyre when she applied for the job at the club. Her appearance and manners impressed me quite favorably and she appeared to be just what we wanted. Yes, I must admit that after the initial interview with her, she definitely was the front-runner for the job and I would have hired her if I hadn't received further information about her. I may have called her later that day to get some basic information necessary to have her enrolled as an employee.

No, I didn't hire her right on the spot, because there were other applications to review and, also, it's our standard practice to do a thorough background check before we hire any employee. I told Miss MacIntyre that and explained to her that a lot would depend on her character references because we could not hire anyone who was not absolutely honest and trustworthy. I told her that guests often leave valuables in their coats or specifically check items for safekeeping in the cloakroom, and that it was imperative that the club maintain an outstanding reputation for security and safekeeping in the cloakroom.

Miss MacIntyre told me that she was living at the St. James Home for Women, and that she knew Reverend MacKenzie Taylor. I belong to St. James Parish, and I've known Reverend Taylor for some time and have admired his work. He counsels young people and helps them get employment. I have contributed money to his work, and yes, I guess I did tell Miss MacIntyre that I had done so.

When Miss MacIntyre mentioned Reverend Taylor, I told her that if she knew Reverend Taylor, there wasn't much for her to worry about. No, I didn't ask her for any other references or anything about her previous employment. I certainly didn't suspect that she had difficulties with the law and so, of course, I didn't ask her anything about having a criminal record. Yes, she gave the address at the St. James Home, but that alone didn't necessarily suggest to me that she was an ex-convict. I knew that Reverend Taylor works with parolees from prison, but he also does a lot of work with other young women who don't have criminal records. It's my understanding that the St. James Home is not exclusively for parolees from prison. I do contribute to the Weston Foundation, a not-for-profit corporation that works with ex-offenders and has a special emphasis in placing ex-offenders in jobs. I am aware of the evidence cited in their literature that shows recidivism has a strong negative correlation with employment upon release. That's just good common sense.

I didn't ask Miss MacIntyre for other references or anything about her prior employment, as I suppose I was satisfied with Reverend Taylor's name and I knew he would give me a full, complete, and accurate rundown on her character and background. The afternoon that Miss MacIntyre applied, I phoned him, but I couldn't reach him. I then made a mental note to talk to him after church services that Sunday.

As it turned out, however, I never did speak to him about Miss MacIntyre. The next day, Saturday, July 23, 2002 Mr. Ross Easterfield came into the club to have lunch and, when I saw him, I joined him. I have known him and his wife for several years, and he is a member of our Board of Directors. Also, at one time he served as President of the club, and he has always been very active in the club. He owns the Easterfield Realty Company and is one of the wealthiest men in the city. He lives at 221 Rolling Hills Lane, Nita City, a very exclusive part of town.

During lunch, Mr. Easterfield and I had a rather general conversation about sports, politics, and how things were going at the club. I happened to mention that I was hiring a new hatcheck/ coatroom attendant and that the advertisements we'd placed had produced some excellent applicants. When I mentioned hiring the hatcheck attendant, Mr. Easterfield warned me to be careful in my selection and reminded me of the trouble we had with an employee a few years ago. When Easterfield was president of the club, a cashier stole approximately $1,000 from club funds and we never caught her or got the money back.

I told Mr. Easterfield that I had interviewed four or five of the applicants, it looked like I'd found the right person for the job, she appeared to be the perfect person for the position, and if her character references were satisfactory I was going to hire her. He asked me to tell him a little bit about her, and so I told him that she was living at the St. James Home and had given Reverend Taylor as a reference. He remarked that it was quite a coincidence, because a girl from the St. James Home, whom Reverend Taylor had sponsored, had worked for him as a housekeeper until she quit last Sunday. He asked me the girl's name and when I told him Jesse MacIntyre, he looked surprised and was momentarily taken aback.

Mr. Easterfield said that this was the same girl who had worked for them as a housekeeper until she quit last Sunday, and that he had originally hired her on the recommendation and urging of Reverend Taylor. He said that she had served time in the state prison for attempted armed robbery of a gas station and had been paroled to Reverend Taylor. Mr. Easterfield said that he knew of her past criminal record before hiring her, but, at Reverend Taylor's urging, he decided to help her and give her a chance to start over. He also mentioned that, when Miss MacIntyre was hired, they didn't really need another housekeeper, but Reverend Taylor had been so convincing, that he was just too softhearted to refuse.

Then Mr. Easterfield told me about the circumstances under which Miss MacIntyre had quit her job at the Easterfields' that past Sunday. Mrs. Easterfield had worn her very expensive diamond brooch to the club the night before and on Sunday morning, it was missing. Mr. Easterfield said that he had simply asked Miss MacIntyre if she had seen it or knew anything about where the brooch could be, when suddenly she got all upset, stormed out of the room, packed her bags, and walked out, quitting her job with the Easterfields. He said that she had acted very suspiciously and he wouldn't be surprised it she had taken the brooch.

I asked Mr. Easterfield if he had reported this to the police, and he said no. He said that, from the way she acted and all the surrounding circumstances, there was probably enough to have her arrested, but that he knew a little about the law of false arrest and he didn't want to get into any trouble—get into a messy situation.

Mr. Easterfield also remarked about how Miss MacIntyre's conduct during the previous week had aroused his suspicions. He said his wife had overheard the girl in a phone conversation with some person, and that she was being threatened if she did not come across with $500. He said his wife heard her say she'd get the money, even if she had to steal for it. He also mentioned that Miss MacIntyre had tried to borrow $500 from him and that he had turned her down.

I told Mr. Easterfield that his comments put a whole new light on things. I remember he said something to the effect that, since he was a member of the Board of Directors, he had a duty to speak out on all matters connected with the club's affairs.

Because of what he had told me on Saturday, I made no further attempt to reach Reverend Taylor or Miss MacIntyre. I hired another applicant that Monday afternoon, a Miss Martha Van Kirk, who is now working for us, so the job was filled right after I talked to Easterfield.

The next day, Tuesday, July 26, 2002, Jesse MacIntyre called me and inquired about the job. I told her that the job had been filled and there were no other jobs available at the club at the present time. Later that same day, MacIntyre came to see me at the club. She asked me if I had spoken to Reverend Taylor and I told her that I hadn't. I explained to her that, before I had a chance to talk to Reverend Taylor, some other circumstances had come up and the job was filled by another person. She pressed me quite hard on what had happened and why she hadn't gotten the job, but I had to tell her that the information was confidential club business and I couldn't reveal it to her.

I asked her if she had a criminal record, and she flared up and asked me how I had found out about it. I told her that it was a matter of public record. She admitted that she had been convicted of a crime and said something to the effect that if I had contacted Reverend Taylor he would have explained what had happened.

Jesse MacIntyre was obviously annoyed and almost angry at me. She started talking about Mr. Easterfield and the club and was quite upset. She said that if Mr. Easterfield had accused her of stealing his wife's jewelry it was a lie, and that both Mr. Easterfield and I had made a terrible mistake. She said something to the effect that Mrs. Easterfield is always misplacing her jewelry and accusing the employees of stealing it, but that it turns up where she had left it. MacIntyre got very upset at Mr. Easterfield and stated that he should have thought of his wife's carelessness before accusing others of stealing. She started to cry and ran out of the club.

I have never been in the Easterfields' home. I know nothing about Mrs. Easterfield having a habit of misplacing her jewelry and then accusing an employee of stealing it. Mr. Easterfield has never mentioned anything about that to me. The first and only time I ever heard anything about it was when Miss MacIntyre mentioned it the day we talked in the club.

Yes, I hired Martha Van Kirk for the position. I had no idea at that time that she had a criminal record, if indeed she had one. No, I didn't ask her. Usually, you can assume that people don't have records.

Well, yes, there were some rumors surrounding the Easterfields at the club. I had heard that the Easterfields had had serious marital problems from time to time, including last year. Yes, yes, there was the rumor that Mrs. Easterfield would have divorced Mr. Easterfield long ago if it weren't for her fear of adjusting to a lower standard of living. There was a rumor that Mrs. Easterfield had become involved with George Williams, one of the tennis instructors at the club and that he was demanding some money to get out of her life and not to tell Mr. Easterfield. The word was that she was trying to sell some of her jewelry in order to pay him. I confronted him about this relationship with the wife of one of our most prominent members and he told me to mind my own business. He threatened to be "a good deal less discreet" if I pushed it and so I backed off. Well, that gentleman died in a canoeing accident on August 1, 2002. Mrs. Easterfield's mood did seem to improve just after that, I must say.

Around August Third or Fourth, I received a phone call from Mr. Easterfield, and he told me that the missing diamond brooch had been found. He explained that it had been found by their other housekeeper, Ms. Kelly Emerson, in the library behind a book, and oddly enough, a book with an author named MacIntyre.

When Miss MacIntyre applied for the job at the club, she didn't say anything about having a prior criminal record. Also, she didn't tell me the name of her former employer or anything about the missing brooch and the circumstances of her leaving her job with the Easterfields.

It has been a long-standing policy of the club not to hire anyone who has a prior criminal record or any involvement or difficulty with the law in any respect at all. It is absolutely necessary that the club maintain its outstanding reputation, and our members and guests feel comfortable in the club and be able to fully and completely trust the employees. It's a private club, not a commercial establishment, and we have high standards to live up to. I am sure that I would not have hired Jesse had I known about the criminal record. In fact, I remember having a conversation with Mrs. Easterfield several years ago, before I had even heard of Jesse MacIntyre. She told me about the trouble they had with their chef, Alice Brown, stealing from them. I told her that we were very careful about hiring at the club and I'm sure I told her that we would never hire someone with a criminal record, for example. No, I never told Reverend Taylor we would hire someone with a criminal record. He must have misunderstood me.

Yes, there was a rumor around that Mr. Easterfield had been instrumental in the firing of the Executive Director before me. The rumor was this. The guy was a single fellow who started dating one of the waitresses whom Easterfield himself was seeing. The rumor was that Easterfield had told him to "find himself another girlfriend. Cross me on this and you're through." When he refused, Easterfield had him fired. No reasons. The board just fired him. I called this guy, Arnold Weblow to check out the rumor and he said he didn't want to talk about it. He said he might need a reference sometime. I did have one dispute with Mr. Easterfield concerning a pay matter, but we resolved it amicably. I ended up with an 8 percent increase when I had been given a 3 percent increase and expected a 10 percent increase. I wrote the letter dated "February 5" during that dispute. It is below at page 127.

Among the officers and members of the club with whom I am associated in the course of my duties, I can say that Mr. Easterfield enjoys the highest reputation for honesty, integrity, and fair dealing. I never believed the rumor about Mr. Arnold Weblow. In my dealings with him, I have always found him to be completely truthful and an honest man to deal with. I would believe him under any circumstances, whether under oath or not.

The Deposition was concluded and Marlow was excused.

This Deposition was transcribed, and then it was signed by the Deponent, Lee Marlow.

Certified by

A. Marie Lane

_____

Certified Shorthand Reporter (CSR)
Nita City, Nita

EXHIBITS

Floorplan of Easterfield's House

THIRD FLOOR

SECOND FLOOR

FIRST FLOOR

PHOTOGRAPH EASTERFIELD'S HOME—OUTSIDE

Photograph of Easterfield's Home—Dining Room

PHOTOGRAPH OF EASTERFIELD'S HOME—LIBRARY

NITA CITY TRANSIT AUTHORITY BUS SCHEDULE

NITA CITY TRANSIT AUTHORITY

Bus Schedule

LINE 44: Rolling Hills Lane

Line 44 runs East-West on Rolling Hills Lane from 4th Avenue West to 26th Avenue

SUNDAY SCHEDULE

4th /	6th /	9th /	11th /	14th /	18th /	21st /	26th
9:45	9:48	9:52	9:55	9:58	10:02	10:06	10:09
10:10	10:16	10:20	10:23	10:26	10:29	10:32	10:37
10:35	10:41	10:45	10:48	10:52	10:56	10:59	11:04
11:10	11:15	11:19	11:23	11:28	11:32	11:36	11:43

STATE OF NITA   )

)   SS

COUNTY OF DARROW   )

    I, Francis W. Burns, Secretary of Records of the NITA City Transit Company, hereby certify that the above is a true and accurate copy of the Schedule for Line 44 in Nita City in effect on July 17, 2002.

Francis W. Burns

CHURCH CERTIFICATION AND MASS SCHEDULE

St. James Parish Episcopal Church

Schedule of Services

Summer 2002

8:30   *Mass in the Small Chapel*

9:30   *Mass in the Main Church*

10:30   *High Mass in Main Church*

6:15   *Evensong*

12 Cockle Shell Court   Nita City, Nita

O GLORIOUS SAINT JAMES, because of your fervor and generosity Jesus chose you to witness his glory on the Mount and his agony in the Garden. Obtain for us strength and consolation in the unending struggles of this life. Help us to follow Christ constantly and generously, to be victors over all our difficulties, and to receive the crown of glory in heaven. Amen.

DARROW DIOCESE
ST. JAMES PARISH

I, Reverend Thomas Stearns Lewis, pastor of St. James Parish do certify that the above is a true and accurate copy of our Mass schedule for July 17, 2002. In testament thereof, I do affix the seal of St. James Parish.

Rev. Thomas Stearns Lewis

Reverend Thomas Stearns Lewis

St. James Parish
Darrow Diocese

IN THE CIRCUIT COUR OF DARROW COUNTY
CRIMINAL DIVISION

PEOPLE OF THE STATE OF NITA   )
)
       v.   )   Nos.   1999 Cr 44454 &
)   1999 Cr 44455
FRANK HOLMAN &   )
JESSE MacINTYRE   )

REPORT OF PROCEEDINGS

      The following is a partial transcript of the proceedings in the above captioned case held in the Nita Circuit Court, Criminal Division on June 16, 1999. I certify them to be true and correct.

George Lancaster

————————————————————

George Lancaster
Certified Court Reporter

Sworn to and Subscribed
Before Me this 13th day of
November, 1999

Sarah McGinty

————————————————————
NOTARY PUBLIC

* * *

THE COURT.	Mr. Prosecutor, may I have the basis?
STATE.	The evidence would show that on the night of May 16, 1999, the defendant, JESSE MacINTYRE, went with defendant, FRANK HOLMAN, to the Service Station at McCormack and Dempster. That he was armed with a .22 caliber pistol which the State would introduce into evidence. Dr. George of the Nita County Criminal Laboratory would testify that a bullet fired from that same .22 pistol was removed from the shoulder of Peter Moskol, the owner of that Service Station, in the early morning hours of May 17 at the St. Polycarp Hospital. That the defendant was aware of HOLMAN'S purpose in going to the station. That the defendant, MacINTYRE, and HOLMAN conspired to commit the robbery and that she positioned herself behind the wheel in the front seat of his vehicle with the intention of aiding his escape from the station. That according to their plan, HOLMAN entered the station, pointed the aforementioned pistol at Moskol and ordered Moskol to open the drawer of his cash register. That HOLMAN then reached into the drawer with his hand and took out approximately $465.00 and backed toward the door intending to flee and permanently deprive Frank Moskol of those $465.00. That Moskol then reached for his gun and there was an exchange of fire in which both Moskol and HOLMAN were hit. All this occurred in the City of Nita, County of Darrow.
THE COURT.	So stipulated, Mr. Johnson?
MR. JOHNSON.	Yes, Your Honor, that would be the evidence.
MR. HOLMAN.	May I say something, Your Honor?
THE COURT.	Yes.
MR. HOLMAN.	I just want to say that the girl didn't know what I was going to do. She shouldn't have to take a fall.
THE COURT.	That's noble of you, Mr. Holman. I think she and her lawyer can make their own decisions.

IN THE CIRCUIT COURT OF DARROW COUNTY, NITA

JESSE S. MacINTYRE)
)
v.)
)
ROSS J. EASTERFIELD)

I, Georgette Leeds, certified court reporter do certify that the attached is a partial transcript of the deposition of ALICE ADAMS, conducted this 7th day of November, 2002, in SACRAMENTO COUNTY, CALIFORNIA.

Georgette Leeds

_____

MR. MOEHN. Did you tell Jesse MacIntyre anything about Frank Holman when you introduced her to him?

MS. ADAMS. Well, just general things. That he seemed to be a nice guy. You know. Oh, I also told her that he had done time for a couple of robberies. I thought she should know that.

* * * * * * * * * * * * * * * *
CROSS-EXAMINATION BY MS. DEMETRAL

Q.   Now, Ms. Adams, I suppose you saw Jesse often during the time you worked together?

A.   Yes.

Q.   You had many conversations with her?

A.   Yes.

Q.   Too many to count, really?

A.   Yes.

Q.   Some of those conversations took place after you introduced her to Frank Holman?

A.   Yes.

Q.   And a few before?

A.   Right.

Q.   And you continued to talk with her, even after she had been arrested?

A.   Yes.

Q.   And I suppose that's when you and she really started talking about Holman?

A.   Sure.

Q.   Now, you really can't remember in which of those many conversations, you said that about Holman, can you?

A.   Well, no.

Q.   I suppose you felt kind of guilty introducing Jesse and Holman?

A.   Yeah, I suppose I did.

Q.   You wished you weren't responsible for what happened to Jesse?

A.   That's right.

Q.   And as you try to remember now when you told Jesse about Holman's record you still have that wish?

A.   Yes.

Q.   Ms. Adams, it's possible that you didn't mention Holman's record until after Jesse was arrested, isn't it?

A.   Yes, it's possible.

Q.   Thank you for your honesty, Ms. Adams.

A.   You're welcome.

APPLICATION FOR PERSONAL LOAN

FIDELITY LOAN COMPANY
PERSONAL LOAN APPLICATION—
FOR LESS THAN ONE THOUSAND DOLLARS

APPLICATION DATE: June 6, 2001

NAME Jesse MacIntyre

ADDRESS 221 Rolling Hills Lane
Nita City, Nita

EMPLOYER Mr. Ross Easterfield

WEEKLY INCOME $150

ASSETS Cash—less than $100, personal effects

PRESENT INDEBTEDNESS NONE

PURPOSE FOR PERSONAL LOAN Legal fees—Misc.

AMOUNT REQUESTED $800.00

REPAYMENT PLAN REQUESTED BY APPLICANT A B C D <u>E</u> F G

LOAN INTAKE CLERK Bev Coy #24

I hereby affirm under penalty of perjury that the information on this application is true, correct, and complete. It is a criminal offense to knowingly supply false information in an application for a loan from a Nita loan company.

Jesse MacIntyre 6-6-01

Loan Applicant Signature Date

Co-applicant Signature(s) Date   Co-applicant Signature(s) Date

NITA REVISED STATUTES

Ch. 38, § 14 (a)

No person shall knowingly supply false information to a Nita chartered loan company in order to induce such company to extend a loan.

Violation of this provision is a Class 3 felony.

Ch. 38, § 1008(b)(4)

A Class 3 felony is punishable by a maximum of five (5) years' imprisonment.

Ch. 38, § 16A-4 Presumptions. If any person:

(a)   conceals upon his or her person or among his or her belongings, unpurchased merchandise displayed, held, stored or offered for sale in a retail merchantile establishment; and

(b)   removes that merchandise beyond the last known station for receiving payments for that merchandise in that retail mercantile establishment such person shall be presumed to have possessed, carried away or transferred such merchandise with the intention of retaining it or with the intention of depriving the merchant permanently of the possession, use or benefit of such merchandise without paying the full retail value of such merchandise.

STATEMENT OF JESSE MacINTYRE

I was just out on a date with Frank Holman, whom I have dated a few times. I was sitting in the passenger side of the car waiting for him to come out of the Standard Station. He told me that he was just going in to get cigarettes. I didn't have any idea that he had a gun or intended to rob the station.

That's all I know.

Jesse MacIntyre

_____

Jesse MacIntyre

Sworn to and subscribed before me
this 16th day of May, 1999.

Mary Boehne

_____

NOTARY PUBLIC

LETTER TO REVEREND TAYLOR

Dear Reverend Taylor,

I can't tell you face to face. One lye has led to another. They shouldn't have treted me this way. I can't turn back now. I have to go thru with this. God forgive me. I'll make it up somehow.

Jesse

LETTER FROM REVEREND TAYLOR

St. JamesParish Episcopal Church

March 12, 2002

Dear Mr. Easterfield,

I enjoyed visiting you and your gracious wife
today and seeing that Jessse was doing so well.
I really remain appreciative to you for giving
her a chance.

If I could I would like to make one little suggestion. You told me how pleased you were
with Jesse's work. Jesse told me that she wasn't sure how pleased you were with her
work. I think you should tell her. Ordinarily you might not feel this to be necessary.
Jesse, however, is extremely sensitive to your judgments of approval or disapproval.
You can understand why, given her personal history. We all must be especially sensitive
to her need for acceptance and approval. I understand this heightened sensitivity
requires a kind of attention that is demanding, but I think that it will really do a lot for
Jesse.

Gratefully,

Reverend MacKenzie Taylor

12 Cockle Shell Court   Nita City, Nita

O GLORIOUS SAINT JAMES, because of your fervor and generosity Jesus chose you to witness his
glory on the Mount and his agony in the Garden. Obtain for us strength and consolation in the
unending struggles of this life. Help us to follow Christ constantly and generously, to be victors
over all our difficulties, and to receive the crown of glory in heaven. Amen.

Statement of Mike Stiko

CITY OF NITA   )
) SS

COUNTY OF DARROW   )

My name is Mike Stiko. I did time with Frank Holman when he was in the penitentiary for robbery. I was doing time for burglary. In early May of 1999, I got a call from Frank who said that he wanted to talk with me. We met at the Welcome Inn Bar and Grill over on 9th Avenue. He told me that he was planning to do a job at a gas station and wanted a driver. I told him that I wanted no part of it. By then we'd had a few drinks. He told me that he knew just who he'd get to drive. Said he was dating "some bimbo who's real lights out—a real six year old." I asked if she would be willing to take that kind of chance for him. He laughed, and said, "Hell, I'm not going to tell her. I'll take her out to a movie and make a little unannounced stop." He pushed back his chair and just laughed and laughed.

Mike Stiko

Mike Stiko

Sworn to and subscribed before me
this 1st day of July, 2001

Jill Williams

NOTARY PUBLIC

NITA PRISONER REVIEW BOARD

IN RE THE MATTER OF: :
                                   :

The Application of :
                                   :

JESSE MacINTYRE :   No. 2000-33
                                   :

for Parole :

ORDER

We find that Jesse MacIntyre has conducted herself in an exemplary manner while a resident at the Nita Women's Facility, receiving only 3 Disciplinary Points while incarcerated. Our resolution favorable to the Petitioner is motivated in part by our conviction that there exists under all the circumstances here some possibility that Petitioner's original incarceration was the result of a miscarriage of justice.

DATE: July 9, 2000

ENTER: *Barbara Kelly*

                    Chairperson

CERTIFICATION

I, Ronald MacDougle, secretary of the Prisoner Review Board, do certify that the attached Order is a true and accurate copy of the Order entered IN THE MATTER OF THE APPLICATION OF JESSE MacINTYRE on the 15th day of July, 2000.

Ronald MacDougle

SEAL

Letter From Reverend Taylor to Nita Transit

St. James Parish Episcopal Church

August 25, 2002

George Curtan
Personnel Director
Nita Transit
445 East Milwaukee
Nita City, Nita 56783

Dear Mr. Curtan:

This is in response to your request for a letter of reference for Jesse MacIntyre. I have known Jesse for approximately three years. I have been her chaplain, counselor, and employer during that period of time. I think I know her quite well.

I know that she has explained to you the circumstances surrounding her imprisonment. My own extensive investigations have shown her to be telling the whole truth in this matter and I regard her imprisonment, in the words of the Prisoner Review Board, as a "miscarriage of justice." In any event, I could not speak more highly of her honesty, integrity, and diligence.

Nonetheless, I do not think this is the job for Jesse at this time. The pressure of driving in heavy traffic and of the interpersonal tensions that the job involves probably are not right for her at this time. I think I could recommend her fully in a year's time.

Sincerely,

Reverend MacKenzie Taylor

12 Cockle Shell Court   Nita City, Nita

O Glorious Saint James, because of your fervor and generosity Jesus chose you to witness his glory on the Mount and his agony in the Garden. Obtain for us strength and consolation in the unending struggles of this life. Help us to follow Christ constantly and generously, to be victors over all our difficulties, and to receive the crown of glory in heaven. Amen.

NITA CRIMINAL CODE

Section 4(A)(2)(a)

Criminal Real Estate Fraud

> A person who knowingly misrepresents material facts with the intent thereby to induce another to purchase real estate commits the offense of Criminal Real Estate Fraud.

> Criminal Real Estate Fraud is a Class 4 Felony.

Section 27(A)(2)(b)

> Class 4 Felonies are punishable by not more than two (2) years imprisonment.

STATEMENT OF REEVE WINSOR

STATEMENT FORM

My name is Reeve Winsor. I am
assistant Manager at ABC
Employment Agency. I am being
interviewed by Paul Pirro who
is an investigator for Ross
Easterfield's lawyer. I spoke
with Easterfield in July,
2002. My memory of the
conversation is not too good.
Easterfield may have said
J. MacIntyre quit in a huff.
She did not cooperate
in their own investigation
of missing jewelry. That was
issue between them.

↑ brooch RW

WITNESS _Paul Pirro_   SIGNED _R. Winer_

DATE _11-4-02_

NITA NATIONAL BANK AND TRUST COMPANY
Joint Account Summary Statement

Ross Easterfield
221 Rolling Hills Lane
Nita City, Nita

This statement reflects a summary of all activity from October 1, 2003 through December 31, 2003 on the following accounts:

Now Account	0009877788
Money Market Account	991123399
Jumbo CDs	44545
	77898
	99899
	14983

NOW ACCOUNT 0009877788

Opening Balance	$18,980.12
Deposits	12,090.10
Debits	6,998.98
Interest	120.99

NEW BALANCE $24,192.23

CHECKS			
Date	Number	Amount	Payee
11-6-03	8989	$1,998.98	First Bank of Nita
11-8-03	9890	$5,000.00	Libertarian Party of Nita

MONEY MARKET ACCOUNT 991123339

Opening Balance	$112,900.54
Deposits	223,090.99
Interest	3,123.44

NEW BALANCE $339,114.97

PAGE 1 OF 2

Ross Easterfield
Summary Statement
PAGE 2 of 2

JUMBO CD 44545

Opening Balance	$750,000.00
Interest	20,789.09
NEW BALANCE	$770,789.09

JUMBO CD 77898

Opening Balance	$1,234,445.98
Interest	38,998.42
NEW BALANCE	$1,273,444.40

JUMBO CD 99899

Opening Balance	$987,993.34
Interest	25,998.27
NEW BALANCE	$1,013,991.61

JUMBO CD 14983

Opening Balance	$880,982.98
Interest	22,345.22
NEW BALANCE	$903,328.20

DEPOSITION TRANSCRIPT OF MARIA ZANONI

[After Ross Easterfield described a conversation with Peter Zanoni that caused the Plaintiffs' lawyers some concern, they decided to take the deposition of Maria Zanoni, Mr. Zanoni's widow, in order to preserve her testimony. She has since moved to Texas. The following is an excerpt from her deposition.]

Yes, I remember Peter telling me about the events of July 17. He told me that he had seen Jesse coming out of the Easterfields' bedroom and that Jesse had looked a little annoyed when she came out. He told me that Jesse always reminded him of our grown daughter Theresa and he used to enjoy teasing her gently. He told me that he said to her, "Well, don't you look like you have some sad little secret. Or are you mad at someone?" She relaxed, gave him a broad smile and said, "Nah, I'm okay." Then she went upstairs. Ross Easterfield asked my husband whether Jesse had anything with her when she left the bedroom and my husband told him that she didn't.

Certified by:

John Luck

Certified Shorthand Reporter (CSR)
Nita City, Nita

BILL OF SALE FOR BROOCH

Carol's Fine Jewelry

Written Appraisals
Fine Jewelry Repair
Expert Watchmaker and Clock maker
Estate and New Jewelry

Date: 5-15-75

Sold To: ROSS EASTERFIELD
461 LAKE SHORE DR
PENDLETON OHIO

Item: ONE 1.78 ct. t.w. DIAMOND
BROOCH SS C-1 $2450.—

Shopping Mecca Plaza   444 Friar Boulevard   Nita City

ROSS EASTERFIELD'S DESK CALENDAR

12
AUGUST 2002

@ 11:30
CALLED ABL 475-6943
RE: J.M. - LEFT MSG.
to call me. HAVE MORE
INFO.

⇛·Ross Easterfield
221 Rolling Hills Lane
Nita City, Nita

Providential Insurance
1122 South Main Street
Nita City, Nita 60942

Dear Sir:

I wish to report the loss of a diamond brooch insured by your company pursuant to Policy Number 4435544. My wife probably lost the brooch on the evening of July 16, 2002 or the morning of July 17, 2002. A thorough search has failed to turn it up.

I look forward to speaking with your claimsperson.

Sincerely,

Ross Easterfield

Ross Easterfield

APPLICATION TO ABC EMPLOYMENT AGENCY

ABC EMPLOYMENT AGENCY
315 N. MICHIGAN
NITA CITY, NITA 46556

MacIntyre   Jesse   S.
Last Name   First   Middle Initial

St. James Home   1406 8th Street
Address

232-4488   385-44-1202
Phone   Social Security Number   Age

F
Birthdate   Sex Race circle One (W)B S O   Height   Weight

Domestic Work in Hotels or Private Homes; sales cl
Type of Job Applying for

Just those of domestic worker
Any Skills You Have

List Former Employers-Include Names & Addresses-Position Held-How Long

1. Ross Easterfield 221 Rolling Hills Lane - 2yrs

2.

3.

DO NOT WRITE BELOW THIS LINE

AGENCY COMMENTS:

-- Called former employer, Mr. Ross Easterfield
-- Applicant let go - very expensive jewelry missing - theft.
-- Employer gave bad character reference and negative
   recommendation for the applicant.
-- For benefit of the Agency's good name in the industry, should avoid
   placing applicant in a position where trust is necessary, where there
   is access to valuables, or where money is handled.

SENSITIVE FILE * HANDLE WITH DISCRETION AND CARE
Route to Supervisor Before Placement for Approval

Interviewer R. Papr   Supervisor: R. Winsor

APPLICANT'S SIGNAT Jesse MacIntyre

DATE: 7-21-02

PETER STEINFEL'S OPINION LETTER AND RESUME

FAMILY PRACTICE ASSOCIATES OF NITA CITY

1221 NORTH BROADWAY
NITA CITY, NITA 45554

PETER STEINFELS, M.D.

December 12, 2002

Mr. Brian Moehn, Esq.
Berry, Moehn, Foley, & Madden, P.C.
Suite 1120, First National Bank Building
Nita City, Nita

Dear Mr. Moehn,

At your request, I have conducted a psychiatric evaluation of Ms. Jesse MacIntyre. although I would have preferred to conduct a clinical interview of Ms. MacIntyre, I believe that I had more than adequate opportunity to evaluate her. Indeed, the eight hours I spent in Ms. MacIntyre's presence during her deposition provided me a far better opportunity than the 45 minutes typically devoted to the personal evaluation of a criminal defendant by the court-affiliated Psychiatric Institute here in Nita. I have also reviewed the entire transcript of her deposition, which has afforded me much useful information about her personal history. The picture that emerges is really quite clear.

Ms. MacIntyre suffers from a relatively mild form of Borderline Personality Disorder (DSM-III-R). This is a pervasive pattern of instability of mood, interpersonal relationships, and self-image. At the heart of the disorder is a marked and persistent identity disturbance. She manifests the characteristic swings between overidealization and devaluation in interpersonal relations, the affective instability evidenced by marked mood shifts, irritability, and inappropriate anger and anxiety. Her criminal record evinces the impulsiveness characteristic of the disorder. Both the dependence on the boyfriend who actually did the robbery and the attorney who pressured her into pleading guilty are also characteristic. At the depositions I saw signs of the same inappropriate anger which she manifested when Mr. Easterfield made innocent inquiries as to the missing jewelry last July. She shows characteristic uncertainty about life goals, type of friends desired, and preferred values. Her school records indicate early shoplifting (uncharged), self-destructive promiscuity, frequent lying, and tendency to drug and alcohol abuse that is typical of borderlines.

Borderlines are prone to theft, usually shoplifting. In Ms. MacIntyre's case, stealing from her employer would have been simpler but served as an equivalent expression of symptomology. Theft of the jewelry would be perfectly consistent with her symptomology.

Their feelings of poor self-definition often give rise to extremely manipulative behavior such as lying, and I believe that she was lying at various times during her deposition and would be a very untrustworthy witness. Stress, such as the sort that Ms. MacIntyre was undergoing when she misinterpreted Mr. Easterfield's inquiries, could easily have caused transient psychotic functioning, which would, of course, render her completely unreliable as a witness of what occurred, even putting her tendency to lie aside.

In sum, attempting to steal the brooch, misinterpreting Mr. Easterfield's inquiries, grossly distorting the subsequent conversation, and lying about either or both of those things is highly likely in Ms. MacIntyre's case.

Also, as you asked me, I reviewed Reverend Taylor's deposition testimony. He is displaying typical symptoms of persons who were themselves children in dysfunctional families. A prominent characteristic is the need to "rescue" persons who are themselves victims of one sort or another. Jesse fits the latter profile perfectly. Thus Taylor's opinions of Jesse and even his "factual" testimony are distorted by this very common and well-understood pathology. This kind of interaction often leads to a romantic relationship, whether or not expressed physically, and I would not be surprised to see some manifestation of this.

Sincerely,

Peter Steinfels, M.D.

Peter Steinfels, M.D.

Peter Steinfels, M.D.
Northwestern Psychiatric Group
1221 North Broadway
Nita City, Nita

RESUME

PROFESSIONAL EXPERIENCE

1980   Private Practice of Psychiatric Medicine; Hospital Privileges at Nita Hospital; Member American Psychiatric Association; American Medical Association; Nita Psychiatric Association; Past Secretary Nita Psychiatric Association

1984   Board Certification in General Psychiatry

EDUCATION

1978–1980   Residency in General Psychiatry, Nita Hospital

1977–1978   Internship, University of Chicago Hospitals

1973–1977   Medical School, Georgetown University Medical School

1969–1973   Undergraduate education, Fairfield College. B.S. cum laude

JESSE MACINTYRE'S SCHOOL RECORD

SCHOOL DISTRICT 021
NITA CITY, NITA

PSYCHOLOGICAL-COUNSELING REPORT
NAME: Jesse MacIntyre
AGE: 13
GUARDIAN: Lutheran Charities
GRADE: 9th
SECTION: C
HOMEROOM: Mrs. Pilsen
DATE: February 7, 1992

REMARKS:
Loss of parents becoming central issue; identity disturbances. Self-directed anger:

—suspected substance abuse (admits alcohol—evasive on "pills")
—promiscuity
—rumored pilfering of school stationery.

Seeking reputation as "fast."

Jane Damske, Ph.d.

JANE DAMSKE, Ph.D.

NITA TRIBUNE CLASSIFIED AD

[The following is the ad that ran in the *Nita City Tribune* during the week of July 17, 2002. Assume that you have a copy of the newspaper for July 18, 2002.]

COATROOM ATTENDANT
NITA COUNTRY CLUB

Quali cations: reliability
and honesty. Good bene ts.
Ideal for day student: hours
are 4 P.M. to 1 A.M. We will
check all references in every
case carefully. Persons
without references should
not apply.

VIDEOTAPE INTERVIEW—MARTHA VAN KIRK

[The following is the transcript of a videotaped interview with Martha Van Kirk. It was given at the law offices of the plaintiff's attorneys. No one else was present. It was given on October 4, 2002. Martha Van Kirk worked at the Nita Country Club from July 2002 until October 2002 when she quit to go to California. No one has any idea where she is living now.]

Well, I had a face-to-face interview with Marlow. She asked me general questions about work history. That sort of thing. She seemed favorable to me. I thought I should tell her about the one bad mark on my record, a criminal conviction eight years ago for retail theft. I served thirty days in the county jail. She told me to forget about it, that it wouldn't hurt my chances. A few days later she called me and said that they had given the job to someone else. Then she called back yet again and said they wanted me. I started working there soon after.

LETTER FROM LEE MARLOW

Nita City Athletic Club

February 5, 2002

Board of Directors
Nita City Athletic Club
615 South Street
Nita City, Nita 65998

To the Board of Directors:

I am writing to complain about the failure of the Board of Directors to provide me with a pay increase of more than 3 percent for the 2000 fiscal year. Mr. Easterfield promised me not more than thirty days ago that my increase would be 10 percent. Because of that promise I turned down another very attractive possibility. I consider this a real breach of faith, a betrayal. Please meet with me as soon as possible about this.

Sincerely,

Lee Marlow
312 Post Avenue
Nita City, Nita

(555) 468-3364   227 Pumpkin Iron Drive   Nita City, Nita

IN THE CIRCUIT COURT OF
DARROW COUNTY, NITA
CIVIL DIVISION

JESSE E. MacINTYRE,	)	
Plaintiff,	)	
	)	
v.	)	No.
	)	
ROSS J. EASTERFIELD,	)	
Defendant.	)	

MEMORANDUM ORDER

This cause coming to be heard on Defendant's Motion for Partial Summary Judgment on Defendant's Second and Fourth Affirmative Defenses, the court having heard the representations of the parties and having reviewed the depositions herein, the court hereby determines that no substantial issue of material fact exists as to the following and so finds:

1. There is a sufficient factual basis to support Defendant's claim of qualified privilege with regard to the alleged communications between Defendant and Lee Marlow (Second Affirmative Defense); and

2. There is a sufficient factual basis to support Defendant's claim of qualified privilege with regard to the alleged communications between Defendant and the ABC Employment Agency (Fourth Affirmative Defense);

Now, therefore, it shall be and hereby is ordered as follows:

A. That Defendant's motion for partial summary judgment is granted, and the court will instruct the jury that Defendant is protected by a qualified privilege with regard to alleged communications between Defendant and Lee Marlow and between Defendant and the ABC Employment Agency; and

B. That nothing in this order shall be regarded as limiting the Plaintiff's right to argue or introduce evidence that the Defendant abused said privileges, and the court will instruct the jury that the defense of qualified privilege may be lost if the privilege has been abused.

Enter:

Prentice Landers

Judge Prentice Landers

JURY INSTRUCTIONS

1.   The Court will now instruct you on the claims and defenses of each party and the law governing the case. You must arrive at your verdict by unanimous vote.

2.   The Plaintiff, Jesse MacIntyre, claims that the Defendant, Ross Easterfield, defamed her in three specific instances:

    a.   Statements made to her within the hearing of Kelly Emerson on July 17, 2002;

    b.   Statements made to Lee Marlow on July 23, 2002;

    c.   Statements made to the ABC Employment Agency on July 22, 2002.

3.   In order to recover on her claim of defamation in any of the three alleged instances, Plaintiff must prove the following:

    a.   That Defendant made the alleged statement;

    b.   That the statement tended to harm Plaintiff's reputation, lower her in the opinion of others, or discourage others from associating with her or dealing with her;

    c.   That Defendant intentionally or negligently communicated the defamatory statement to a person other than Plaintiff herself or the Defendant's spouse.

    d.   That Plaintiff was damaged; and

    e.   That Plaintiff's damages were caused by Defendant's defamatory statement.

4.   Substantial truth is a defense to defamation. Substantially true means that the substance or gist of the statement is true. The burden is on Defendant to prove that his statements were substantially true. If the Defendant proves that a statement was substantially true, then your verdict must be for the defendant with regard to that statement.

5.   Husband-wife privilege is a defense. A defamatory statement made to one's spouse is absolutely privileged with regard to defamation. The privilege does not apply, however, when the statement is communicated, either intentionally or negligently, to others.

6. Qualified Privilege. The court has ruled, as a matter of law, that the statements made by Defendant to Lee Marlow and to the ABC Employment Agency are protected by a qualified privilege. There are very important legal, moral, business, and social interests served by having honest and forthright character references. There are also important interests served by allowing employers to reprimand employees, if the reprimand concerns the subject of employment and is made on business premises.

Because Defendant's statements are protected by a qualified privilege, Plaintiff may only recover if she proves that the Defendant abused the qualified privilege by making statements with malice toward her or with reckless disregard for her interests.

7. Abuse of Qualified Privilege. A person acts with malice if he makes a false statement with knowledge of its falsity, or if he makes it for the specific purpose of injuring another person. A person acts with reckless disregard if he consciously disregards and is indifferent to the truth or falsity of the statement.

It is not necessary for the Plaintiff to prove that Defendant deliberately intended to injure her. It is sufficient if Defendant acted with reckless disregard of the truth or falsity of his statements.

8. In determining whether Defendant acted with malice or reckless disregard, you may consider the following factors:

  a. Did Defendant reasonably rely on the circumstances known to him when he made the statements;

  b. Did the Defendant make the statement in good faith and believing it to be true;

  c. Did the Defendant act with spite or ill will toward the Plaintiff; did he intend to injure her reputation, good name or feelings;

  d. Did Defendant attempt to minimize any harm to Plaintiff by apologizing or retracting a statement within a reasonable time after determining a statement to be false?

9.   Burdens of Proof:

  a.   Plaintiff has the burden of proving her claim of defamation, namely, that Defendant made a statement that defamed her; that it was communicated to another person (other than the Defendant's spouse or the Plaintiff herself); that she was injured by the defamatory statement; and that the Defendant made the statement with malice or reckless disregard. If you find that Plaintiff has proven each of these elements, then your verdict must be for Plaintiff, unless you find that the statement was true.

  b.   Defendant has the burden of proving the defense of truth. If you find that a statement was true, then your verdict must be for Defendant with regard to that statement.

10. Damages. If you find for Plaintiff on any of her claims of defamation, then you shall determine her damages in an amount that will justly and fairly compensate her for the harm caused by Defendant's defamatory statement or statements. In determining damages you may consider the injury to Plaintiff's reputation and good name, any physical or mental suffering she may have sustained, and any loss of earnings or harm to business and employment relations.

You may also, in your discretion, assess punitive damages against Defendant as punishment and as a deterrent to others. If you find that punitive damages should be assessed against Defendant, you may consider the financial resources of Defendant in fixing the amount. Punitive damages are awarded to punish the Defendant, not to compensate the Plaintiff.

Verdict Forms

IN THE CIRCUIT COURT OF
DARROW COUNTY, NITA
CIVIL DIVISION

JESSE E. MacINTYRE, Plaintiff,	))))	
v.	)))	JURY VERDICT [Alternative Verdict] Form #1*
ROSS J. EASTERFIELD, Defendant.	))	

The jury is to answer the following interrogatories.[1] The foreperson is to answer the interrogatories for the jury and sign the verdict.

Interrogatory No. 1: Did Defendant make a defamatory statement about Plaintiff?

YES _____

NO _____

Interrogatory No. 2: Did Defendant publish the defamatory statement to a person other than Plaintiff?

YES _____

NO _____

Interrogatory No. 3: Did Defendant make the defamatory statement with malice toward the Plaintiff, or with a reckless disregard for her interests?

YES _____

NO _____

1. The interrogatories may be used either separately as a distinct form of verdict, or in conjunction with a general verdict form. See Vercidt form #2 for a general verdict form.

Interrogatory No. 4: Was the defamatory statement true?

YES _____

NO _____

Interrogatory No. 5: Was the defamatory statement protected by a husband-wife privilege?

YES _____

NO _____

Interrogatory No. 6: If the answer to No. 1 is Yes, then did the defamatory statement injure Plaintiff?

YES _____

NO _____

Interrogatory No. 7: Please determine the amount of damages necessary to justly and fairly compensate Plaintiff:

Amount $_____

Interrogatory No. 8: If the answer to No. 3 is yes, then you may assess punitive damages against Defendant. Please indicate the amount of punitive damages, if any, you assess against Defendant:

Amount $_____

The members of the jury have unanimously answered the Interrogatories in the manner I have indicated.

_____

Foreperson

IN THE CIRCUIT COURT OF
DARROW COUNTY, NITA
CIVIL DIVISION

JESSE E. MacINTYRE,	)	
Plaintiff,	)	
	)	
v.	)	JURY VERDICT[1]
	)	[Alternative Verdict]
	)	Form #2*
ROSS J. EASTERFIELD,	)	
Defendant.	)	

I.

We, the jury, find for the Plaintiff and assess damages as follows:

Compensatory - $_____

Punitive - $_____

Total Damages - $_____

_____
Foreperson

II.

We, the jury, find for the Defendant.

_____
Foreperson

1. This general verdict form may be used either separately or in conjunction with the interrogatories in Verdict Form #1.

MEMORANDUM OF LAW

MEMORANDUM OF LAW

To: TRIAL JUDGE

From: LAW CLERK

Re: *MacIntyre v. Easterfield*—Research on Defamation.

Plaintiff alleges three specific instances in which Defendant made a defamatory statement concerning her. They are:

(1) Statement(s) made by Defendant to Plaintiff in the library of his home which were allegedly overheard by a housekeeper, Kelly Emerson;

(2) Statement(s) made by Defendant to Lee Marlow as General Manager of the Nita City Athletic Club;

(3) Statement(s) made by Defendant to the ABC Employment Agency.

Plaintiff claims that each of these three statements defamed her and caused her to be injured. Defendant denies that he made any defamatory statements, and, even if they were defamatory, he asserts the defenses of truth, a husband-wife privilege, and a qualified privilege.

This case raises the following legal/factual issues with respect to each of the three instances of defamation alleged by Plaintiff:

    I.   Did Defendant defame Plaintiff—Proof of <u>prima facie</u> case of defamation;

    II.   Defense of Truth;

    III.   Defense of a Husband-Wife Privilege;

    IV.   Defense of a Qualified Privilege;

    V.   Damages.

This memorandum will discuss the applicable law and the relative roles of the court and the jury for each of these issues.

I.   PRIMA FACIE CASE OF DEFAMATION.   The law is well settled in Nita that there are 5 basic elements necessary to prove a <u>prima facie</u> case of defamation: (1) Defendant made the alleged statement; (2) it was defamatory; (3) it was published to someone other than the Plaintiff; (4) Plaintiff was injured; and (5) Plaintiff's injuries were caused by Defendant's defamatory statement.

A. Defendant Made the Alleged Statement.

The complaint must specifically allege that the defamatory statement or statements were made, so the Defendant has notice of the claim. Plaintiff's complaint raises three instances in which it is alleged that Defendant made a defamatory statement or statements.

From the pleadings and the discovery, it appears that what the Defendant did in fact say will be disputed by the parties. What the Defendant said and whether the allegedly defamatory statements were made are questions of fact for the jury.

B. The Alleged Statement Is Defamatory.

Nita, like most jurisdictions, has a broad definition of "defamatory" as a reflection of the high value placed on one's reputation and good name, relying on the defenses of truth and privilege to prevent any hardships or inequities to the speaker.

A defamatory statement has been uniformly defined in the cases as any statement which tends to harm a person's reputation and thereby lower him in the opinion of others, in either social or business respects.

A statement which accuses another person of criminal conduct is defamatory per se. The cases have held that not only is such a statement defamatory as a matter of law, but it is presumed that the person has been injured by the statement. All that is presumed as a matter of law is some injury, with the extent of the injury and the amount of damages being left to the jury. The juries in some fairly notorious cases have awarded only nominal damages.

The jury decides whether a statement is defamatory. The complaint alleges statements accusing Plaintiff of criminal conduct.

C. Publication of the Defamatory Statement.

To be liable for damages, the Defendant must have published the defamatory statement to a person other than Plaintiff. Publication has historically been a fundamental element of defamation, because without it, a person's reputation or good name has not been injured. The focus of publication, and thereby injury, has been on the hearing of the defamatory statement, rather than the act of speaking itself. Thus, publication may be either a direct or a circumstantial communication, as long as the statement was heard by third person and such hearing was reasonably foreseeable to the speaker. A defamatory statement has been sufficiently published if it was made directly to a third person, or even when it was made only to the person defamed, if the speaker knew or should have known that others might hear it.

In addition to the original publication, Defendant is liable for any foreseeable republication or repetition of a defamatory statement by third persons. Republication is considered an element of damages, rather than an essential element for stating a prima facie case of defamation.

Publication and republication are questions of fact for the jury.

D.   Injury To Plaintiff.

The requirement that Plaintiff be injured by Defendant's defamatory statement is an essential element for stating a prima facie case of defamation. For a discussion of the injuries compensable to Plaintiff, see Section V, infra. Injury to Plaintiff and the amount of damages are questions of fact for the jury.

E.   Causation.

Plaintiff's injuries must have been caused by Defendant's defamatory statement or statements -. This is a necessary element for stating a prima facie case of defamation, and a causal connection must also be shown for any damages awarded. Causation is a question of fact for the jury.

The courts have noted that proximate cause analysis is inappropriate in defamation cases because its basic principles have been essentially incorporated into the doctrine of publication. The courts have likewise held that the defense of intervening cause is incorporated into the requirement of publication. The principles of superseding cause have also been essentially incorporated into the doctrine of republication.

II.   DEFENSE OF TRUTH

Truth is an absolute defense to a claim for defamation. Thus, even if Plaintiff proves a prima facie case of defamation, Defendant is not liable if the defamatory statement is true. As noted supra, "defamatory" is defined quite broadly, and any inequities to the speaker are precluded by the defense of truth.

"Substantial truth" is sufficient to prove the defense of truth. Substantial truth does not require that every word be true, but rather, the focus is on the substance or gist of the statement. If Plaintiff proves that Defendant made and published a defamatory statement, then substantial truth of the statement is an absolute defense.

The burden is on Defendant to prove that the statement he made was substantially true.[1] Substantial truth is question of fact for the jury.

---

1. In the First Amendment area of publication by the press regarding public officials, the burden of proof regarding truth has effectively been shifted to the plaintiff to prove that the publication was false. See *New York Times Co. v. Sullivan*, 376 U.S. 254 (1964) and its progeny. In this case, that body of law is inapplicable.

III. DEFENSE OF HUSBAND-WIFE PRIVILEGE.

A defamatory statement that is made and published to one's spouse is privileged. The husband-wife privilege is an absolute defense to a defamation action. The theory that the courts and commentators espouse as the basis for this defense is that a statement made within the scope of the privilege should be protected because of the value placed on interspousal communications and the need for free communication between spouses. If a statement to one's spouse is privileged, then a statement made within the scope of the privilege has not been published to a third person. Since publication is an essential element in a defamation case, the privilege is an absolute defense.

The husband-wife privilege is a defense only for those statements that are made within the scope of the privilege. Furthermore, it does not protect statements which have been republished outside the scope of interspousal communications. In those cases, the defamatory matter has been published to third persons, and the defense is not applicable.

The burden is on Defendant to establish the defense of interspousal privilege. Thus, Defendant has the burden of proving that the husband-wife privilege exists, <u>and</u> that the defamatory statement was made within scope of the privilege without further republication.

Whether a defamatory statement has been made within the scope of the husband-wife privilege, or has been later republished outside the scope of the privilege, is an issue of fact to be decided by the jury.

IV. DEFENSE OF QUALIFIED PRIVILEGE.

In Nita, as in most jurisdictions, the case law on defamation recognizes a qualified privilege for statements made within certain business and social relationships. The privilege is qualified because it is not an absolute defense. The privilege can be abused, and in those instances it is not available to the Defendant.

A.   Definition of a Qualified Privilege.

Under the case law in Nita, a qualified privilege has been defined as a privilege that protects a statement made on a subject in which the speaker has an important interest or duty, either legal, moral, business, or social, provided that the statement was made to another person having a like interest or duty. Thus, a qualified privilege exists if <u>both</u> parties to a communication have an important interest or duty with regard to the statement.

The qualified privilege relating to an important interest or duty of the publisher and the recipient of a defamatory statement has been classified into three general categories.

1. The statement relates to a Common Interest between the Publisher and the Recipient;

2. The statement relates to an Interest of the Recipient and the Publisher has a Duty, either legal, moral, business or social, to provide the Recipient with that information;

3. The statement relates to an Interest of the Publisher and the Recipient can be of Service in Protecting that Interest.

For all three categories, the privilege protects only those statements that were made for the purpose and within the scope of the common interest or duty between the parties.

Defendant asserts the existence of a qualified privilege because the alleged defamatory statements were made within the context of a character reference, or, with respect to at least one of the three instances, because they were made in the course of an employer-employee relationship.

Negative character references, or even references which are less than enthusiastic, are by definition "defamatory" under the broad definition of defamatory which exists in Nita and most jurisdictions. The courts have recognized the common interest or duty between the parties to a communication pertaining to a character reference, and also the obvious societal interests in encouraging honest and forthright character references. Thus, the courts have specifically recognized the existence of a qualified privilege for character references. Likewise, the courts have also recognized the existence of a qualified privilege for statements made in the course of an employer-employee relationship.

B.   Qualified Privilege Defense: Has Privilege Been Abused?

This privilege is a qualified rather than an absolute privilege. Thus, it is a qualified, not an absolute, defense to a defamation action. The privilege is qualified because providing carte blanche or absolute protection would readily lead to abuses of the privilege, in which case the original societal interest in protecting the speaker would no longer be present. The qualified privilege protects the speaker until he abuses the privilege, and the privilege then no longer applies.

The standard for determining whether a qualified privilege has been abused is "malicious conduct." The courts have defined "malicious conduct" as the speaker's acting with "malice" or with a "reckless disregard" for the interests of another person.

1. Malice

In the defamation area, the courts have held that a person acts with "malice" when:

(a) he makes a false statement concerning another person, knowing it to be false, <u>or</u>

(b) he makes a false statement concerning another person, without knowledge of its falsity, but with the intent to hurt or injure the person.[2]

This form of malicious conduct has sometimes been referred to by the courts as an "actual malice." The courts have not used the term "actual" as a modifier for malice to state additional requirement for a finding that a person acted with malice. The phrase "actual malice" has been used simply as a means of distinguishing acting with "malice" as a form of malicious conduct from the lesser standard of acting with a "reckless disregard."

2. <u>Reckless Disregard.</u>

The courts have held that a person acts with a "reckless disregard" for the interests of another person when he makes a false statement recklessly without regard for:

(a) the truth or falsity of the statement, <u>and</u>

(b) the probable consequences of his act.

"Reckless disregard" is conduct that demonstrates an indifference to the rights of another person and whether wrong or injury is done to them. Although it is not necessary to show that the speaker deliberately intended to injure the person that was the subject of his statement, more than mere negligence must be shown. A "reckless disregard" is a breach of the standard of care that is greater than ordinary negligence. It is reckless conduct, rather than a mere lack of due care.

C. <u>Consequences of Abusing the Qualified Privilege</u>

If a qualified privilege exists, but the speaker had abused it by acting with "malice" or with a "reckless disregard" for the interests of another person, then the privilege no longer applies and its protections are lost. While the existence of a qualified privilege in a particular case is a matter to be determined by the court, whether the speaker has abused the privilege by acting with "malice" or with a "reckless disregard" is classic question of fact that the courts have submitted to the jury.

---

2. This type of "malice" has sometimes been defined by the courts as the speaker acting with "spite" or "ill will" toward another person. This was particularly true in the early cases dealing with qualified privileges. In recent years, the courts have adopted the broader and more descriptive concept of "intent to injure," in lieu of the more limited and somewhat dated concept of "spite" and "ill will."

D. Burdens Of Proof.

The burden of proving the existence of a qualified privilege is on the Defendant, or the one seeking the protection of the privilege. The Plaintiff has the burden of proving that the speaker acted with "malice" or a "reckless disregard" and has lost the protection of the privilege.

E. Summary.

A qualified privilege is a defense to defamation, and therefore Plaintiff must prove a prima facie case of defamation before the qualified privilege is necessary as a defense. The privilege protects defamatory statements that are made within the purpose and scope of a common interest or duty between the parties to the communication, but it does not protect statements which are made with "malice" or with a "reckless disregard" for the interests of another person.

The burdens of proof are:

1. Plaintiff must prove a prima facie case of defamation (5 elements, see section I), and then the questions of defamation and damages are submitted to the jury;

2. Defendant has the burden of establishing the defense of a qualified privilege—that the alleged defamatory statement is protected by a qualified privilege;

3. Plaintiff has the burden of proving that the privilege was abused—that Defendant made the alleged defamatory statement with "malice" or with a "reckless disregard" for the interests of Plaintiff.

V. DAMAGES.

A. Compensatory Damages.

In a defamation case, the Plaintiff may recover for the following damages:

1. Injury to general reputation and good name in the community;

2. Injury to feelings and psychological harm, with or without any physical manifestations;

3. Physical harm or suffering;

4. Loss of earnings or economic injury;

5. Damages from republication or repetition by third persons that were foreseeable by Defendant's publication.

The jury may consider certain mitigating factors in determining the amount of damages. Such mitigating factors would be: Defendant never intended to injure Plaintiff's reputation, good name, or feelings; Defendant reasonably relied on the circumstances known to him when he made the defamatory statement; Defendant made the defamatory statement in good faith and believing it to be true; and Defendant apologized or retracted the defamatory statement within a reasonable period of time.

B.   Punitive Damages.

The jury may assess punitive damages if it finds that Defendant acted maliciously. If a prima facie case of malicious conduct is proven by Plaintiff, then a punitive damage instruction is given.

Punitive damages may be appropriate, regardless of whether a qualified privilege exists. Qualified privilege and punitive damages are separate and distinct concepts with the common basis of a finding of malicious conduct.